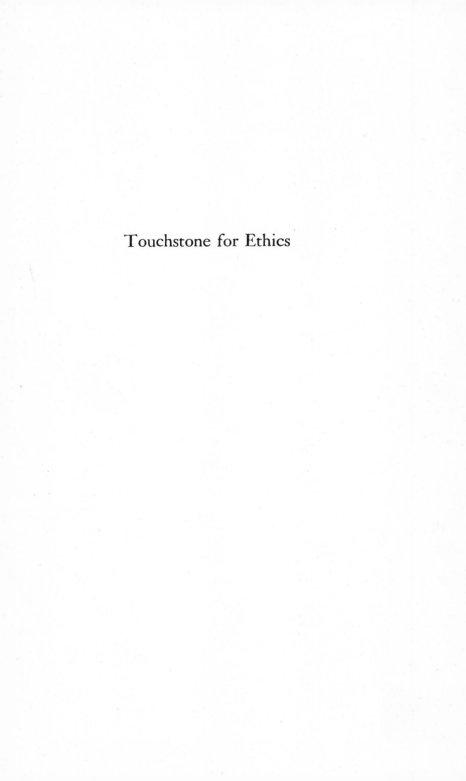

# Touchstone for Ethics

# TOUCHSTONE
## FOR
# ETHICS

### 1893-1943

THOMAS H. HUXLEY AND JULIAN HUXLEY

*Essay Index Reprint Series*

**BOOKS FOR LIBRARIES PRESS**
PLAINVIEW, NEW YORK

067383
0242936

Copyright 1947 by Julian Huxley
All rights reserved
Reprinted 1971 by arrangement with
Harper & Row, Publishers, Inc.

INTERNATIONAL STANDARD BOOK NUMBER:
0-8369-2402-9


LIBRARY OF CONGRESS CATALOG CARD NUMBER:
74-156661


PRINTED IN THE UNITED STATES OF AMERICA

# Contents

067383

024293

# Preface

ETHICS and morality pose some of the basic and perennial questions to which, in any and every age, man must attempt to find an answer. At the present moment, the questions demand their answer with peculiar insistence and urgency. The ethical problem confronts us in this acute form because the behaviour of our enemies, with the Japanese atrocities and the final horrors of the Nazi camps, have revealed that what we have regarded as self-evident principles of morality have not been in the least self-evident to large sections of the human species. Evidently, men and women can be conditioned, trained, and selected until they become capable not merely of sporadic acts but of systematic policies which fill us with horror. But they are men and women, not creatures of another and inherently different race or species from ourselves; and we do well to remember that there, but for the grace of God, go we.

Furthermore, we are now confronted with a task unique in history—of attempting to ensure that in the place of German and Japanese fascism new civilizations should arise, whose moral principles should be in some sort of harmony with ours. This raises ethical problems of every kind—how far can we be certain of the rightness of our own principles? how far can we hope to impose a system of morality on an entire nation, or how far can we succeed by encouraging in it a general type of social structure and trusting to the natural flowering of a better ethic? Should we deliberately inculcate what we believe to be the right (running the risk, always involved in propaganda, of defeating our own aims), or should we merely forbid what we are sure is wrong (running not merely the risk already mentioned, but that of creating a moral vacuum into which seven new and unexpected devils may creep for each one that is ejected)?

At such a time, any serious discussion of the basic problems of ethics should be useful. Accordingly I make no apology for republishing in one volume my own and my grandfather's Romanes Lectures on the relations between Ethics and Evolution, together with an introduction. In this I have endeavoured to bring out some of the historical bases of evolutionary naturalism in ethics prior to 1893, together with some of the relevant changes in fact and in approach between then and 1943, and have concluded with a more general summing up than was possible in my lecture. I have also added an article on the *Vindication of Darwinism*, which will, I hope, make clearer the modern position on the mechanism of biological evolution. For permission to reprint this, I have to thank the editors of the *Rationalist Annual* (1946) and the Oxford University Press for permission to reprint my Romanes Lecture. J. S. H.

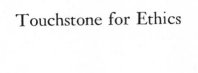

Touchstone for Ethics

# Introduction

## THE PROBLEM: INTUITIONAL ETHICS

Is there any external standard for morals? any touchstone by which goodness may be recognized, any yardstick by which it may be measured? Does there exist any natural foundation on which our human superstructure of right and wrong may safely rest, any cosmic sanction for ethics?

It is with that central question of moral philosophy that my grandfather and I, each in his own way, were concerned in the two Romanes Lectures which are here reprinted. In spite of our both approaching the question from the same direction and with the same background of evolutionary biology, we gave markedly different replies. I should like to stress the nature of our differences, and some of the reasons for them.

Thus, in the first place, it appeared to me that all purely intuitive theories of ethics can now be ruled out. They are ruled out by recent advances in psychology, notably as to how the precursor of our conscience (which I have ventured to christen the proto-ethical mechanism) develops in each individual human being. Even the development of a moral sense is not given irrevocably by heredity, but depends on the infant's environment; and the so-called intuitions of right and wrong through which our moral sense operates are not intuitions in the strict sense, but dependent and conditioned mental acts. Furthermore, the recent developments of social anthropology and social history have added their weighty contribution. Even if an intuitional component of ethics existed in early life,

3

it must be capable of being over-laid, distorted, and even contradicted by social factors.

T. H. Huxley, in his Lecture, advances a curious argument on this subject. He points out that if a bee could philosophize, it would have to be 'an intuitive moralist of the first water', since the workers begin to work, in the most socially-minded and self-sacrificing way, immediately they are hatched, and without any possibility of experience or of reflection on experience. 'On the other hand', he continues, the biologist sees in the bees' behaviour 'simply the perfection of an automatic mechanism, hammered out by the blows of the struggle for existence. . . .'

The antithesis involved in his phrase 'on the other hand', appears to me to be ill-founded. If our ethics did really have an intuitive basis, then, on any modern evolutionary theory, that basis would, of necessity, have had to be provided by heredity shaped by natural selection. Indeed T. H. Huxley continues, 'I see no reason to doubt that, at its origin, human society was as much a product of organic necessity as that of the bees'. He then points out the fundamental difference between insect and human societies, namely that in the former the individual is predetermined for his (or her or its) place and work in society by heredity, of instincts as well as of structure, whereas in the latter he is not; and proceeds to enumerate other aspects of human nature which have implications for our ethical problem. However, he never explicitly enunciates what seems to me the fundamental point—that man is inevitably (and alone among all organisms) subject to mental conflict as a normal factor in his life, and that the existence of this conflict is the necessary basis or ground on which conscience, the moral sense, and our systems of ethics grow and develop.

In support of this view, or rather in support of a particular exemplification of it, I referred in my lecture to modern work on 'morally defective' children, which brings out the fact that most such moral defectives have been separated from their mothers (or mother-substitutes) during a certain critical period—of early babyhood, but after they were 6-12 months old. Thus it is not only true that conflict is a necessary prerequisite for ethics, and that its existence has determined some of the characteristics of the developing human mind, such as repression: it seems further, that the existence of the particular conflict of love and hate over the mother (who is at once the fountain of the infant's satisfactions and the source of thwarting authority) is indispensable, or at least normally requisite, for the development of the primitive super-ego or proto-ethical mechanism.

A still more recent study of the subject[1] supports this thesis in general, while modifying it in various particulars. The author now prefers the term 'affectionless character' to 'moral defective' (though children of this type are very defective morally), and has somewhat altered his views as to the various ways in which such affectionless and morally defective characters arise. However, the main point which interests us remains—namely that without the normal relation between mother (or mother-substitute) and infant, with its attendant primal conflict, there will not (or probably will not) develop any functioning super-ego, and consequently any normal conscience or moral sense, or any significant system of ethical feelings and ideas, however inchoate or unformulated. These conclusions need to be supplemented by others drawn from genetical science, which emphasize the share of hereditary predisposition in giving rise to our moral sense and its variations. To this point I shall return. Meanwhile, facts of this sort should be enough to dispose at once of all purely intuitive theories of ethics.

Although T. H. Huxley was opposed to formal intuitional theories of ethics, he had not, it seems, freed himself explicitly from some of the intuitional preconceptions that are probably inevitable when one first sets oneself to think out the ethical problem. One obvious effect of such preconceptions is the un-

[1] Bowlby, J., 1944, *Forty-four Juvenile Thieves.* Internat. J. Psychoanal. 25, 1-57.

conscious assumption that the current ethical theories of the day
are not only eternal but self-evident. T. H. Huxley nowhere
claims explicitly that the ethics of his time are self-evident, but he
often appears to assume it. Thus, he constantly uses terms like
*good*, and *evil*, and *morality*, as if there were general agreement
as to their connotation, and without feeling it necessary to discuss
how the moral sense arises.

He does, it is true, agree that the moral sentiments must have
originated 'in the same way as other natural phenomena, by a
process of evolution', and then gives a specific case of the later
evolution of a particular moral sentiment, in the shape of justice:
'during historical times the idea of justice thus underwent a
gradual sublimation from punishment and reward according to
acts, to punishment and reward according to desert; or, in other
words, according to motive'.

But he never explicitly relates the origin of ethical ideas in
general to the inevitable conflicts of infancy. This can in no way
be ascribed to him for error or for blame. The data were not there
for the construction of a social-evolutionary theory of ethics; Freud
had not shed the light of his new conceptions on the dim realm of
mental embryology; nor had neo-mendelian analysis and mathematical selection-theory illuminated the genetic bases of social life
and the processes of evolution itself.

II

THE EARLY HISTORY OF NATURALISTIC ETHICS

It is not enough to analyse our ethical disagreements in the light
of general princip'.es, for the principles are not sufficiently general,
but change with time. Thus it is only through a historical approach
that we can really illuminate the question. It alone will enable my
readers to see my own and my grandfather's lectures as contributions, inevitably limited and particular, to the general trend of
naturalistic thought on the subject of morality, which, emanating

from the young plant of modern science, has for three centuries grown with its growth. Though it is destined to grow and change still further with new discovery and with new organization of scientific ideas, we can, I think, by now be sure of its general shape and its definitive direction. In this light, and with the aid of the reflective tranquillity of intellectual digestion, we can later reformulate in more general terms both the general problem which I attacked and the conclusions which I reached in my lecture.

Up till a decade or two ago, the naturalistic theory of ethics suffered from the incompleteness of the body of scientific knowledge to which it owed its origin and from which it inevitably took its complexion. The absence of knowledge—as we have seen with regard to evolution in pre-darwinian and with regard to deep psychology in pre-freudian days—led to the skating over of certain crucial difficulties of the ethical problem, or even the refusal to face the fact of their existence: the sudden access of new general principles—again as in evolution—led to an over-emphasis on the importance of the new ideas as magic or universal keys: and the multiplicity of new detailed knowledge—as with the social anthropology of morals—led to the obscurement of principle in a jungle of facts. Furthermore, the progress of science was uneven in different fields, so that the connection between separate fields of knowledge often remained obscure until revealed by deeper analysis or new discovery.

The result was an irregular development of naturalistic ethical theory, with both over- and under-emphasis swinging now here now there. If we are to try to give a broad picture of this erratic and adventurous course, it will be something as follows. There was first the rationalist point of view, derived from Renaissance humanism rather than from post-Renaissance science—an attempt to consider man, society, and ethics in the light of reason rather than of evolution, authority, or tradition. Machiavelli, Hobbes, and Spinoza are among the chief representatives of this tendency. Next, as a justifiable reaction against over-reliance on reason, came Shaftesbury, with his emphasis on studying the natural make-up of man, and the first enunciation of the idea of an innate, or at least in-grained, 'moral sense'. This was the original ancestor of the modern idea of conscience, though Shaftesbury himself would doubtless have indignantly denied any relationship, and its implica-tions are quite different. Then there was the use of the empirical and inductive outlook of modern science, and its combination in varying degrees with that of rationalism. Leibnitz exhibited this scientific tendency to a certain degree, though his rationalist or indeed rationalizing spirit is seen in his famous dictum that we inhabit 'the best of all possible worlds'. The result of this philo-sophic optimism, as Voltaire emphasized through the creation of Dr. Pangloss, and F. H. Bradley through the addition of his own gloss, 'and everything in it is a necessary evil', is to make nonsense of any concrete system of ethics, and indeed of the facts of society and history.

Locke was the first philosopher in whom the scientific spirit played a major part. The resultant rationalist empiricism, pursued by Berkeley, culminated in Hume, who, as Bertrand Russell says, 'by making it self-consistent made it incredible'. Less rationalism and more empiricism, and above all more scientific facts and more induction, were needed to give naturalism a rebirth. The less of rationalism, however, was first brought about by the romantic movement. Its claims on behalf of 'sensibility' and the emotions were a direct challenge to that pre-eminence of pure reason on which the previous century had insisted, and first opened the door to a psychological (as opposed to a merely intellectual) analysis of conscience and morality. The late seventeenth and most of the eighteenth century exalted intellect and order as safeguards against fanaticism and the ideological wars (like the religious wars of Europe and the Civil War in England) which had resulted from it. But by 1750 or thereabouts intellect had grown inbred and arid, order was in many countries becoming synonymous with the existing order and with repression against the rise of any other order, and many people were growing tired of too much security, especially when linked with security police, and were craving not only for more freedom but for emotional excitement.

The result of this psychological climate was to discredit the philosophical ideas which men had read into the Newtonian system, of a cosmic order in which every particle and planet followed the laws prescribed by a divine Governor, and prepared their minds for the irrational actuality, the disorderly variety and plethora of facts, to be disclosed by geology and biology, and by latter-day astronomy.

Rousseau is the epitome of this anti-rational, anti-logical, anti-orderly, intuitional movement, and carried emotional romanticism in philosophy and ethics to a pitch where, like Hume's rationalist empiricism, it defeated itself, although Hegel was able to develop certain of Rousseau's ideas to a higher degree of elaboration. It remained for Kant to combine an intellectualist with an intuitional approach, and so, in a new synthesis, to prepare the way for a fresh growth of philosophy in the nineteenth century. His particular theory of ethics, with its famous 'categorical imperative', concerns us only in so far as it was the first attempt to proclaim the autonomy of human morality and its independence both of divine intervention, through the implantation of conscience in human nature or otherwise, and of utilitarian considerations. In this he foreshadows certain aspects of the modern psychological approach to ethics, though on the other hand, he is opposed to it in maintaining that morality depends on *a priori* concepts rooted in reason.

Hegel's major contribution to the problem is, I suppose, the view that the raw data of experience, the 'facts' of the empirical philosopher, are essentially irrational, and only become capable of rational interpretation when viewed in all their relations with each other and with the whole. His method of establishing these relations, the famous dialectic, is equally important, since, quite apart from having been taken over (and inverted into materialist terms) as the basis of Marxist philosophy, it introduced the notion of conflict as the fruitful parent of synthesis, emphasized the 'altogetherness of everything', the universal web of interrelatedness which is at the basis both of modern scientific thought and of Whitehead's philosophy, and, with its insistence that the synthesis of the antithesis of Being and Not-Being is Becoming, prepared the ground for the dynamic type of philosophy necessitated by the acceptance of evolution. In respect of ethics, his emphasis on the Whole, combined with his glorification of the State as 'the actually realized moral life', 'the Divine Idea as it exists on earth' and 'the embodiment of rational freedom, realizing and recognizing itself [!] in an objective form', led him into the demonstrably false position of denying the importance of the individual, and of asserting the intrinsically higher value of the State as against that of its members.

The falsity of this moral doctrine, as I have pointed out in my lecture, can be demonstrated on purely biological and evolutionary grounds, as well as on human and social ones. However, before the facts were available for its disproof, it became a philosophic convenience to dictators anxious to conduct the world into Fascism, and served almost without attention as the intellectual justification for their systems, as we may perceive by reading Mussolini's article on *Fascismo* in the Fascist Encyclopædia. It needed the pragmatic test of a world war to defeat this thesis; and we cannot yet be sure that it is dead. All the more reason therefore for proclaiming the scientific evidence for its falsity, which I have also summarized in my lecture.

Kant in his metaphysics and ethics, and Hegel in his whole philosophy, were little influenced by the discoveries or the methodology of science. The currents of scientific naturalism, however, had continued to flow, although in minor channels, throughout the late eighteenth and early nineteenth century; during this period Condorcet and Helvetius kept the flow alive. Condorcet, though largely a Romantic in outlook, was the first to produce a theory of population; through Malthus' father, he was the direct inspirer of that gloomy clergyman's doctrine, which in turn exercised such a decisive effect on all subsequent thought through having led Darwin to the theory of Natural Selection. Helvetius was equally important, for he was the father of nineteenth-century Utilitarianism, through his influence both on Jeremy Bentham and James Mill. The two currents affected a partial junction, since for a time at least, utilitarianism could be conceived of as the psychological equivalent in the individual of natural selection in the biology of the race.[1]

But from early Victorian times onward, the decisive effects in the field which here concerns us have been exerted by new discoveries and new principles in the field of natural science rather than by new philosophical insight. Let us enumerate a few. First came the discoveries of the geologists, beginning with William Smith's proof of a definite time-sequence for geological formations and culminating in Lyell's uniformitarianism, which knocked out creationism, gave a mortal blow to the doctrine of scriptural infallibility, enlarged the time-scale for man and earth to what seemed at first a frightening extent, and with its demonstration of the gigantic cumulative effect of small and gradual changes, prepared men's minds for the same doctrine of gradualism in biological evolution.

Then came Darwin. He had several effects upon the treatment of our problem. In the first place, his demonstration of the fact of evolution made it imperative to apply the evolutionary approach to ethics, as to other facts of human life. Secondly, he demonstrated the unity of all life, however various, and the need for a rational and scientific explanation of that unity and that variety. Thus his

---

[1] From the angle of the out-and-out ethical relativists, utilitarianism is sometimes regarded as the inevitable outcome of a commercially-minded epoch— "the ethics of bourgeois book-keeping", as Trotsky called it. This attitude, however, while it may explain why utilitarianism met with special favour during the early nineteenth century, does not tell us anything about the truth or untruth of its propositions.

work led to an extension and a reinterpretation of that of the great comparative anatomists, paleontologists, and embryologists of the first half of the century. Their discovery of 'archetypal plans' common to large and apparently heterogeneous groups was at once explicable in terms of common ancestry; while the principle of common ancestry could be readily extended to cover the entire realm of life; the obvious general similarity but equally obvious particular difference between extinct and existing animals could at once be interpreted in terms of evolution instead of in those of repeated cataclysms and repeated creation—that curious 'epicyclic' complication of creationist theory embodied in the doctrine of Catastrophism; and von Baer's discovery that the embryos of higher forms often resemble lower forms became explicable if the development of the higher type in some sense recapitulated that of its ancestors.

In the third place, his promulgation of natural selection as a possible (and, as it turned out, the main actual) method of evolution led at once to a naturalistic approach to the whole of biology, and made both vitalism and creationism or divine intervention almost infinitely less plausible or tenable.

This last tendency was reinforced by the discoveries of Pasteur on the reproduction of micro-organisms. Those discoveries are often described in negative terms, as the disproof of spontaneous generation or the like. In reality, they are the keystone of a positive generalization of the highest importance—namely the fact that reproduction is based on continuity of substance between parent and offspring. In the light of evolution, this at once implies the eventual continuity of all living substance whatsoever: and as a result of the further discoveries of men like Fleming, van Beneden, the Hertwigs, Boveri, E. B. Wilson, T. H. Morgan, Darlington, and Muller, it led to detailed knowledge of what precisely this self-reproducing substance was (namely, the genes in the chromosomes), and of how it varied (by mutation) so as to produce the raw material out of which selection fashioned evolutionary changes.

In the inorganic field, the chemists and physicists contributed their quota to a unified world outlook. On the material side Dalton, Avogadro, and Berzelius paved the way by showing that all matter consists of elemental units or atoms, grouped together in units of substance or molecules; Mendeleeff showed that there must be some relationship between the atoms of the various elements; Rutherford, Bohr, Moseley, and the long line of modern atomic physicists demonstrated that that relationship was dependent on their all being composed of the same basic units, only in different numbers and proportions. Meanwhile, building on the pioneer work of Rumford, Davy, Carnot, Joule, Faraday, and many other workers in different branches of physics, Kelvin and Clerk Maxwell unified all the diverse activities and transformations of matter into the comprehensive theory of energy, with conservation of total sum but progressive dissipation of amount available, as its twin pillars. And during the present century Einstein opened the door to a still further unification, so that today, instead of envisaging physical phenomena as the joint activities of two categories of reality—matter and energy—we can describe them as manifestations of a unitary world-stuff—'matter-cum-energy'— of which the two aspects are mutually convertible.

Meanwhile the chemists, beginning with Wöhler, had discovered that organic compounds, though they are normally to be found only in plant or animal bodies, did not owe their formation to any special 'vital force', but could be produced equally well in the laboratory—a discovery at the base of the remarkable synthetic chemistry of today. They and the physiologists also showed that animals and plants exhibited no kind of matter and no transformations of energy beyond those familiar in the inorganic world, so that living substance in its physical aspects could eventually be seen as part of the same world-stuff as the rest of the cosmos. This once accomplished, the way lay open for a reverse effect of biology upon physics. Acceptance of the principle of evolution, together with that of the material identity of substance in life and not-life, made it clear that the phenomena of life are merely the properties of a particular portion of the world-stuff which is endowed with the capacity for self-reproduction. But then, as I indicate elsewhere, the existence of mind in the higher ranges of life, together with the principle of continuity of substance during evolution, made it necessary to add a third category, in the shape of mind, or mind-like (psychoid) qualities, to the properties of the world-stuff, so that it becomes 'matter-cum-life-cum-mind'.

With this, the essential unity of phenomena both in space and time was established, and the way lay open to the modern generalized theory of evolution, the necessary scientific background for a unified world outlook in general, as well as for a universal and scientific theory of ethics in particular.

III

THE RISE OF AN EVOLUTIONARY THEORY OF ETHICS

THE recent publication by Professor Quillian[1] of a careful but essentially hostile survey of the nineteenth-century developments of naturalistic ethics along evolutionary lines, prompts me to summarize this aspect of the subject more fully than I should have otherwise intended, or been able, to do.

Professor Quillian's survey makes it clear that the philosophic movement which he calls Evolutionary Naturalism represents a natural development of the Utilitarian school of Jeremy Bentham and John Stuart Mill and the Positivism of Auguste Comte (which latter was essentially evolutionary in its approach), themselves in turn offshoots of the main stream of empiricist and humanist thought which arose as the result of the Renaissance and especially of the birth of modern science in the seventeenth century. In this

[1] W. F. Quillian, *The Moral Theory of Evolutionary Naturalism.* (Yale Studies in Religious Education XVII.) Yale University Press, 1945.

nineteenth-century development of the movement, natural evolution was seized upon as the central integrating and explanatory
idea.

The chief exponents of what Quillian calls Evolutionary
Naturalism (as of Utilitarianism and of Empiricism, back to the
time of Francis Bacon) were British—Charles Darwin, Herbert
Spencer, W. K. Clifford, Leslie Stephen, L. T. Hobhouse, Francis
Galton, Henry Drummond, and T. H. Huxley (though his Romanes
Lecture was opposed to some of the main conclusions of the school)
—or, if not British by origin, did their main work in Britain,
like the Finn, Edward Westermarck; though Frenchmen like J. F.
Guyau and Germans like Haeckel were also among its adherents.

Quillian's analysis, however, is very much weakened by the
fact that he does not include any modern members of the school.
He is thus able very conveniently to advance criticisms of the
general thesis which have been rendered quite irrelevant by later
advances of knowledge. Thus he rightly disagrees with Herbert
Spencer (and other early proponents of an evolutionary theory of
ethics) for basing his views on the lamarckian theory of the
inheritance of acquired characters, in this case certain conscious
experiences. For instance, Spencer in his *Principles of Ethics*
categorically states that 'moral intentions are the results of accumulated experiences of utility gradually organized and inherited',
until they 'have come to be quite independent of conscious experience'. But in Spencer's time it was perfectly legitimate to adopt a
lamarckian viewpoint, so that Quillian's criticism of Spencer on
this point is largely irrelevant. On the other hand, to-day we know
that lamarckian inheritance does not exist, and that evolution on
the pre-human level proceeds mainly or wholly by the natural
selection of small mutations and their recombinations; and all
modern evolutionary theories of ethics start from this presupposition. Yet Quillian uses the lamarckian views of the early
members of the school as a stick with which to belabour all
theories of evolutionary ethics.

All modern theories on the subject also start from the pre-supposition that mutations are, biologically speaking, random, and bear no special relation to changes in the environment or the conditions of life, so that a second criticism by Quillian, that Darwin and others relate variation (mutation) to the external world, equally falls to the ground.

Similarly, as set forth in the next section of this introduction, any modern naturalistic theory of ethics must take account of the facts of infantile conflict and repression to which Freud was the first to draw attention, for it is these alone, or at least in the main, which give us an understanding of the categorical sense of obligation associated with morality. Yet Quillian does not even mention Freud[1]; and he reproaches the whole school of Evolutionary Naturalism for not giving any adequate explanation of this sense of moral obligation, when none of the thinkers he criticizes lived to hear of Freud's work. It is like rebuking Darwin for being ignorant of the genetic work of Morgan and Darlington!

Finally, he criticizes many of these thinkers for explicitly or implicitly assuming that man is 'only' a developed animal, and that his behaviour and evolution are governed by the same principles and laws as apply to lower animals. This is a just criticism— but fails to mention that modern evolutionary analysis has shown that the attainment of the distinctively human condition marks a critical point in evolution, and that after this point quite new principles apply and new evolutionary mechanisms become dominant.

In fact, his title is misleading. He is not analysing the theory of Evolutionary Naturalism, but only the theory of Evolutionary Naturalism during the nineteenth century. The early pioneers were bound to make mistakes in the then largely uncharted wilderness of biology: but by confuting their mistakes and omitting even to

---

[1] Though he cites Waddington, who deals with the interrelations of ethics with psycho-analysis and with Darwinism, in his bibliography, he does not discuss his essay in the text.

mention the work of their successors, he contrives to give the impression that he has confuted any and every evolutionary or naturalistic theory of ethics. If not disingenuous, this is at least unfortunate.

The crucial problems for any naturalistic theory of ethics would seem to be the following:—the existence and nature of conscience; the compulsive sense of moral obligation and duty; the 'moral law'; ethical and moral standards and their objectivity (or otherwise); and the relation between private or personal and public or social morality. Quillian has certainly rendered a service in summarizing, analyzing, and criticizing the ways in which the evolutionary naturalists of the nineteenth century attempted to solve these problems, and often (for want of scientific knowledge or of philosophical method) failed in their attempts.

The nineteenth-century adherents of the school rightly perceived that evolutionary biology must be able to give a naturalistic explanation of ethics; but in the absence of the knowledge we now possess they were often driven into forced or untenable positions. Their ignorance and their errors alike serve to delimit the problem more clearly and to warn us, their successors, against facile 'complete' explanations. In the light of the past, we can see that our present efforts cannot claim to provide a definitive or static solution, but may justly attempt to find a right direction along which analysis may advance.

The primary question of any naturalistic ethics is, as Quillian says, 'to resolve the puzzle of [the existence of] social conduct in originally egoistic individuals'. Hobbes advanced what seems to us the very transparent fiction[1] of a pre-existing social contract or covenant between the members of a community to delegate power to a single ruler or ruling body. It was to this contract, explicitly or implicitly recognized, that Hobbes ascribed the sense of obligation in morality—an ascription which will not work psychologically

---

[1] Betrand Russell suggests that Hobbes himself did not consider this covenant as an actual historical event, but as 'an explanatory myth'.

and is clearly not a true explanation. Locke, on the other hand (to whose views, by a remarkable oversight, Quillian does not refer at all), was the forerunner of the utilitarian theory of morals. 'Things are good or evil only in relation to pleasure or pain. That we call "good", which is apt to cause or increase pleasure, or diminish pain in us'— we seem to be hearing the voice of Jeremy Bentham, well over a century later.

In Bentham's philosophy the early naturalistic school attained its highest expression. This phase of naturalism inevitably looks primitive and over-simplified to our modern eyes, partly because of its lack of a full background of knowledge about nature in general, partly because of the lack of depth in its analysis of human nature in particular. Both were, I think, unavoidable in what we may justly call the pre-biological epoch, before Darwin had pointed the way to a history of life, Pasteur that to the essence of life, Claude Bernard that to an understanding of its mechanism, and Mendel, Bateson, and Morgan that to an understanding of its transmission—and one which was *a fortiori* pre-anthropological, before T. H. Huxley had underlined 'Man's Place in Nature', before Boucher de Perthes had opened a window on pre-history and Frazer on the primitive origin and bizarre development of ritual and religion, before Robertson Smith and Rivers and Malinowski had shown that human cultures could be a proper subject for scientific analysis, before Freud, Columbus-like, had discovered the New World of human mind in the shape of the Unconscious, and before the realization that with the advent of man, evolution had reached a new level, in which the biological agency of natural selection, operating through the mechanisms of heredity, had been largely suspended by the specifically human agency of social selection operating through the mechanisms of tradition.

The chief defect, by modern standards, of the early naturalistic school was that they tended to ignore (and indeed were largely ignorant of) the complexity of man's emotional structure, and accordingly not only took Reason at its face value or at its own value, but exaggerated its importance and its rôle. The apogee of this naïvely rationalist naturalism was reached by the Utilitarians. For Bentham, human psychology could be summed up in two principles—the principle of association, and the pleasure or happiness principle. The principle of association was supposed to account for the general structure of the mind, while the pleasure principle, according to which we consistently and consciously desire and pursue the end which we think will give us most pleasure or happiness, was supposed to account for its dynamics.

In passing, we may note that the first principle is inadequate, being only one of many components of mental structure; while the second is simply erroneous, for, as Bertrand Russell well puts it, 'Everybody's main activities are determined by desires' (or, one might preferably say, by impulses) 'which are anterior to the calculation of pleasures and pains'.

In his theory of ethics, Bentham fell into two further errors. In the first place, though the pleasure principle is intended as a statement of fact, he gave it an illegitimate ethical twist by saying that what gives pleasure or happiness is automatically what is good. He then proceeds to assert that the *summum bonum*, the ethical standard by which we must judge virtue in general, is the 'greatest happiness of the greatest number'. In spite of the attractiveness at first sight of this simple and apparently scientific formulation, it involves a fallacy, for it provides no means of bridging the gap between the individual and society. If each man inevitably pursues his own happiness, and if that happiness is good, we are still faced by the all-too-familiar fact that in pursuing their individual happinesses, men and women often come into conflict. And there cannot be any simple arithmetical balance of individual pleasures and pains to constitute a total social happiness. At the very least some objective standard, such as social well-being, is required; and to give effect to this you need a lawgiver or moralist of almost superhuman powers and one who will not be thinking in terms of his own happiness. The greatest happiness of the greatest number is, even on Bentham's own principles, no real standard at all: and Utilitarianism leaves unsolved one of the basic problems of ethics, the conflict between man as an individual and man as a social being, the antagonism of selfishness and altruism.

With the emergence of evolution as the central principle of biology, the situation at once changed. Even before the publication of the *Origin of Species*, Herbert Spencer had indicated the evolutionary theory of ethics which he later developed in his *Principles of Ethics*. He was the first to maintain the genetic principle that 'we must interpret the more developed by the less developed'. This, however, while at first sight appearing as a necessary corollary of evolution, and as such having been adopted by various evolutionary philosophers, is in fact a fallacy. This was clearly pointed out by Edward Caird over half-a-century ago, when he wrote in his *Evolution of Religion*, 'It lies in the very nature of the case that the earliest form of that which lives and develops is the least adequate to its nature, and therefore that from which we can get the least distinct clue to the main principle of that nature. Hence, to trace a living being [or, we may add, any product of a living being, such as ethics or religion] back to its beginning, and to explain what follows by such beginning, would be simply to omit almost all that characterizes it, and then to suppose that in what remains we have the secret of its existence. That is not really to explain it, but to explain it away'.

Most evolutionary naturalists of the present century have recognized the fallacy. I myself have on numerous occasions attacked the crude reasoning of the 'nothing-but' school—those, for instance, who on realizing that man is descended from a primitive ancestor, say that he is only a developed monkey; or on being persuaded that Freud's theories are correct, interpret all our higher mental activities in terms of sex. I shall not refer to it again here, except to say that Quillian seems to think that it is inherent in all evolutionary naturalistic systems. In this he is incorrect: as we shall see, the search for origins which not unnaturally so preoccupied the earlier evolutionists has now given place to the search for directions.

Herbert Spencer, like most ethical philosophers, attempted to find some fixed standard by which to measure good. His standard was the increasing length, and the increasing breadth or quantity, of life attained. This was, so far as I am aware, the first attempt to use a biological or evolutionary standard for human ethics. It cannot, however, be accepted—for one thing because it cannot in point of fact be measured or estimated, for another because even if it were, it would not distinguish between some of the less and the more desirable directions of evolution.

Darwin, on the other hand, sought the ethical yardstick in man's relation to society. He considered that obedience to the social instincts, as he called them, was moral, in contradistinction to the following of individual instincts, and ascribed the sense of moral obligation (the feeling that a man 'ought to regret his conduct' when he has followed one kind of instinct rather than the other, though both are equally 'natural') to the fact that the other-regarding instincts, though not more powerful than the self-regarding, are more permanent. Darwin thus faced the crucial problem of the feeling of duty. And though his solution of it was, it must be confessed, a feeble one, it was impossible for him or anyone else of his epoch to give an adequate naturalistic explanation of it.

W. K. Clifford, in his *Lectures and Essays*, put some of the implications of Darwin's views in more philosophical terms. The brilliance and wide range of intellect which he showed before his untimely death at the age of thirty-four makes one wonder what he might have achieved in the way of maturer synthesis if he had lived. His chief innovation was the introduction of the idea of a 'tribal self' which represents the biological needs of the tribe or other social unit as opposed to those of the individual. Clifford accepted the lamarckian view that sentiments could become hereditary and instinctive by long repetition (although he also ascribes considerable power to natural selection, in determining what particular sentiments shall become 'tribalized' in this way). Accordingly the 'tribal self' becomes embodied in conscience. And conscience is for him an instinct—'an instinctive desire for those things which conduce to the welfare of society'. Elsewhere he expressly asserts that 'the spring of virtuous action is the social instinct'.

In this the modern evolutionary naturalist finds three separate errors. First, instincts are quite certainly not inherited habits or sentiments; secondly, conscience is not an instinct in any sense in which that word can properly be used; and thirdly, he denies any virtue to purely individual activities. Nevertheless, it is his merit to have clearly pointed out the importance of the sentiments current in the social group for the development of conscience and of the social element in morality. He was thus among the first of the evolutionary social biologists.

Leslie Stephen developed this viewpoint in a very interesting way. For one thing, he rightly rejected all lamarckian views as to the origin of the moral sense. He uses the term 'social tissue' to denote the activities of men-in-society, of groups of individuals as social beings, not as units abstracted from their social surroundings. This is a somewhat unfortunate term, which Stephen used as a result of his acceptance of Comte's idea that a society is truly an organism; in point of fact, the organismic concept of society is largely metaphorical, and apt to mislead its adherents into forcing social concepts into a too narrowly biological mould. If Stephen, with his robust rationalism, could have had at his disposal the facts of modern social anthropology and sociology, we may hazard that he would have developed a much more satisfying view of the cohesive forces and transmissive mechanims of social existence. Even so, there is no sign that he realized the difficulty of that other basic problem of ethics—the compulsive nature of the sense of moral obligation. Here his rationalism was too robust.

He could write that 'morality is the sum of the preservative instincts of society, and presumably of those which imply a desire for the good of the society itself', without apparently noticing that such a definition leaves some of the most characteristic features of morality untouched.

For some unexplained reason, the only twentieth-century representatives of evolutionary naturalism adequately discussed by Quillian are Westermarck and L. T. Hobhouse. Westermarck's *Origin and Development of Moral Ideas* (1912-1917) was the first comprehensive treatment of morality on an anthropological basis, though Hobhouse in his *Morals in Evolution* (1915) wrote an important essay along similar lines. This school gives, first and foremost, an empirical account of the evolution of morality within human societies, rather than a philosophical explanation of the evolution of human morality from its pre-human origins.

Hobhouse is pre-eminent among the evolutionary naturalists in rejecting the 'nothing-but' line of approach, the attempt to explain the more developed entirely by the less developed. On the contrary, he refers to 'those most intimate and sure experiences which reveal the true capabilities of the human soul'. However, although his contributions to the theory of ethics include a strong ground storey, in the shape of a natural history of primitive morals, he did not join this up satisfactorily with his philosophic superstructure, nor was he specially concerned with the firmness of its biological and psychological foundations.

The same may broadly be said of Westermarck, though in his case the factual material from anthropology was much more extensive, and the philosophic superstructure quite different. In fact, the chief conclusion which he drew was the sceptical one of ethical relativity (fully developed in his book of 1932 with that title). Moral judgments are based on emotions; emotions lack objectivity; and the particular questions involved are derived from the particular social context in which they arise. 'Society is the birthplace of the moral consciousness. . . . The first moral judg-

067383

ments expressed emotions felt by the society at large'. In general, he denies any ultimate validity to any particular moral judgment.

I have discussed this question of ethical relativity in my lecture and in the notes thereon. We may summarize the modern position by saying that though the detailed development of studies on the natural history of morals seemed at one time to point to ethical chaos rather than true ethical relativity, their further analysis showed that this only applies to minor variations of ethical expression. On a broader view, systems of ethics are definitely correlated with the major type of society in which they are found. This relativity, however, does not imply mere arbitrariness and lack of objective validity for ethics. But in order to disentangle essential correlations from unessential variations, we must learn to think in terms of direction rather than of static and immutable standards. Here, it seems, Westermarck was confused by the multiplicity and variety of the valuable facts of moral natural history which he himself had done so much to discover and put on record.

This error was a natural and perhaps an inevitable one in the early history of a complex and largely inductive subject. It was precisely the same error which led many biologists, impressed by the multiplicity and variety of the evolutionary facts and principles unearthed since Darwin's day, to refuse validity to the idea of progress in evolution, and even to deny any meaning to the terms 'higher' and 'lower' in biology, in spite of the fact that these spring automatically to the mind in considering the difference between a mammal and a polyp, a daisy and a liverwort, a man and a fish.

In discussing this school of thought, with obvious intent to refute it, Quillian lays his chief stress on what he calls 'the crucial point in the moral theory of Evolutionary Naturalism'—'the transition from a purely descriptive account of the development of moral phenomena to a normative interpretation of morality'. That it is here he intends to make his stand is clear from the next sentence:—'Upon the validity of this transition depends the success of the attempt made by this school of philosophy to develop a non-religious theory of morality'. To illustrate his point concretely he writes of ethics as one of the normative sciences, 'The important question for ethics is: what is the distinguishing character of that which we judge to be morally good or right? Here the mediate, 'good', enters as a new notion which is superadded to, and is derived from, the logical or casual relations established by means of description'—though, as he later points out, a normative science may *also* be descriptive.

Personally, I should have thought that the important questions for ethics were, first, why right and wrong is accompanied by a sense of obligation, with its peculiar compulsive quality, and secondly, whether there is any standard, apart from our own judgments or those of our society, for such peculiar assumptions. I have already pointed out that Quillian appears to imagine that, because he has to his own satisfaction confuted the earlier crude advocates of the theory, no later extension of knowledge or refinement of analysis will be of avail. This is in truth nonsense: it is precisely the new discoveries of deep psychology and the refinement of analysis employed by modern evolutionary theory which have for the first time made it possible to put forward a satisfactory naturalistic theory of ethics.

Again, in one place he makes the extraordinary assertion that 'one element in the moral consciousness which cannot be explained by a genetic account and which is of highest importance is the rational element'. If this means anything, it means that human reason cannot be supposed to have originated naturally in the course of evolution, but must be due to Divine intervention—a conclusion with which few educated men would today agree!

He devotes a whole section to the fact that none of the 'evolutionary naturalists' whom he discusses can explain the sense of obligation, but does not mention that recent representatives of the school, notably Waddington and myself, have paid particular attention to the problem, and have suggested explanations which would account for it on naturalistic grounds.[1]

---

[1] If this were due to ignorance, it might be more excusable; but he cites Waddingon's work in his bibliography!

Finally, he dismisses all attempts to derive some external standard for rightness and wrongness from the facts of evolution by confuting some of the earlier and cruder ones, such as those based on utilitarianism. In particular, he makes no reference to recent analyses of the meaning of progress as an objective biological or evolutionary concept.

However, I do not propose to spend more time on Quillian's views. His work is only useful in bringing out the early history of the evolutionary theory of ethics, with all its errors and its inevitable imperfections. Further, he omits to mention certain other important contributions to a naturalistic and evolutionary system of ethics which were made during the late nineteenth century. Of these we must specially mention Marx's 'dialectical materialism' and its later development at the hands of Lenin, Trotsky, and other Russian Marxists. This was naturalistic in that it expressly repudiated any supernatural basis and any Absolute, and it was evolutionary in that it postulated existence as an irreversible process in time, each stage leading on to the next by the 'dialectical' mechanism of conflict and the reconciliation of opposites in a higher synthesis. But on both counts it was limited. In spite of the fact that Marx's main works were written well after the publication of the *Origin of Species*, the evolutionary concept is applied or illustrated almost exclusively from human society,[1]

[1] It is true that Engels later, in his *Dialectics of Nature*, adopted the view that matter, life, mind, and [human] society represented four successive evolutionary levels in the development of nature, and stressed the 'impossibility of carrying over biological laws bag and baggage from animals into human society. The fact of [human] production means that the supposed struggle for existence is no longer concerned solely with the means of existence as such, but more with the means of enjoyment and development'. (On this last point, by the way, Engels' remark is very similar to that of my grandfather, where he spoke of the 'struggle for enjoyment'). Further, as Needham points out in his *History Is on Our Side*, modern Marxism has regarded socialism as the inevitable continuation of the evolution of life as a whole. However, the Marxists never took the trouble to analyse the process of biological evolution in detail as a help in forming a general theory of evolution, but have preferred to 'interpret' them in terms of that general theory, namely, dialectical materialism—which has

0242034

and even within this field, Marx's naturalistic analysis was too restricted, in limiting the mechanism of social evolution to a class struggle, and one based only on economics. If only Marxism, before solidifying into a dogmatic system, could have assimilated the data and ideas of modern sociology and social anthropology, and had been willing to learn from biology instead of attempting to force biological facts into a dialectical strait-waistcoat, it would have been in an immensely stronger position. Its chief strength lay, and still lies, in applying a naturalistic theory of evolution to the interpretation of human history. And if the Marxists are to be blamed for these shortcomings, the evolutionary biologists of the nineteenth century deserve equal blame for failing to perceive that social evolution is a process differing radically from biological evolution, with its own laws and mechanisms and modalities, and not capable of explanation on purely biological postulates. Curiously enough this recognition of the limitations of biology was not adequately made until well on in the present century (e.g., by H. S. Jennings), though now the autonomy of social evolution is generally admitted.

In regard to the particular problem of ethics, though Marx regarded the 'dialectical' movement of history as pre-ordained and inevitable in broad outline, he also stressed the necessary rôle of human thought and will, human effort and sacrifice in bringing it about; and he further considered the fore-ordained end of the movement, the classless society, to be in some way good in itself, as well as providing the fullest bases for human well-being and happiness. Further, through his belief in the dialectical process, he considered that no real distinction was to be drawn between

the convenient property of being so elastic that it is applicable *post hoc* to almost any conceivable process of change.

While on this subject it should be pointed out that Engels' inclusion of mind as one of his emergent evolutionary levels is logically inadmissible. Mind is a subjective concept, and cannot take its place in a series of objective stages. What Engels presumably meant was the capacity of learning by experience or some similar comparatively high level of psycho-physical achievement; and if so, this would be perfectly admissible.

means and ends, since an objective which at one stage of the process is an end, may become a means once it is achieved. In this he is certainly correct—so long as existence is considered only as a progress in time and its final state accordingly regarded as the highest end. This is, however, to limit the idea of *end* to one aspect only—namely, the state which comes latest in time. Marxism fails to take account of the most basic of all the contradictions of our existence, which must somehow be reconciled in thought if we are to have a satisfactory philosophy, and in action if we are to lead a satisfactory life—namely, that between *end* as latest event and *end* as highest value; between individual life as part of a larger process, and as a series of events conferring varying degrees of satisfaction and fulfilment; between existence as a historical sequence in time and as a set of experiences to any of which time is largely irrelevant.

It is this failure which enabled the Russian Marxists of the early revolution, like Lenin and Trotsky[1], to take such a one-sided view of ethics. Thus Lenin could assert that: 'For us morality is wholly subordinated to the interests of the proletarian class struggle', and that 'We deny all morality taken from . . . non-class conceptions'. Again, Trotsky, in his interesting pamphlet, writes: 'A means can be justified only by its end. But the end in its turn needs to be justified. From the Marxist point of view . . . the end is justified if it leads to increasing the power of man over Nature and to the abolition of the power of man over man'. And of morality he says that we must acknowledge 'that morality is a product of social development; that there is nothing immutable about it; that it serves social interests; and these interests are contradictory; that morality more than any other form of ideology has a class character'. With most of this there will be general agreement, as with his argument that in war and revolution much of ordinary morality, including even the most universal command-

[1] See V. I. Lenin, *Religion*. London (Laurence and Wishart). L. Trotsky, *Their Morals and Ours*. New York (Pioneer Publishers).

ments such as those against killing and lying, is inevitably and rightly suspended, so that we cannot speak of any eternal or general laws of morality. But he disregards the origin of the moral sense in the development of each one of us, as well as the fact that some moral laws have a general basis (e.g., respect for the dignity of the individual) and that some ends are of the 'timeless' sort I have just referred to, which have value in themselves instead of as steps in the process of social evolution and therefore as means to something else.[1]

This reduction of morality to an organ useful to a particular group of men in a particular stage of society is, of course, part of Marx's general 'materialist conception of history', according to which the outlook and cultural achievement of any period, including its ethics, are resultants of its economic system. Here the Marxists seem to have exaggerated a real and important thesis into a dangerous 'nothing-but' principle. Man's ethics, like his art, *are* influenced by the economic state of society; but they are *not* wholly determined by it. A truly naturalistic theory must seek out every cause which contributes to form our ethics, and not concentrate on one alone.

IV

The modern period of evolutionary naturalism may be dated very precisely from the turn of the century, with the novel outlook of Freud in psychology and the Mendelians in biology.

If Freud hardly merits the title of the Newton of psychology, we may perhaps claim that he was its Copernicus, introducing into his science a radically new conception, though one which

[1] As a counterpart to Dean Swift's definitions of morality (p. 124) I cannot forbear from citing Trotsky's remarks on some of his social democratic opponents: 'The morals of these gentlemen consist of conventional precepts, and turns of speech which are supposed to screen their appetites, interests, and fears. . . . In the holy sphere of personal interests the end to them justifies any means. But it is precisely because of this that they require special codes of morals, variable and at the same time elastic, like good suspenders'.

was erroneous in many important details. For we must acknowledge that the greatest change since 1893 in our attitude towards the great problems of ethics has been due to the new facts and the new approach provided by modern psychology; and that in its turn owes its rise to the genius of Freud. It was two years after my grandfather's Romanes Lecture that Breuer and Freud, in their *Studien über Hysterie*, gave us the first crude map of the new psychological world of the Unconscious; and it was the last year of the nineteenth century which witnessed the publication of Freud's first independent book, in which he abandoned hypnosis for the slower but more effective methods of what we now call psycho-analysis.

The full effect of Freud's work did not begin to be felt until after the first World War. It then provoked counter-movements such as the schools of Jung and Adler, and led to spirited reactions on the part of more academic psychologists such as McDougall. But even where the conclusions of Freud were most vigorously denied or attacked, his genius had permeated. It is no longer possible for a psychologist to dispense with Freudian ideas, any more than it is possible for a biologist to dispense with Darwinian ideas.

I have treated in my lecture of the bearings of psycho-analysis on ethics. But there is another side to the picture—that of genetics. It is an interesting historical fact that the origin and early development of what we might call 'neo-psychology' was almost precisely contemporaneous with that of neo-Mendelism; and both, though in quite different ways, had the most profound effects not merely within their special sphere of research, but on general scientific thought and broad human outlook.

Freud's *Traumdeutung* was published in 1900, the same year that saw the re-discovery of Mendel's Laws. His theory reached the stage of general development in his *Vorlesungen zur Einführung in die Psychologie* in 1916, while neo-Mendelism reached the stage of generalization a year previously, with the publication of *The Mechanism of Mendelian Heredity* by Morgan, Sturtevant, Muller, and Bridges. The inter-war period saw the permeation of many fields and schools of psychology, and indeed of general sociology, by Freud's basic ideas of the unconscious and of repression, as well as witnessing the detailed development of psychoanalysis in the strict sense. In a similar way the same period witnessed an amazing development of neo-mendelian analysis, together with the permeation of other branches of biology, such as taxonomy, cytology, plant and animal breeding, eugenics, and general evolution theory, by the basic neo-mendelian ideas of particulate inheritance, mutation, and selection.

For our present purpose, modern genetics is of importance in several ways. It stresses the *fact* of man's immense genetic variability, and also the *value* of that fact, both for biological reasons and for its own sake. Ethics must include a respect for human difference; and the student of ethics must learn to discount the predispositions of those who, for inherent reasons of their genetic make-up, tend to attach either too much or too little importance to feelings of guilt and sin, or to desires for rational completeness of moral outlook. Further, it warns us against exclusive preoccupation either with environment or with heredity in studying the growth of the moral sense or in assessing moral praise or blame. For while it seems certain that environment (in the shape of a particular relation with a mother or mother-substitute during a particular period of infancy) is necessary for the formation of an effective moral sense, yet it is at least equally certain, on the basis both of what we know about psychological development in general and of observation and scientific analysis, that differences in moral sense may often be due, wholly or in part, to differen es in inherited (genetic) predisposition. Thus, in general, typical extroverts tend to have a different moral attitude from typical introverts: and Kretschmer and his followers have made out a good case for a general correlation of rigid puritanical morality with the (genetically determined) asthenic type of body-build.

To mention a recent example, E. and P. Slater[1] have shown that genetic predisposition exists towards neuroses and psychopathies, as well as summarizing similar evidence for schizophrenic and manic-depressive states. Different types of morality are associated with these various conditions: thus neurotics and psychopaths when tested were found to disapprove of more things, to be afraid of more things, and to enjoy fewer things, than normal people.

The relevance of all this is that while better upbringing in early infancy, better social and economic conditions, better education, a better and more rational moral code, and greater freedom and opportunity would undoubtedly do away with much unrealistic guilt and much exaggeration or distortion of moral sense, yet there will always exist differences of what we may call 'moral temperament'. Accordingly, there will be a considerable number of people who are 'sub-moral', or perhaps it would be better to say relatively amoral, with weak ethical tendencies; and the burden of prodding these up to an adequate intensity and level of ethical standards will always devolve on those with stronger moral predisposition. Per contra, there will always be a certain proportion of ultra-moral people, whose ethical zeal outruns society's needs, and requires to be moderated or restrained by those with a more reasonable moral temperament.

Modern genetics has also been important, in providing the basis for a comprehensive selectionist theory of evolution. Though the earlier Mendelians were anti-selectionist, the younger generation, with H. J. Muller as their protagonist, speedily perceived not only the logical necessity of natural selection, but its applicability in a mendelian universe. This was followed up by other workers, such as J. B. S. Haldane and Sewall Wright, and gereralized in 1930 by R. A. Fisher in his notable work *The Genetical Basis of Natural Selection*. The net result has been to establish

[1] *A Heuristic Theory of Neurosis*, J. Neurol. Neurosurg. Res. and Psychiatry 7:49 (1944); E. Slater, *Genetics and Psychiatry*, J. Ment. Sci. 90:17 (1944). See also M'Gill, V. J., *Types of Men and their Relation to Ethics*, Philos. and Phenom. 3: (1942-43).

selection not only as a positive factor in evolution, guiding and determining the type of change produced, but as the major factor. Mutation provides the raw material of evolution, but has little or no effect upon its direction or results. All other suggested natural agencies of evolution, such as Lamarckism or orthogenesis, have been shown to be untenable; and all non-naturalistic agencies, such as an *élan vital* or other vitalistic immanent tendencies, or Divine guidance, have been demonstrated to be quite unnecessary.

The further analysis of selection and its results led to additional progress. In the first place, as Muller first adequately pointed out, natural selection is 'a mechanism for generating an extremely high degree of improbability', to use R. A. Fisher's later epigram. Thus the existence of co-adaptations neither leads us, with the natural theologians, to postulate a Divine Designer, nor, with the later sceptics, to doubt the power of selection or to demand, like Cuénot, an 'unconscious purpose' (whatever that may mean!) in nature. On the contrary, the more complex or apparently improbable they are—like the human eye or a bird's wing—the better proof do they become for the moulding power of selection on evolving life.

Then it has been demonstrated that 'natural selection' is not uniform, but covers a number of agencies of biological change, differing in their methods and their results, and agreeing only in all leading to the differential survival of one type of individual or set of genes as against others. There is first the distinction between intra- and extra- (inter-) specific selection. The latter may involve a struggle for existence against the adverse forces of nature, or against other species, such as enemies or parasites. It in general promotes biological efficiency. Intra-specific selection, on the other hand, involves a struggle between members of the same species for something of which there is a limited supply, such as food, space, mates, or breeding territory; further, it is almost always unduly wasteful, it need not promote biological efficiency, and it may indeed (as with the intra-sexual struggle

for mates in polygamous forms) produce results which are deleterious from the standpoint of the general biology of the species.
Selection may also differ in sign according to conditions, being
negative or change-resisting in certain conditions, positive or
change-promoting in others.

A parallel development has been the analysis of the results of
evolution—the various trends observable within it. Once more,
it turned out that there is not one kind of trend only, but many.
The most important are the following: the non-adaptive, biologically random trends to be seen in small isolated populations;
small-scale adaptations; long-range adaptations or specializations
(including so-called degeneration, which is always an adaptation
to a special mode of life, such as parasitism); and true biological
progress. Of the large-scale adaptations, specialization is sharply
marked off from progress through its always and inevitably coming
to a limit, after which nothing but small-scale change is possible;
whereas after a progressive trend has been effected, the way is
still open to other large-scale changes.

Analysis of the particular line of progress leading to ourselves
shows that man is, even biologically speaking, a quite peculiar
and indeed unique organism (Huxley, *op. cit.*). Furthermore,
once he was definitely evolved, new methods of evolution came
to dominate the scene, taking over the major rôle in producing
change. In man, selection may still operate, but it is (except to
a minor degree) no longer natural selection in the proper sense,
involving differential survival of certain genetic types. Most
change is now produced by the differential survival of ideas or
machines or social systems. The (intra-specific) struggle for
existence between these may be very intense—as between rival
nomadic warlike tribes, or between modern 'super-states' in the
conditions of total war. Machin[1] gives many examples (notably
among the Red Indians) of the former and of its effects in developing a particular type of ethics and social code; and we have just

[1] Machin, Alfred, *What is Man?*

seen how powerful the results of the latter may be, in the virtually complete wiping out of the social system concerned with modern German culture in Europe.

Further, as my grandfather pointed out (p. 64), the struggle between individuals in human society is not a struggle for existence at all, but a 'struggle for the means of enjoyment'; and the winners in this struggle may be the losers in the subsidiary biological struggle for differential survival, as illustrated by the differential birth-rate as between classes of different wealth and status in recent industrial societies.

A further important contribution to the scientific background of ethics was made during the twentieth century by the social anthropologists, who pointed out, first the immense variety of ethical systems actually in vogue, many of them flatly contradicting each other in regard to the objects to which they attach the labels of right and wrong; secondly, the considerable rôle of chance or randomness in this; but thirdly, the existence of a broad general correlation between type of society and type of ethical system.

Thus the way was opened for an analysis of the evolution of human ethics, both as regards the trends which it has exhibited and the methods by which it has been brought about.

I have not referred to any influence of modern physics on our problem, for I do not consider that the influence is destined to remain. A. S. Eddington may have sought to safeguard the doctrine of free will and moral responsibility by appealing to the (extremely small!) degree of indeterminism resulting from Heisenberg's Uncertainty Principle: but I agree with Professor Stebbing in thinking that his reasoning was unsound and that neither Heisenberg's Principle nor any other of the peculiarities of modern quantum physics have any real relevance for the patterns of free will or morality.

On the contrary, it is the growth of biology which is shedding light on our problem. Modern physics is now seen to be a science of the highest degree of abstractness, abstracting from reality everything which cannot be dealt with mathematically. Biology, on the other hand, by demonstrating that man, albeit an extremely peculiar organism, has evolved from lower organisms by natural means, that all life is part of a single process, and that life must have developed from "not-life" during a peculiar phase of our planet's history, forces us to pay attention to a great many other attributes of reality—such as sensation, perception, emotion, rational insight, and purpose. We cannot abstract these from the biological facts without sacrificing something of biological reality, for they play an important rôle in the later reaches of biological evolution. Furthermore, in the final stage of evolution constituted by man, not only mind but values play an essential part. And if, as is undoubtedly the case, the biological facts are but part of a true unity of nature, then in failing to pay attention to these attributes, both those of mind and those of value, physicists are sacrificing something of reality in general. In a sense this is not their fault, for physics is a domain in which these attributes of reality are particularly imperceptible. However, now that biology has drawn attention to their validity as attributes of reality (or the world-stuff, if you prefer) when it has attained a certain level and type of organization, the physicists must give up trying to draw ultimate and general conclusions from physics alone. The field of physics is the best in which to study the properties of sub-atomic particles; but the field of animal and human biology is the best in which to study those of mind.

Finally, the introduction of the evolutionary idea has not only become basic to biology, by demonstrating that the whole of the phenomena of life can be looked at as a single process: it is becoming part of the general background of science as a whole. It is now possible to outline a generalized theory of evolution, which applies not only to plants and animals but also to inorganic matter on the one hand, and human societies on the other. Evolution in this extended sense is still a single process, though divisible into very distinct sectors. And in this single process both mind and values play their part in due course and ethics is seen not only as a product but also as an agency in the later history of the process.

Furthermore, since in the process of evolution values emerge, they must be taken into account by the scientist. We find values not merely emerging from the evolutionary process, but playing an active part in its latest phase; we know as an immediate and obvious fact that there are higher and lower values; we discover as a result of scientific analysis that there are more and less desirable or valuable directions in evolution. And so it comes about that, since the extended scientific world-view based on the theory of evolution must take account of mind and values, it is capable of performing a function which a purely physical world-view can never achieve: in addition to providing us with knowledge and an intellectual outlook and approach, it can give us guidance. It can thus aid in the construction of a scientific morality, whereas the contribution of physics to any new religious or general outlook is limited to one section of what we may call the theological aspect.

To these generalizations and their implications I shall return in the concluding section. Here, after this historical introduction, we can turn to what my grandfather actually wrote in 1893.

# I

## T. H. Huxley

# Evolution and Ethics

### (1) PROLEGOMENA

### [1894]

IT MAY be safely assumed that, two thousand years ago, before
Cæsar set foot in southern Britain, the whole country-side visible
from the windows of the room in which I write, was in what is
called 'the state of nature'. Except, it may be, by raising a few
sepulchral mounds, such as those which still, here and there,
break the flowing contours of the downs, man's hands had made
no mark upon it; and the thin veil of vegetation which overspread
the broad-backed heights and the shelving sides of the coombs
was unaffected by his industry. The native grasses and weeds,
the scattered patches of gorse, contended with one another for
the possession of the scanty surface soil; they fought against the
droughts of summer, the frosts of winter, and the furious gales
which swept, with unbroken force, now from the Atlantic, and
now from the North Sea, at all times of the year; they filled up,
as they best might, the gaps made in their ranks by all sorts of
underground and overground animal ravagers. One year with
another, an average population, the floating balance of the unceasing struggle for existence among the indigenous plants, maintained itself. It is as little to be doubted, that an essentially similar
state of nature prevailed, in this region, for many thousand years
before the coming of Cæsar; and there is no assignable reason

for denying that it might continue to exist through an equally prolonged futurity, except for the intervention of man.

Reckoned by our customary standards of duration, the native vegetation, like the 'everlasting hills' which it clothes, seems a type of permanence. The little Amarella Gentians, which abound in some places to-day, are the descendants of those that were trodden underfoot by the prehistoric savages who have left their flint tools about, here and there; and they followed ancestors which, in the climate of the glacial epoch, probably flourished better than they do now. Compared with the long past of this humble plant, all the history of civilized men is but an episode.

Yet nothing is more certain than that, measured by the liberal scale of time-keeping of the universe, this present state of nature, however it may seem to have gone and to go on for ever, is but a fleeting phase of her infinite variety; merely the last of the series of changes which the earth's surface has undergone in the course of the millions of years of its existence. Turn back a square foot of the thin turf, and the solid foundation of the land, exposed in cliffs of chalk five hundred feet high on the adjacent shore, yields full assurance of a time when the sea covered the site of the 'everlasting hills'; and when the vegetation of what land lay nearest, was as different from the present Flora of the Sussex Downs, as that of Central Africa now is.[1] No less certain is it that, between the time during which the chalk was formed and that at which the original turf came into existence, thousands of centuries elapsed, in the course of which, the state of nature of the ages during which the chalk was deposited, passed into that which now is, by changes so slow that, in the coming and going of the generations of men, had such witnessed them, the contemporary conditions would have seemed to be unchanging and unchangeable.

But it is also certain that, before the deposition of the chalk,

---

[1] See 'On a Piece of Chalk' in the preceding volume of these Essays (vol. viii, p. 1).

a vastly longer period had elapsed, throughout which it is easy to follow the traces of the same process of ceaseless modification and of the internecine struggle for existence of living things; and that even when we can get no further back, it is not because there is any reason to think we have reached the beginning, but because the trail of the most ancient life remains hidden, or has become obliterated.

Thus that state of nature of the world of plants, which we began by considering, is far from possessing the attribute of permanence. Rather its very essence is impermanence. It may have lasted twenty or thirty thousand years, it may last for twenty or thirty thousand years more, without obvious change; but, as surely as it has followed upon a very different state, so it will be followed by an equally different condition. That which endures is not one or another association of living forms, but the process of which the cosmos is the product, and of which these are among the transitory expressions. And in the living world, one of the most characteristic features of this cosmic process is the struggle for existence, the competition of each with all, the result of which is the selection, that is to say, the survival of those forms which, on the whole, are best adapted to the conditions which at any period obtain; and which are, therefore, in that respect, and only in that respect, the fittest.[1] The acme reached by the cosmic process in the vegetation of the downs is seen in the turf, with its weeds and gorse. Under the conditions, they have come out of the struggle victorious; and, by surviving, have proved that they are the fittest to survive.

That the state of nature, at any time, is a temporary phase of a process of incessant change, which has been going on for

[1] That every theory of evolution must be consistent not merely with progressive development, but with indefinite persistence in the same condition and with retrogressive modification, is a point which I have insisted upon repeatedly from the year 1862 till now. See *Collected Essays*, vol. ii, pp. 461-89; vol. iii, p. 33; vol. viii, p. 304. In the address on 'Geological Contemporaneity and Persistent Types' (1862), the paleontological proofs of this proposition were, I believe, first set forth.

innumerable ages, appears to me to be a proposition as well established as any in modern history. Paleontology assures us, in addition, that the ancient philosophers who, with less reason, held the same doctrine, erred in supposing that the phases formed a cycle, exactly repeating the past, exactly foreshadowing the future, in their rotations. On the contrary, it furnishes us with conclusive reasons for thinking that, if every link in the ancestry of these humble indigenous plants had been preserved and were accessible to us, the whole would present a converging series of forms of gradually diminishing complexity, until, at some period in the history of the earth, far more remote than any of which organic remains have yet been discovered, they would merge in those low groups among which the boundaries between animal and vegetable life become effaced.[1]

The word 'evolution', now generally applied to the cosmic process, has had a singular history, and is used in various senses.[2] Taken in its popular signification it means progressive development, that is, gradual change from a condition of relative uniformity to one of relative complexity; but its connotation has been widened to include the phenomena of retrogressive metamorphosis, that is, of progress from a condition of relative complexity to one of relative uniformity.

As a natural process, of the same character as the development of a tree from its seed, or of a fowl from its egg, evolution excludes creation and all other kinds of supernatural intervention. As the expression of a fixed order, every stage of which is the effect of causes operating according to definite rules, the conception of evolution no less excludes that of chance. It is very desirable to remember that evolution is not an explanation of the cosmic process, but merely a generalized statement of the method and results of that process. And, further, that, if there is proof that

---

[1] 'On the Border Territory between the Animal and the Vegetable Kingdoms', Essays, vol. viii, p. 162.
[2] See 'Evolution in Biology', Essays, vol. ii, p. 187.

the cosmic process was set going by any agent, then that agent will be the creator of it and of all its products, although supernatural intervention may remain strictly excluded from its further course.

So far as that limited revelation of the nature of things, which we call scientific knowledge, has yet gone, it tends, with constantly increasing emphasis, to the belief that, not merely the world of plants, but that of animals; not merely living things, but the whole fabric of the earth; not merely our planet, but the whole solar system; not merely our star and its satellites, but the millions of similar bodies which bear witness to the order which pervades boundless space, and has endured through boundless times; are all working out their predestined courses of evolution.

With none of these have I anything to do, at present, except with that exhibited by the forms of life which tenant the earth. All plants and animals exhibit the tendency to vary, the causes of which have yet to be ascertained; it is the tendency of the conditions of life, at any given time, while favouring the existence of the variations best adapted to them, to oppose that of the rest and thus to exercise selection; and all living things tend to multiply without limit, while the means of support are limited; the obvious cause of which is the production of offspring more numerous than their progenitors, but with equal expectation of life in the actuarial sense. Without the first tendency there could be no evolution. Without the second, there would be no good reason why one variation should disappear and another take its place; that is to say, there would be no selection. Without the third, the struggle for existence, the agent of the selective process in the state of nature, would vanish.[1]

Granting the existence of these tendencies, all the known facts of the history of plants and of animals may be brought into rational correlation. And this is more than can be said for any other hypothesis that I know of. Such hypotheses, for example,

[1] *Collected Essays*, vol. ii, *passim*.

as that of the existence of a primitive, orderless chaos; of a passive and sluggish eternal matter moulded, with but partial success, by archetypal ideas; of a brand-new world-stuff suddenly created and swiftly shaped by a supernatural power; receive no encouragement, but the contrary, from our present knowledge. That our earth may once have formed part of a nebulous cosmic magma is certainly possible, indeed seems highly probable; but there is no reason to doubt that order reigned there, as completely as amidst what we regard as the most finished works of nature or of man.[1] The faith which is born of knowledge, finds its object in an eternal order, bringing forth ceaseless change, through endless time, in endless space; the manifestations of the cosmic energy alternating between phases of potentiality and phases of explication. It may be that, as Kant suggests,[2] every cosmic magma predestined to evolve into a new world, has been the no less predestined end of a vanished predecessor.

## II

Three or four years have elapsed since the state of nature, to which I have referred, was brought to an end, so far as a small patch of the soil is concerned, by the intervention of man. The patch was cut off from the rest by a wall; within the area thus protected, the native vegetation was, as far as possible, extirpated; while a colony of strange plants was imported and set down in its place. In short, it was made into a garden. At the present time, this artificially treated area presents an aspect extraordinarily different from that of so much of the land as remains in the state of nature, outside the wall. Trees, shrubs, and herbs, many of them appertaining to the state of nature of remote parts of the globe, abound and flourish. Moreover, considerable quantities of vegetables, fruits, and flowers are produced, of kinds which

[1] *Ibid.*, vol. iv, p. 138; vol. v, pp. 71-73.
[2] *Ibid.*, vol. viii, p. 321.

neither now exist, nor have ever existed, except under conditions
such as obtain in the garden; and which, therefore, are as much
works of the art of man as the frames and glass-houses in which
some of them are raised. That the 'state of Art', thus created in
the state of nature by man, is sustained by and dependent on him,
would at once become apparent, if the watchful supervision of
the gardener were withdrawn, and the antagonistic influences of
the general cosmic process were no longer sedulously warded off,
or counteracted. The walls and gates would decay; quadrupedal
and bipedal intruders would devour and tread down the useful
and beautiful plants; birds, insects, blight, and mildew would
work their will; the seeds of the native plants, carried by winds
or other agencies, would immigrate, and in virtue of their long-
earned special adaptation to the local conditions, these despised
native weeds would soon choke their choice exotic rivals. A century or two hence, little beyond the foundations of the wall and
of the houses and frames would be left, in evidence of the victory
of the cosmic powers at work in the state of nature, over the
temporary obstacles to their supremacy, set up by the art of the
horticulturist.

It will be admitted that the garden is as much a work of art,[1]
or artifice, as anything that can be mentioned. The energy localized
in certain human bodies, directed by similarly localized intellects,
has produced a collocation of other material bodies which could
not be brought about in the state of nature. The same proposition
is true of all the works of man's hands, from a flint implement
to a cathedral or a chronometer; and it is because it is true, that
we call these things artificial, term them works of art, or artifice,
by way of distinguishing them from the products of the cosmic
process, working outside man, which we call natural, or works
of nature. The distinction thus drawn between the works of nature

---

[1] The sense of the term 'Art' is becoming narrowed; 'work of Art' to most
people means a picture, a statue, or a piece of *bijouterie*; by way of compensation
'artist' has included in its wide embrace cooks and ballet girls, no less than
painters and sculptors.

and those of man, is universally recognized; and it is, as I conceive, both useful and justifiable.

III

No doubt, it may be properly urged that the operation of human energy and intelligence, which has brought into existence and maintains the garden, by what I have called 'the horticultural process', is, strictly speaking, part and parcel of the cosmic process. And no one could more readily agree to that proposition than I. In fact, I do not know that any one has taken more pains than I have, during the last thirty years, to insist upon the doctrine, so much reviled in the early part of that period, that man, physical, intellectual, and moral, is as much a part of nature, as purely a product of the cosmic process, as the humblest weed.[1]

But if, following up this admission, it is urged that, such being the case, the cosmic process cannot be in antagonism with that horticultural process which is part of itself—I can only reply, that if the conclusion that the two are antagonistic is logically absurd, I am sorry for logic, because, as we have seen, the fact is so. The garden is in the same position as every other work of man's art; it is a result of the cosmic process working through and by human energy and intelligence; and, as is the case with every other artificial thing set up in the state of nature, the influences of the latter are constantly tending to break it down and destroy it. No doubt, the Forth bridge and an ironclad in the offing, are, in ultimate resort, products of the cosmic process; as much so as the river which flows under the one, or the sea-water on which the other floats. Nevertheless, every breeze strains the bridge a little, every tide does something to weaken its foundations; every change of temperature alters the adjustment of its parts, produces friction and consequent wear and tear. From time to time, the

[1] See 'Man's Place in Nature', *Collected Essays,* vol. vii ,and 'On the Struggle for Existence in Human Society' (1888).

bridge must be repaired, just as the ironclad must go into dock; simply because nature is always tending to reclaim that which her child, man, has borrowed from her and has arranged in combinations which are not those favoured by the general cosmic process.

Thus, it is not only true that the cosmic energy, working through man upon a portion of the plant world, opposes the same energy as it works through the state of nature, but a similar antagonism is everywhere manifest between the artificial and the natural. Even in the state of nature itself, what is the struggle for existence but the antagonism of the results of the cosmic process in the region of life, one to another?[1]

IV

Not only is the state of nature hostile to the state of art of the garden; but the principle of the horticultural process, by which the latter is created and maintained, is antithetic to that of the cosmic process. The characteristic feature of the latter is the intense and unceasing competition of the struggle for existence. The characteristic of the former is the elimination of that struggle, by the removal of the conditions which give rise to it. The tendency of the cosmic process is to bring about the adjustment of the forms of plant life to the current conditions; the tendency of the horticultural process is the adjustment of the conditions to the needs of the forms of plant life which the gardener desires to raise.

The cosmic process uses unrestricted multiplication as the means whereby hundreds compete for the place and nourishment adequate for one; it employs frost and drought to cut off the weak and unfortunate; to survive, there is need not only of strength, but of flexibility and of good fortune.

The gardener, on the other hand, restricts multiplication; pro-

[1] Or to put the case still more simply. When a man lays hold of the two ends of a piece of string and pulls them, with intent to break it, the right arm is certainly exerted in antagonism to the left arm; yet both arms derive their energy from the same original source.

vides that each plant shall have sufficient space and nourishment; protects from frost and drought; and, in every other way, attempts to modify the conditions, in such a manner as to bring about the survival of those forms which most nearly approach the standard of the useful, or the beautiful, which he has in his mind.

If the fruits and the tubers, the foliage and the flowers thus obtained, reach, or sufficiently approach, that ideal, there is no reason why the *status quo* attained should not be indefinitely prolonged. So long as the state of nature remains approximately the same, so long will the energy and intelligence which created the garden suffice to maintain it. However, the limits within which this mastery of man over nature can be maintained are narrow. If the conditions of the cretaceous epoch returned, I fear the most skilful of gardeners would have to give up the cultivation of apples and gooseberries; while, if those of the glacial period once again obtained, open asparagus beds would be superfluous, and the training of fruit trees against the most favourable of south walls, a waste of time and trouble.

But it is extremely important to note that, the state of nature remaining the same, if the produce does not satisfy the gardener, it may be made to approach his ideal more closely. Although the struggle for existence may be at end, the possibility of progress remains. In discussions on these topics, it is often strangely forgotten that the essential conditions of the modification, or evolution, of living things are variation and hereditary transmission. Selection is the means by which certain variations are favoured and their progeny preserved. But the struggle for existence is only one of the means by which selection may be effected. The endless varieties of cultivated flowers, fruits, roots, tubers, and bulbs are not products of selection by means of the struggle for existence, but of direct selection, in view of an ideal of utility or beauty. Amidst a multitude of plants, occupying the same station and subjected to the same conditions, in the garden, varieties arise. The varieties tending in a given direction are preserved, and the rest are destroyed. And the same process takes place among the varieties until, for example, the wild kale becomes a cabbage, or the wild *Viola tricolor* a prize pansy.

V

The process of colonization presents analogies to the formation of a garden which are highly instructive. Suppose a shipload of English colonists sent to form a settlement, in such a country as Tasmania was in the middle of the last century. On landing, they find themselves in the midst of a state of nature, widely different from that left behind them in everything but the most general physical conditions. The common plants, the common birds and quadrupeds, are as totally distinct as the men from anything to be seen on the side of the globe from which they come. The colonists proceed to put an end to this state of things over as large an area as they desire to occupy. They clear away the native vegetation, extirpate or drive out the animal population, so far as may be necessary, and take measures to defend themselves from the re-immigration of either. In their place, they introduce English grain and fruit trees; English dogs, sheep, cattle, horses; and English men; in fact, they set up a new Flora and Fauna and a new variety of mankind, within the old state of nature. Their farms and pastures represent a garden on a great scale, and themselves the gardeners who have to keep it up, in watchful antagonism to the old régime. Considered as a whole, the colony is a composite unit introduced into the old state of nature; and, thenceforward, a competitor in the struggle for existence, to conquer or be vanquished.

Under the conditions supposed, there is no doubt of the result, if the work of the colonists be carried out energetically and with intelligent combination of all their forces. On the other hand, if they are slothful, stupid, and careless; or if they waste their energies in contests with one another, the chances are that the old state of nature will have the best of it. The native savage will destroy the immigrant civilized man; of the English animals and plants some will be extirpated by their indigenous rivals, others will pass into the feral state and themselves become components of the state of nature. In a few decades, all other traces of the settlement will have vanished.

VI

Let us now imagine that some administrative authority, as far superior in power and intelligence to men, as men are to their cattle, is set over the colony, charged to deal with its human elements in such a manner as to assure the victory of the settlement over the antagonistic influences of the state of nature in which it is set down. He would proceed in the same fashion as that in which the gardener dealt with his garden. In the first place, he would, as far as possible, put a stop to the influence of external competition by thoroughly extirpating and excluding the native rivals, whether men, beasts, or plants. And our administrator would, select his human agents, with a view to his ideal of a successful colony, just as the gardener selects his plants with a view to his ideal of useful or beautiful products.

In the second place, in order that no struggle for the means of existence between these human agents should weaken the efficiency of the corporate whole in the battle with the state of nature, he would make arrangements by which each would be provided with those means; and would be relieved from the fear of being deprived of them by his stronger or more cunning fellows. Laws, sanctioned by the combined force of the colony, would restrain the self-assertion of each man within the limits required for the maintenance of peace. In other words, the cosmic struggle for existence, as between man and man, would be rigorously suppressed; and selection, by its means, would be as completely excluded as it is from the garden.

At the same time, the obstacles to the full development of the capacities of the colonists by other conditions of the state of nature than those already mentioned, would be removed by the creation of artificial conditions of existence of a more favourable character. Protection against extremes of heat and cold would be afforded by houses and clothing; drainage and irrigation works would antagonize the effects of excessive rain and excessive drought; roads, bridges, canals, carriages, and ships would overcome the natural obstacles to locomotion and transport; mechanical engines would supplement the natural strength of men and of their draught animals; hygienic precautions would check, or remove, the natural causes of disease. With every step of this progress in civilization, the colonists would become more and more independent of the state of nature; more and more, their lives would be conditioned by a state of art. In order to attain his ends, the administrator would have to avail himself of the courage, industry, and co-operative intelligence of the settlers; and it is plain that the interest of the community would be best served by increasing the proportion of persons who possess such qualities, and diminishing that of persons devoid of them. In other words, by selection directed towards an ideal.

Thus the administrator might look to the establishment of an earthly paradise, a true garden of Eden, in which all things should work together towards the well-being of the gardeners: within which the cosmic process, the coarse struggle for existence of the state of nature, should be abolished; in which that state should be replaced by a state of art; where every plant and every lower animal should be adapted to human wants, and would perish if human supervision and protection were withdrawn; where men themselves should have been selected, with a view to their efficiency as organs for the performance of the functions of a perfected society. And this ideal policy would have been brought about, not by gradually adjusting the men to the conditions around them, but by creating artificial conditions for them; not by allowing the free play of the struggle for existence, but by excluding that struggle; and by substituting selection directed towards the administrator's ideal for the selection it exercises.

## VII

But the Eden would have its serpent, and a very subtle beast too. Man shares with the rest of the living world the mighty instinct of reproduction and its consequence, the tendency to multiply with great rapidity. The better the measures of the administrator achieved their object, the more completely the destructive agencies of the state of nature were defeated, the less would that multiplication be checked.

On the other hand, within the colony, the enforcement of peace, which deprives every man of the power to take away the means of existence from another, simply because he is the stronger, would have put an end to the struggle for existence between the colonists, and the competition for the commodities of existence, which would alone remain, is no check upon population.

Thus, as soon as the colonists began to multiply, the administrator would have to face the tendency to the reintroduction of the cosmic struggle into his artificial fabric, in consequence of the competition, not merely for the commodities, but for the means of existence. When the colony reached the limit of possible expansion, the surplus population must be disposed of somehow; or the fierce struggle for existence must recommence and destroy that peace, which is the fundamental condition of the maintenance of the state of art against the state of nature.

Supposing the administrator to be guided by purely scientific considerations, he would, like the gardener, meet this most serious difficulty by systematic extirpation, or exclusion, of the superfluous. The hopelessly diseased, the infirm, aged, the weak or deformed in body or in mind, the excess of infants born, would be put away, as the gardener pulls up defective and superfluous plants, or the breeder destroys undesirable cattle. Only the strong and the healthy, carefully matched, with a view to the progeny best adapted to the purposes of the administrator, would be permitted to perpetuate their kind.

VIII

Of the more thoroughgoing of the multitudinous attempts to apply the principles of cosmic evolution, or what are supposed to be such, to social and political problems, which have appeared of late years, a considerable proportion appear to me to be based upon the notion that human society is competent to furnish, from its own resources, an administrator of the kind I have imagined. The pigeons, in short, are to be their own Sir John Sebright.[1] A despotic government, whether individual or collective, is to be endowed with the preternatural intelligence, and with what, I am afraid, many will consider the preternatural ruthlessness, required for the purpose of carrying out the principle of improvement by selection, with the somewhat drastic thoroughness upon which the success of the method depends. Experience certainly does not justify us in limiting the ruthlessness of individual 'saviours of society'; and, on the well-known grounds of the aphorism which denies both body and soul to corporations, it seems probable (indeed the belief is not without support in history) that a collective despotism, a mob got to believe in its own divine right by demagogic missionaries, would be capable of more thorough work in this direction than any single tyrant, puffed up with the same illusion, has ever achieved. But intelligence is another affair. The fact that 'saviours of society' take to that trade is evidence enough that they have none to spare. And such as they possess is generally sold to the capitalists of physical force on whose resources they depend. However, I doubt whether even the keenest judge of

[1] Not that the conception of such a society is necessarily based upon the idea of evolution. The Platonic state testifies to the contrary.

character, if he had before him a hundred boys and girls under fourteen, could pick out, with the least chance of success, those who should be kept, as certain to be serviceable members of the polity, and those who should be chloroformed, as equally sure to be stupid, idle, or vicious. The 'points' of a good or of a bad citizen are really far harder to discern than those of a puppy or a short-horn calf; many do not show themselves before the practical difficulties of life stimulate manhood to full exertion. And by that time the mischief is done. The evil stock, if it be one, has had time to multiply, and selection is nullified.

IX

I have other reasons for fearing that this logical ideal of evolutionary regimentation—this pigeon-fanciers' polity—is unattainable. In the absence of any such a severely scientific administrator as we have been dreaming of, human society is kept together by bonds of such a singular character, that the attempt to perfect society after his fashion would run serious risk of loosening them.

Social organization is not peculiar to men. Other societies, such as those constituted by bees and ants, have also arisen out of the advantage of co-operation in the struggle for existence; and their resemblances to, and their differences from, human society are alike instructive. The society formed by the hive bee fulfils the ideal of the communistic aphorism 'to each according to his needs, from each according to his capacity'. Within it, the struggle for existence is strictly limited. Queen, drones, and workers have each their allotted sufficiency of food; each performs the function assigned to it in the economy of the hive, and all contribute to the success of the whole co-operative society in its competition with rival collectors of nectar and pollen and with other enemies, in the state of nature without. In the same sense as the garden, or the colony, is a work of human art, the bee polity is a work of apiarian art, brought about by the cosmic process, working through the organization of the hymenopterous type.

Now this society is the direct product of an organic necessity, impelling every member of it to a course of action which tends to the good of the whole. Each bee has its duty and none has any rights. Whether bees are susceptible of feeling and capable of thought is a question which cannot be dogmatically answered. As a pious opinion, I am disposed to deny them more than the merest rudiments of consciousness.[1] But it is curious to reflect that a thoughtful drone (workers and queens would have no leisure for speculation) with a turn for ethical philosophy, must needs profess himself an intuitive moralist of the purest water. He would point out, with perfect justice, that the devotion of the workers to a life of ceaseless toil for a mere subsistence wage, cannot be accounted for either by enlightened selfishness, or by any other sort of utilitarian motives; since these bees begin to work, without experience or reflection, as they emerge from the cell in which they are hatched. Plainly, an eternal and immutable principle, innate in each bee, can alone account for the phenomena. On the other hand, the biologist, who traces out all the extant stages of gradation between solitary and hive bees, as clearly sees in the latter, simply the perfection of an automatic mechanism, hammered out by the blows of the struggle for existence upon the progeny of the former, during long ages of constant variation.

## X

I see no reason to doubt that, at its origin, human society was as much a product of organic necessity as that of the bees.[2] The human family, to begin with, rested upon exactly the same conditions as those which gave rise to similar associations among

[1] *Collected Essays*, vol. i, 'Animal Automatism'; vol. v., 'Prologue', pp. 45 *et seq.*
[2] *Collected Essays*, vol. v., Prologue, pp. 50-54.

animals lower in the scale. Further, it is easy to see that every increase in the duration of the family ties, with the resulting co-operation of a larger and larger number of descendants for protection and defence, would give the families in which such modification took place a distinct advantage over the others. And, as in the hive, the progressive limitation of the struggle for existence between the members of the family would involve increasing efficiency as regards outside competition.

But there is this vast and fundamental difference between bee society and human society. In the former, the members of the society are each organically predestined to the performance of one particular class of functions only. If they were endowed with desires, each could desire to perform none but those offices for which its organization specially fits it; and which, in view of the good of the whole, it is proper it should do. So long as a new queen does not make her appearance, rivalries and competition are absent from the bee polity.

Among mankind, on the contrary, there is no such predestination to a sharply defined place in the social organism. However much men may differ in the quality of their intellects, the intensity of their passions, and the delicacy of their sensations, it cannot be said that one is fitted by his organization to be an agricultural labourer and nothing else, and another to be a landowner and nothing else. Moreover, with all their enormous differences in natural endowment, men agree in one thing, and that is their innate desire to enjoy the pleasures and to escape the pains of life; and, in short, to do nothing but that which it pleases them to do, without the least reference to the welfare of the society into which they are born. That is their inheritance (the reality at the bottom of the doctrine of original sin) from the long series of ancestors, human and semi-human and brutal, in whom the strength of this innate tendency to self-assertion was the condition of victory in the struggle for existence. That is the reason of the *aviditas vitæ*[1]—the insatiable hunger for enjoyment—of all mankind, which is one of the essential conditions of success in the war with the state of nature outside; and yet the sure agent of the destruction of society if allowed free play within.

The check upon this free play of self-assertion, or natural liberty, which is the necessary condition for the origin of human society, is the product of organic necessities of a different kind from those upon which the constitution of the hive depends. One of these is the mutual affection of parent and offspring, intensified by the long infancy of the human species. But the most important is the tendency, so strongly developed in man, to reproduce in himself actions and feelings similar to, or correlated with, those of other men. Man is the most consummate of all mimics in the animal world; none but himself can draw or model; none comes near him in the scope, variety, and exactness of vocal imitation; none is such a master of gesture; while he seems to be impelled thus to imitate for the pure pleasure of it. And there is no such another emotional chameleon. By a purely reflex operation of the mind, we take the hue of passion of those who are about us, or, it may be, the complementary colour. It is not by any conscious 'putting one's self in the place' of a joyful or a suffering person that the state of mind we call sympathy usually arises;[2] indeed, it is often contrary to one's sense of right, and in spite of one's will, that 'fellow-feeling makes us wondrous kind' or the reverse. However complete may be the indifference to public opinion, in a cool, intellectual view, of the traditional sage, it has not yet been my fortune to meet with any actual sage who took its hostile manifestations with entire equanimity. Indeed, I doubt

[1] See below. Romanes Lecture, note 7.

[2] Adam Smith makes the pithy observation that the man who sympathizes with a woman in childbed, cannot be said to put himself in her place. ('The Theory of the Moral Sentiments', Part vii, sec. iii, chap. i.) Perhaps there is more humour than force in the example; and, in spite of this and other observations of the same tenor, I think that the one defect of the remarkable work in which it occurs is that it lays too much stress on conscious substitution, too little on purely reflex sympathy.

if the philosopher lives, or ever has lived, who could know himself to be heartily despised by a street boy without some irritation. And, though one cannot justify Haman for wishing to hang Mordecai on such a very high gibbet, yet, really, the consciousness of the Vizier of Ahasuerus, as he went in and out of the gate, that this obscure Jew had no respect for him, must have been very annoying.[1]

It is needful only to look around us, to see that the greatest restrainer of the anti-social tendencies of men is fear, not of the law, but of the opinion of their fellows. The conventions of honour bind men who break legal, moral, and religious bonds; and, while people endure the extremity of physical pain rather than part with life, shame drives the weakest to suicide.

Every forward step of social progress brings men into closer relations with their fellows, and increases the importance of the pleasures and pains derived from sympathy. We judge the acts of others by our own sympathies, and we judge our own acts by the sympathies of others, every day and all day long, from childhood upwards, until associations, as indissoluble as those of language, are formed between certain acts and the feelings of approbation or disapprobation. It becomes impossible to imagine some acts without disapprobation, or others without approbation of the actor, whether he be one's self, or any one else. We come to think in the acquired dialect of morals. An artificial personality, the 'man within', as Adam Smith[2] calls conscience, is built up beside the natural personality. He is the watchman of society, charged to restrain the anti-social tendencies of the natural man within the limits required by social welfare.

---

[1] Esther v, 9-13. ' . . . but when Haman saw Mordecai in the king's gate, that he stood not up, nor moved for him, he was full of indignation against Mordecai. . . . And Haman told them of the glory of his riches. . . . and all the things wherein the king had promoted him. . . . Yet all this availeth me nothing, so long as I see Mordecai the Jew sitting at the king's gate'. What a shrewd exposure of human weakness it is!

[2] Theory of the Moral Sentiments', Part iii, chap. 3. *On the influence and authority of conscience.*

## XI

I have termed this evolution of the feelings out of which the primitive bonds of human society are so largely forged, into the organized and personified sympathy we call conscience, the ethical process.[1] So far as it tends to make any human society more efficient in the struggle for existence with the state of nature, or with other societies, it works in harmonious contrast with the cosmic process.[1] But it is none the less true that, since law and morals are restraints upon the struggle for existence between men in society, the ethical process is in opposition to the principle of the cosmic process, and tends to the suppression of the qualities best fitted for success in that struggle.[2]

It is further to be observed that, just as the self-assertion, necessary to the maintenance of society against the state of nature, will destroy that society if it is allowed free operation within; so the self-restraint, the essence of the ethical process, which is no less an essential condition of the existence of every polity, may, by excess, become ruinous to it.

Moralists of all ages and of all faiths, attending only to the relations of men towards one another in an ideal society, have agreed upon the 'golden rule', 'Do as you would be done by'. In other words, let sympathy be your guide; put yourself in the place of the man towards whom your action is directed; and do to him what you would like to have done to yourself under the circumstances. However much one may admire the generosity of such a rule of conduct; however confident one may be that average men may be thoroughly depended upon not to carry it out to its full logical consequences; it is nevertheless desirable to recognize the

[1] Worked out, in its essential features, chiefly by Hartley and Adam Smith, long before the modern doctrine of evolution was thought of. See *Note* below, p. 60.

[2] See the essay 'On the Struggle for Existence in Human Society' below, and *Collected Essays*, vol. i, p. 276, for Kant's recognition of these facts.

fact that these consequences are incompatible with the existence of a civil state, under any circumstances of this world which have obtained, or, so far as one can see, are, likely to come to pass.

For I imagine there can be no doubt that the great desire of every wrongdoer is to escape from the painful consequences of his actions. If I put myself in the place of the man who has robbed me, I find that I am possessed by an exceeding desire not to be fined or imprisoned; if in that of the man who has smitten me on one cheek, I contemplate with satisfaction the absence of any worse result than the turning of-the other cheek for like treatment. Strictly observed, the 'golden rule' involves the negation of law by the refusal to put it in motion against law-breakers; and, as regards the external relations of a polity, it is the refusal to continue the struggle for existence. It can be obeyed, even partially, only under the protection of a society which repudiates it. Without such shelter, the followers of the 'golden rule' may indulge in hopes of heaven, but they must reckon with the certainty that other people will be masters of the earth.

What would become of the garden if the gardener treated all the weeds and slugs and birds and trespassers as he would like to be treated, if he were in their place?

XII

Under the preceding heads, I have endeavoured to represent in broad, but I hope faithful, outlines the essential features of the state of nature and of that cosmic process of which it is the outcome, so far as was needful for my argument; I have contrasted with the state of nature the state of art, produced by human intelligence and energy, as it is exemplified by a garden; and I have shown that the state of art, here and elsewhere, can be maintained only by the constant counteraction of the hostile influences of the state of nature. Further, I have pointed out that the 'horticultural process' which thus sets itself against the 'cosmic process' is opposed to the latter in principle, in so far as it tends to arrest the struggle for existence, by restraining the multiplication which is one of the chief causes of that struggle, and by creating artificial conditions of life, better adapted to the cultivated plants than are the conditions of the state of nature. And I have dwelt upon the fact that, though the progressive modification, which is the consequence of the struggle for existence in the state of nature, is at an end, such modification may still be effected by that selection, in view of an ideal of usefulness, or of pleasantness, to man, of which the state of nature knows nothing.

I have proceeded to show that a colony, set down in a country in the state of nature, presents close analogies with a garden; and I have indicated the course of action which an administrator, able and willing to carry out horticultural principles, would adopt, in order to secure the success of such a newly formed polity, supposing it to be capable of indefinite expansion. In the contrary case, I have shown that difficulties must arise; that the unlimited increase of the population over a limited area must, sooner or later, reintroduce into the colony that struggle for the means of existence between the colonists, which it was the primary object of the administrator to exclude, insomuch as it is fatal to the mutual peace which is the prime condition of the union of men in society.

I have briefly described the nature of the only radical cure, known to me, for the disease which would thus threaten the existence of the colony; and, however regretfully, I have been obliged to admit that this rigorously scientific method of applying the principles of evolution to human society hardly comes within the region of practical politics; not for want of will on the part of a great many people; but because, for one reason, there is no hope that mere human beings will ever possess enough intelligence to select the fittest. And I have adduced other grounds for arriving at the same conclusion.

I have pointed out that human society took its rise in the organic necessities expressed by imitation and by the sympathetic emotions;

and that, in the struggle for existence with the state of nature and with other societies, as part of it, those in which men were thus led to close co-operation had a great advantage.[1] But, since each man retained more or less of the faculties common to all the rest, and especially a full share of the desire for unlimited self-gratification, the struggle for existence within society could only be gradually eliminated. So long as any of it remained, society continued to be an imperfect instrument of the struggle for existence and, consequently, was improvable by the selective influence of that struggle. Other things being alike, the tribe of savages in which order was best maintained; in which there was most security within the tribe and the most loyal mutual support outside it, would be the survivors.

I have termed this gradual strengthening of the social bond, which, though it arrests the struggle for existence inside society, up to a certain point improves the chances of society, as a corporate whole, in the cosmic struggle—the ethical process. I have endeavoured to show that, when the ethical process has advanced so far as to secure every member of the society in the possession of the means of existence, the struggle for existence, as between man and man, within that society is, *ipso facto*, at an end. And, as it is undeniable that the most highly civilized societies have substantially reached this position, it follows that, so far as they are concerned, the struggle for existence can play no important part within them.[2] In other words, the kind of evolution which is brought about in the state of nature cannot take place.

I have further shown cause for the belief that direct selection, after the fashion of the horticulturist and the breeder, neither has played, nor can play, any important part in the evolution of society;

[1] *Collected Essays*, vol. v, Prologue, p. 52.
[2] Whether the struggle for existence with the state of nature and with other societies, so far as they stand in the relation of the state of nature with it, exerts a selective influence upon modern society, and in what direction, are questions not easy to answer. The problem of the effect of military and industrial warfare upon those who wage it is very complicated.

apart from other reasons, because I do not see how such selection could be practised without a serious weakening, it may be the destruction, of the bonds which hold society together. It strikes me that men who are accustomed to contemplate the active or passive extirpation of the weak, the unfortunate, and the superfluous; who justify that conduct on the ground that it has the sanction of the cosmic process, and is the only way of ensuring the progress of the race; who, if they are consistent, must rank medicine among the black arts and count the physician a mischievous preserver of the unfit; on whose matrimonial undertakings the principles of the stud have the chief influence; whose whole lives, therefore, are an education in the noble art of suppressing natural affection and sympathy, are not likely to have any large stock of these commodities left. But, without them, there is no conscience, nor any restraint on the conduct of men, except the calculation of self-interest, the balancing of certain present gratifications against doubtful future pains; and experience tells us how much that is worth. Every day, we see firm believers in the hell of the theologians commit acts by which, as they believe when cool, they risk eternal punishment; while they hold back from those which are opposed to the sympathies of their associates.

### XIII

That progressive modification of civilization which passes by the name of the 'evolution of society', is, in fact, a process of an essentially different character, both from that which brings about the evolution of species, in the state of nature, and from that which gives rise to the evolution of varieties, in the .    of art.

There can be no doubt that vast changes have taken place in English civilization since the reign of the Tudors. But I am not aware of a particle of evidence in favour of the conclusion that this evolutionary process has been accompanied by any modification of the physical, or the mental, characters of the men who have been the subjects of it. I have not met with any grounds for suspecting that the average Englishmen of to-day are sensibly different from those that Shakspere knew and drew. We look into his magic mirror of the Elizabethan age, and behold, nowise darkly, the presentment of ourselves.

During these three centuries, from the reign of Elizabeth to that of Victoria, the struggle for existence between man and man has been so largely restrained among the great mass of the population (except for one or two short intervals of civil war), that it can have had little, or no, selective operation. As to anything comparable to direct selection, it has been practised on so small a scale that it may also be neglected. The criminal law, in so far as by putting to death, or by subjecting to long periods of imprisonment, those who infringe its provisions, it prevents the propagation of hereditary criminal tendencies; and the poor-law, in so far as it separates married couples, whose destitution arises from hereditary defects of character, are doubtless selective agents operating in favour of the non-criminal and the more effective members of society. But the proportion of the population which they influence is very small; and, generally, the hereditary criminal and the hereditary pauper have propagated their kind before the law affects them. In a large proportion of cases, crime and pauperism have nothing to do with heredity; but are the consequence, partly, of circumstances and, partly, of the possession of qualities, which, under different conditions of life, might have excited esteem and even admiration. It was a shrewd man of the world who, in discussing sewage problems, remarked that dirt is riches in the wrong place; and that sound aphorism has moral applications. The benevolence and open-handed generosity which adorn a rich man, may make a pauper of a poor one; the energy and courage to which the successful soldier owes his rise, the cool and daring subtlety to which the great financier owes his fortune, may very easily, under unfavourable conditions, lead their possessors to the gallows, or to the hulks. Moreover, it is fairly probable that the children of a 'failure' will receive from their other parent just that little modification of character which makes all the difference. I sometimes wonder whether people, who talk so freely about extirpating the unfit, ever dispassionately consider their own history. Surely, one must be very 'fit', indeed, not to know of an occasion, or perhaps two, in one's life, when it would have been only too easy to qualify for a place among the 'unfit'.

In my belief the innate qualities, physical, intellectual, and moral, of our nation have remained substantially the same for the last four or five centuries. If the struggle for existence has affected us to any serious extent (and I doubt it) it has been, indirectly, through our military and industrial wars with other nations.

### XIV

What is often called the struggle for existence in society (I plead guilty of having used the term too loosely myself), is a contest, not for the means of existence, but for the means of enjoyment. Those who occupy the first places in this practical competitive examination are the rich and the influential; those who fail, more or less, occupy the lower places, down to the squalid obscurity of the pauper and the criminal. Upon the most liberal estimate, I suppose the former group will not amount to two per cent. of the population. I doubt if the latter exceeds another two per cent.; but let it be supposed, for the sake of argument, that it is as great as five per cent.[1]

As it is only in the latter group that anything comparable to the struggle for existence in the state of nature can take place; as it is only among this twentieth of the whole people that numerous men, women, and children die of rapid or slow starvation, or of the diseases incidental to permanently bad conditions of life; and as there is nothing to prevent their multiplication before they

---

[1] Those who read the last Essay in this volume will not accuse me of wishing to attenuate the evil of the existence of this group, whether great or small.

are killed off, while, in spite of greater infant mortality, they increase faster than the rich; it seems clear that the struggle for existence in this class can have no appreciable selective influence upon the other 95 per cent. of the population.

What sort of a sheep breeder would he be who should content himself with picking out the worst fifty out of a thousand, leaving them on a barren common till the weakest starved, and then letting the survivors go back to mix with the rest? And the parallel is too favourable; since in a large number of cases, the actual poor and the convicted criminals are neither the weakest nor the worst.

In the struggle for the means of enjoyment, the qualities which ensure success are energy, industry, intellectual capacity, tenacity of purpose, and, at least as much sympathy as is necessary to make a man understand the feelings of his fellows. Were there none of those artificial arrangements by which fools and knaves are kept at the top of society instead of sinking to their natural place at the bottom,[1] the struggle for the means of enjoyment would ensure a constant circulation of the human units of the social compound, from the bottom to the top and from the top to the bottom. The survivors of the contest, those who continued to form the great bulk of the polity, would not be those 'fittest' who got to the very top, but the great body of the moderately 'fit', whose numbers and superior propagative power, enable them always to swamp the exceptionally endowed minority.

I think it must be obvious to every one, that, whether we consider the internal or the external interests of society, it is desirable they should be in the hands of those who are endowed with the largest share of energy, of industry, of intellectual capacity, of tenacity of purpose, while they are not devoid of sympathetic humanity; and, in so far as the struggle for the means of enjoyment tends to place such men in possession of wealth and influence, it is a process which tends to the good of society.

[1] I have elsewhere lamented the absence from society of a machinery for facilitating the descent of incapacity. 'Administrative Nihilism'. *Collected Essays*, vol. i, p. 54.

But the process, as we have seen, has no real resemblance to that which adapts living beings to current conditions in the state of nature; nor any to the artificial selection of the horticulturist.

XV

To return, once more, to the parallel of horticulture. In the modern world, the gardening of men by themselves is practically restricted to the performance, not of selection, but of that other function of the gardener, the creation of conditions more favourable than those of the state of nature; to the end of facilitating the free expansion of the innate faculties of the citizen, so far as it is consistent with the general good. And the business of the moral and political philosopher appears to me to be the ascertainment, by the same method of observation, experiment, and ratiocination, as is practised in other kinds of scientific work, of the course of conduct which will best conduce to that end.

But, supposing this course of conduct to be scientifically determined and carefully followed out, it cannot put an end to the struggle for existence in the state of nature; and it will not so much as tend, in any way, to the adaptation of man to that state. Even should the whole human race be absorbed in one vast polity, within which 'absolute political justice' reigns, the struggle for existence with the state of nature outside it, and the tendency to the return of the struggle within, in consequence of over-multiplication, will remain; and, unless men's inheritance from the ancestors who fought a good fight in the state of nature, their dose of original sin, is rooted out by some method at present unrevealed, at any rate to disbelievers in supernaturalism, every child born into the world will still bring with him the instinct of unlimited self-assertion. He will have to learn the lesson of self-restraint and renunciation. But the practice of self-restraint and renunciation is not happiness, though it may be something much better.

That man, as a 'political animal', is susceptible of a vast amount

of improvement, by education, by instruction, and by the application of his intelligence to the adaptation of the conditions of
life to his higher needs, I entertain not the slightest doubt. But,
so long as he remains liable to error, intellectual or moral; so long
as he is compelled to be perpetually on guard against the cosmic
forces, whose ends are not his ends, without and within himself;
so long as he is haunted by inexpugnable memories and hopeless
aspirations; so long as the recognition of his intellectual limitations
forces him to acknowledge his incapacity to penetrate the mystery
of existence; the prospect of attaining untroubled happiness, or of
a state which can, even remotely, deserve the title of perfection,
appears to me to be as misleading an illusion as ever was dangled
before the eyes of poor humanity. And there have been many of
them.

That which lies before the human race is a constant struggle
to maintain and improve, in opposition to the State of Nature,
the State of Art of an organized polity; in which, and by which,
man may develop a worthy civilization, capable of maintaining
and constantly improving itself, until the evolution of our globe
shall have entered so far upon its downward course that the
cosmic process resumes its sway; and, once more, the State of
Nature prevails over the surface of our planet.

## (2) EVOLUTION AND ETHICS

### [*The Romanes Lecture,* 1893]

Soleo enim et in aliena castra transire, non tanquam transfuga sed
tanquam explorator. (L. ANNÆI SENECÆ EPIST. II, 4.)

THERE is a delightful child's story, known by the title of 'Jack
and the Bean-stalk', with which my contemporaries who are

---

*Note* (see p. 58).—It seems the fashion nowadays to ignore Hartley; though,
a century and a half ago, he not only laid the foundations but built up much of
the superstructure of a true theory of the Evolution of the intellectual and moral
faculties. He speaks of what I have termed the ethical process as 'our Progress
from Self-interest to Self-annihilation'. *Observations on Man* (1749), vol. ii,
p. 281.

present will be familiar. But so many of our grave and reverend juniors have been brought up on severer intellectual diet, and, perhaps, have become acquainted with fairyland only through primers of comparative mythology, that it may be needful to give an outline of the tale. It is a legend of a bean-plant, which grows and grows until it reaches the high heavens and there spreads out into a vast canopy of foliage. The hero, being moved to climb the stalk, discovers that the leafy expanse supports a world composed of the same elements as that below, but yet strangely new; and his adventures there, on which I may not dwell, must have completely changed his views of the nature of things; though the story, not having been composed by, or for, philosophers, has nothing to say about views.

My present enterprise has a certain analogy to that of the daring adventurer. I beg you to accompany me in an attempt to reach a world which, to many, is probably strange, by the help of a bean. It is, as you know, a simple, inert-looking thing. Yet, if planted under proper conditions, of which sufficient warmth is one of the most important, it manifests active powers of a very remarkable kind. A small green seedling emerges, rises to the surface of the soil, rapidly increases in size and, at the same time, undergoes a series of metamorphoses which do not excite our wonder as much as those which meet us in legendary history, merely because they are to be seen every day and all day long.

By insensible steps, the plant builds itself up into a large and various fabric of root, stem, leaves, flowers, and fruit, every one moulded within and without in accordance with an extremely complex but, at the same time, minutely defined pattern. In each of these complicated structures, as in their smallest constituents, there is an immanent energy which, in harmony with that resident in all the others, incessantly works towards the maintenance of the whole and the efficient performance of the part which it has to play in the economy of nature. But no sooner has the edifice, reared with such exact elaboration, attained completeness, than it begins to crumble. By degrees, the plant withers and disappears from view, leaving behind more or fewer apparently inert and simple bodies, just like the bean from which it sprang; and, like it, endowed with the potentiality of giving rise to a similar cycle of manifestations.

Neither the poetic nor the scientific imagination is put to much strain in the search after analogies with this process of going forth and, as it were, returning to the starting-point. It may be likened to the ascent and descent of a slung stone, or the course of an arrow along its trajectory. Or we may say that the living energy takes first an upward and then a downward road. Or it may seem preferable to compare the expansion of the germ into the full-grown plant, to the unfolding of a fan, or to the rolling forth and widening of a stream; and thus to arrive at the conception of 'development', or 'evolution'. Here as elsewhere, names are 'noise and smoke'; the important point is to have a clear and adequate conception of the fact signified by a name. And, in this case, the fact is the Sisyphæan process, in the course of which, the living and growing plant passes from the relative simplicity and latent potentiality of the seed to the full epiphany of a highly differentiated type, thence to fall back to simplicity and potentiality.

The value of a strong intellectual grasp of the nature of this process lies in the circumstance that what is true of the bean is true of living things in general. From very low forms up to the highest—in the animal no less than in the vegetable kingdom—the process of life presents the same appearance[1] of cyclical evolution. Nay, we have but to cast our eyes over the rest of the world and cyclical change presents itself on all sides. It meets us in the water that flows to the sea and returns to the springs; in the heavenly bodies that wax and wane, go and return to their places; in the inexorable sequence of the ages of man's life; in that successive rise, apogee, and fall of dynasties and of states which is the most prominent topic of civil history.

As no man fording a swift stream can dip his foot twice into the same water, so no man can, with exactness, affirm of anything in the sensible world that it is.[2] As he utters the words, nay, as he thinks them, the predicate ceases to be applicable; the present has become the past; the 'is' should be 'was'. And the more we learn of the nature of things, the more evident is it that what we call rest is only unperceived activity; that seeming peace is silent but strenuous battle. In every part, at every moment, the state of the cosmos is the expression of a transitory adjustment of contending forces; a scene of strife, in which all the combatants fall in turn. What is true of each part, is true of the whole. Natural knowledge tends more and more to the conclusion that 'all the choir of heaven and furniture of the earth' are the transitory forms of parcels of cosmic substance wending along the road of evolution, from nebulous potentiality, through endless growths of sun and planet and satellite; through all varieties of matter; through infinite diversities of life and thought; possibly, through modes of being of which we neither have a conception, nor are competent to form any, back to the indefinable latency from which they arose. Thus the most obvious attribute of the cosmos is its impermanence. It assumes the aspect not so much of a permanent entity as of a changeful process, in which naught endures save the flow of energy and the rational order which pervades it.

We have climbed our bean-stalk and have reached a wonderland in which the common and the familiar become things new and strange. In the exploration of the cosmic process thus typified, the highest intelligence of man finds inexhaustible employment; giants are subdued to our service; and the spiritual affections of the contemplative philosopher are engaged by beauties worthy of eternal constancy.

But there is another aspect of the cosmic process, so perfect as a mechanism, so beautiful as a work of art. Where the cosmopoietic energy works through sentient beings, there arises, among its other manifestations, that which we call pain or suffering. This baleful product of evolution increases in quantity, and in intensity, with advancing grades of animal organization, until it attains its highest level in man. Further, the consummation is not reached in man, the mere animal; nor in man, the whole or half savage; but only in man, the member of an organized polity. And it is a necessary consequence of his attempt to live in this way; that is, under those conditions which are essential to the full development of his noblest powers.

Man, the animal, in fact, has worked his way to the headship of the sentient world, and has become the superb animal which he is, in virtue of his success in the struggle for existence. The conditions having been of a certain order, man's organization has adjusted itself to them better than that of his competitors in the cosmic strife. In the case of mankind, the self-assertion, the unscrupulous seizing upon all that can be grasped, the tenacious holding of all that can be kept, which constitute the essence of the struggle for existence, have answered. For his successful progress, throughout the savage state, man has been largely indebted to those qualities which he shares with the ape and the tiger; his exceptional physical organization; his cunning, his sociability, his curiosity, and his imitativeness; his ruthless and ferocious destructiveness when his anger is roused by opposition.

But, in propo    on as men have passed from anarchy to social organization, an   a proportion as civilization has grown in worth, these deeply ingrained serviceable qualities have become defects. After the manner of successful persons, civilized man would gladly kick down the ladder by which he has climbed. He would be only too pleased to see 'the ape and tiger die'. But they decline to suit his convenience; and the unwelcome intrusion of these boon companions of his hot youth into the ranged existence of civil life adds pains and griefs, innumerable and immeasurably great, to those which the cosmic process necessarily brings on the mere animal. In fact, civilized man brands all these ape and tiger promptings with the name of sins; he punishes many of the acts which flow from them as crimes; and, in extreme cases, he does his best to put an end to the survival of the fittest of former days by axe and rope.

I have said that civilized man has reached this point; the assertion is perhaps too broad and general; I had better put it that ethical man has attained thereto. The science of ethics professes to furnish us with a reasoned rule of life; to tell us what is right action and why it is so. Whatever differences of opinion may exist among the experts, there is a general consensus that the ape and tiger methods of the struggle for existence are not reconcilable with sound ethical principles.

The hero of our story descended the bean-stalk, and came back to the common world, where fare and work were alike hard; where ugly competitors were much commoner than beautiful princesses; and where the everlasting battle with self was much less sure to be crowned with victory than a turn-to with a giant. We have done the like. Thousands upon thousands of our fellows, thousands of years ago, have preceded us in finding themselves face to face with the same dread problem of evil. They also have seen that the cosmic process is evolution; that it is full of wonder, full of beauty, and, at the same time, full of pain. They have sought to discover the bearing of these great facts on ethics; to find out whether there is, or is not, a sanction for morality in the ways of the cosmos.

Theories of the universe, in which the conception of evolution plays a leading part, were extant at least six centuries before our era. Certain knowledge of them, in the fifth century, reaches us from localities as distant as the valley of the Ganges and the Asiatic coasts of the Ægean. To the early philosophers of Hindostan, no less than to those of Ionia, the salient and characteristic feature of the phenomenal world was its changefulness; the unresting flow of all things, through birth to visible being and thence to not being, in which they could discern no sign of a beginning and for which they saw no prospect of an ending. It was no less plain to some of these antique forerunners of modern philosophy that suffering is the badge of all the tribe of sentient things; that it is no accidental accompaniment, but an essential constituent of the cosmic process. The energetic Greek might find fierce joys in a world in which 'strife is father and king'; but the old Aryan spirit was subdued to quietism in the Indian sage; the mist of suffering which spread over humanity hid everything else from his view; to him life was one with suffering and suffering with life.

In Hindostan, as in Ionia, a period of relatively high and tolerably stable civilization had succeeded long ages of semi-barbarism and struggle. Out of wealth and security had come leisure and refinement, and, close at their heels, had followed the malady of thought. To the struggle for bare existence, which never ends, though it may be alleviated and partially disguised for a fortunate few, succeeded the struggle to make existence intelligible and to bring the order of things into harmony with the moral sense of man, which also never ends, but, for the thinking few, becomes keener with every increase of knowledge and with every step towards the realization of a worthy ideal of life.

Two thousand five hundred years ago, the value of civilization was as apparent as it is now; then, as now, it was obvious that only in the garden of an orderly polity can the finest fruits humanity is capable of bearing be produced. But it had also become evident that the blessings of culture were not unmixed. The garden was apt to turn into a hothouse. The stimulation of the senses, the pampering of the emotions, endlessly multiplied the sources of pleasure. The constant widening of the intellectual field indefinitely extended the range of that especially human faculty of looking before and after, which adds to the fleeting present those old and new worlds of the past and the future, wherein men dwell the more the higher their culture. But that very sharpening of the sense and that subtle refinement of emotion, which brought such a wealth of pleasures, were fatally attended by a proportional enlargement of the capacity for suffering; and the divine faculty of imagination, while it created new heavens and new earths, provided them with the corresponding hells of futile regret for the past and morbid anxiety for the future.[3] Finally, the inevitable penalty of over-stimulation, exhaustion, opened the gates of civilization to its great enemy, ennui; the stale and flat weariness when man delights not, nor woman neither; when all things are vanity and vexation; and life seems not worth living except to escape the bore of dying.

Even purely intellectual progress brings about its revenges. Problems settled in a rough and ready way by rude men, absorbed in action, demand renewed attention and show themselves to be still unread riddles when men have time to think. The beneficent demon, doubt, whose name is Legion and who dwells amongst the tombs of old faiths, enters into mankind and thenceforth refuses to be cast out. Sacred customs, venerable dooms of ancestral wisdom, hallowed by tradition and professing to hold good for all time, are put to the question. Cultured reflection asks for their credentials; judges them by its own standards; finally, gathers those of which it approves into ethical systems, in which the reasoning is rarely much more than a decent pretext for the adoption of foregone conclusions.

One of the oldest and most important elements in such systems is the conception of justice. Society is impossible unless those who are associated agree to observe certain rules of conduct towards one another; its stability depends on the steadiness with which they abide by that agreement; and, so far as they waver, that mutual trust which is the bond of society is weakened or destroyed. Wolves could not hunt in packs except for the real, though unexpressed, understanding that they should not attack one another during the chase. The most rudimentary polity is a pack of men living under the like tacit, or expressed, understanding; and having made the very important advance upon wolf society, that they agree to use the force of the whole body against individuals who violate it and in favour of those who observe it. This observance of a common understanding, with the consequent distribution of punishments and rewards according to accepted rules, received the name of justice, while the contrary was called injustice. Early ethics did not take much note of the animus of the violator of the rules. But civilization could not advance far, without the establishment of a capital distinction between the case of involuntary and that of wilful misdeed; between a merely wrong action and a guilty one. And, with increasing refinement of moral appreciation, the problem of desert, which arises out of this distinction, acquired more and more theoretical and practical importance. If life must be given for life, yet it was recognized that the unintentional slayer did not altogether deserve death; and, by a sort of compromise between the public and the private conception of justice, a sanctuary was provided in which he might take refuge from the avenger of blood.

The idea of justice thus underwent a gradual sublimation from punishment and reward according to acts, to punishment and reward according to desert; or, in other words, according to motive. Righteousness, that is, action from right motive, not only became synonymous with justice, but the positive constituent of innocence and the very heart of goodness.

Now when the ancient sage, whether Indian or Greek, who had attained to this conception of goodness, looked the world, and especially human life, in the face, he found it as hard as we do to bring the course of evolution into harmony with even the elementary requirements of the ethical ideal of the just and the good.

If there is one thing plainer than another, it is that neither the pleasures nor the pains of life, in the merely animal world, are distributed according to desert; for it is admittedly impossible for the lower orders of sentient beings to deserve either the one or the other. If there is a generalization from the facts of human life which has the assent of thoughtful men in every age and country, it is that the violator of ethical rules constantly escapes the punishment which he deserves; that the wicked flourishes like a green bay tree, while the righteous begs his bread; that the sins of the fathers are visited upon the children; that, in the realm of nature, ignorance is punished just as severely as wilful wrong; and that thousands upon thousands of innocent beings suffer for the crime, or the unintentional trespass, of one.

Greek and Semite and Indian are agreed upon this subject. The book of Job is at one with the 'Works and Days' and the Buddhist Sutras; the Psalmist and the Preacher of Israel, with the Tragic Poets of Greece. What is a more common motive of the ancient tragedy in fact, than the unfathomable injustice of the nature of things; what is more deeply felt to be true than its presentation of the destruction of the blameless by the work of his own hands, or by the fatal operation of the sins of others? Surely Œdipus was pure of heart; it was the natural sequence of events—the cosmic process—which drove him, in all innocence, to slay his father and become the husband of his mother, to the desolation of his people and his own headlong ruin. Or to step, for a moment, beyond the chronological limits I have set myself, what constitutes the sempiternal attraction of Hamlet but the appeal to deepest experience of that history of a no less blameless dreamer, dragged, in spite of himself, into a world out of joint; involved in a tangle of crime and misery, created by one of the prime agents of the cosmic process as it works in and through man?

Thus, brought before the tribunal of ethics, the cosmos might well seem to stand condemned. The conscience of man revolted against the moral indifference of nature, and the microcosmic atom should have found the illimitable macrocosm guilty. But few, or none, ventured to record that verdict.

In the great Semitic trial of this issue, Job takes refuge in silence and submission; the Indian and the Greek, less wise perhaps, attempt to reconcile the irreconcilable and plead for the defendant. To this end, the Greeks invented Theodicies; while the Indians devised what, in its ultimate form, must rather be termed a Cosmodicy. For, though Buddhism recognizes gods many and lords many, they are products of the cosmic process; and transitory, however long enduring, manifestations of its eternal activity. In the doctrine of transmigration, whatever its origin, Brahminical and Buddhist speculation found, ready to hand,[4] the means of constructing a plausible vindication of the ways of the cosmos to man. If this world is full of pain and sorrow; if grief and evil fall, like the rain, upon both the just and the unjust; it is because, like the rain, they are links in the endless chain of natural causation by which past, present, and future are indissolubly connected; and there is no more injustice in the one case than in the other. Every sentient being is reaping as it has sown; if not in this life, then in one or other of the infinite series of antecedent existences of which it is the latest term. The present distribution of good and evil is, therefore, the algebraical sum of accumulated positive and negative deserts; or, rather, it depends on the floating balance of the account. For it was not thought necessary that a complete settlement should ever take place. Arrears might stand over as a sort of 'hanging gale'; a period of celestial happiness just earned might be succeeded by ages of torment in a hideous nether world, the balance still overdue for some remote ancestral error.[5]

Whether the cosmic process looks any more moral than at first, after such a vindication, may perhaps be questioned. Yet this plea of justification is not less plausible than others; and none but very hasty thinkers will reject it on the ground of inherent absurdity. Like the doctrine of evolution itself, that of transmigration has its roots in the world of reality; and it may claim such support as the great argument from analogy is capable of supplying.

Everyday experience familiarizes us with the facts which are grouped under the name of heredity. Every one of us bears upon him obvious marks of his parentage, perhaps of remoter relationships. More particularly, the sum of tendencies to act in a certain way, which we call 'character', is often to be traced through a long series of progenitors and collaterals. So we may justly say that this 'character'—this moral and intellectual essence of a man —does veritably pass over from one fleshly tabernacle to another, and does really transmigrate from generation to generation. In the new-born infant, the character of the stock lies latent, and the Ego is little more than a bundle of potentialities. But, very early, these become actualities; from childhood to age they manifest themselves in dullness or brightness, weakness or strength, viciousness or uprightness; and with each feature modified by confluence with another character, if by nothing else, the character passes on to its incarnation in new bodies.

The Indian philosophers called character, as thus defined, 'karma'.[6] It is this karma which passed from life to life and linked them in the chain of transmigrations; and they held that it is modified in each life, not merely by confluence of parentage, but by its own acts. They were, in fact, strong believers in the theory, so much disputed just at present, of the hereditary transmission of acquired characters. That the manifestation of the tendencies of a character may be greatly facilitated, or impeded, by conditions, of which self-discipline, or the absence of it, are among the most important, is indubitable; but that the character itself is modified in this way is by no means so certain; it is not so sure that the transmitted character of an evil liver is worse, or that of a righteous man better, than that which he received. Indian philosophy, however, did not admit of any doubt on this subject; the belief in the influence of conditions, notably of self-discipline, on the karma was not merely a necessary postulate of its theory of retribution, but it presented the only way of escape from the endless round of transmigrations.

The earlier forms of Indian philosophy agreed with those prevalent in our own times, in supposing the existence of a permanent reality, or 'substance', beneath the shifting series of phenomena, whether of matter or of mind. The substance of the cosmos was 'Brahma', that of the individual man 'Atman'; and the latter was separated from the former only, if I may so speak, by its phenomenal envelope, by the casing of sensations, thoughts and desires, pleasures and pains, which make up the illusive phantasmagoria of life. This the ignorant take for reality; their 'Atman' therefore remains eternally imprisoned in delusions, bound by the fetters of desire and scourged by the whip of misery. But the man who has attained enlightenment sees that the apparent reality is mere illusion, or, as was said a couple of thousand years later, that there is nothing good nor bad but thinking makes it so. If the cosmos 'is just and of our pleasant vices makes instruments to scourge us', it would seem that the only way to escape from our heritage of evil is to destroy that fountain of desire whence our vices flow; to refuse any longer to be the instruments of the evolutionary process, and withdraw from the struggle for existence. If the karma is modifiable by self-discipline, if its coarser desires, one after another, can be extinguished, the ultimate fundamental desire of self-assertion, or the desire to be, may also be destroyed.[7] Then the bubble of illusion will burst, and the freed individual 'Atman' will lose itself in the universal 'Brahma'.

Such seems to have been the pre-Buddhistic conception of salvation, and of the way to be followed by those who would attain thereto. No more thorough mortification of the flesh has ever been attempted than that achieved by the Indian ascetic anchorite; no later monachism has so nearly succeeded in reducing the human mind to that condition of impassive quasi-somnambulism, which, but for its acknowledged holiness, might run the risk of being confounded with idiocy.

And this salvation, it will be observed, was to be attained through knowledge, and by action based on that knowledge; just as the experimenter, who would obtain a certain physical or chemical result, must have a knowledge of the natural laws involved and the persistent disciplined will adequate to carry out all the various operations required. The supernatural, in our sense of the term, was entirely excluded. There was no external power which could affect the sequence of cause and effect which gives rise to karma; none but the will of the subject of the karma which could put an end to it.

Only one rule of conduct could be based upon the remarkable theory of which I have endeavoured to give a reasoned outline. It was folly to continue to exist when an overplus of pain was certain; and the probabilities in favour of the increase of misery with the prolongation of existence, were so overwhelming. Slaying the body only made matters worse; there was nothing for it but to slay the soul by the voluntary arrest of all its activities. Property, social ties, family affections, common companionship, must be abandoned; the most natural appetites, even that for food, must be suppressed, or at least minimized; until all that remained of a man was the impassive, extenuated, mendicant monk, self-hypnotized into cataleptic trances, which the deluded mystic took for foretastes of the final union with Brahma.

The founder of Buddhism accepted the chief postulates demanded by his predecessors. But he was not satisfied with the practical annihilation involved in merging the individual existence in the unconditioned—the Atman in Brahma. It would seem that the admission of the existence of any substance whatever—even of the tenuity of that which has neither quality nor energy and of which no predicate whatever can be asserted—appeared to him to be a danger and a snare. Though reduced to a hypostatized negation, Brahma was not to be trusted; so long as entity was there, it might conceivably resume the weary round of evolution, with all its train of immeasurable miseries. Gautama got rid of even that shade of a shadow of permanent existence by a metaphysical *tour de force* of great interest to the student of philosophy, seeing that it supplies the wanting half of Bishop Berkeley's well-known idealistic argument.

Granting the premises, I am not aware of any escape from Berkeley's conclusion, that the 'substance' of matter is a metaphysical unknown quantity, of the existence of which there is no proof. What Berkeley does not seem to have so clearly perceived is that the non-existence of a substance of mind is equally arguable; and that the result of the impartial applications of his reasonings is the reduction of the All to co-existences and sequences of phenomena, beneath and beyond which there is nothing cognoscible. It is a remarkable indication of the subtlety of Indian speculation that Gautama should have seen deeper than the greatest of modern idealists; though it must be admitted that, if some of Berkeley's reasonings respecting the nature of spirit are pushed home, they reach pretty much the same conclusion.[8]

Accepting the prevalent Brahminical doctrine that the whole cosmos, celestial, terrestrial, and infernal, with its population of gods and other celestial beings, of sentient animals, of Mara and his devils, is incessantly shifting through recurring cycles of production and destruction, in each of which every human being has his transmigratory representative, Gautama proceeded to eliminate substance altogether; and to reduce the cosmos to a mere flow of sensations, emotions, volitions, and thoughts, devoid of any substratum. As, on the surface of a stream of water, we see ripples and whirlpools, which last for a while and then vanish with the causes that gave rise to them, so what seem individual existences are mere temporary associations of phenomena circling round a centre, 'like a dog tied to a post'. In the whole universe there is nothing permanent, no eternal substance either of mind or of matter. Personality is a metaphysical fancy; and in very truth, not only we, but all things, in the worlds without end of the cosmic phantasmagoria, are such stuff as dreams are made of.

What then becomes of karma? Karma remains untouched. As the peculiar form of energy we call magnetism may be transmitted from a loadstone to a piece of steel, from the steel to a piece of nickel, as it may be strengthened or weakened by the conditions to which it is subjected while resident in each piece, so it seems to have been conceived that karma might be transmitted from one phenomenal association to another by a sort of induction. However this may be, Gautama doubtless had a better guarantee for the abolition of transmigration, when no wrack of substance, either of Atman or of Brahma, was left behind; when, in short, a man had but to dream that he willed not to dream, to put an end to all dreaming.

This end of life's dream is Nirvana. What Nirvana is the learned do not agree. But, since the best original authorities tell us there is neither desire nor activity, nor any possibility of phenomenal reappearance for the sage who has entered Nirvana, it may be safely said of this acme of Buddhistic philosophy—'the rest is silence'.[9]

Thus there is no very great practical disagreement between Gautama and his predecessors with respect to the end of action; but it is otherwise as regards the means to that end. With just insight into human nature, Gautama declared extreme ascetic practices to be useless and indeed harmful. The appetites and the passions are not to be abolished by mere mortification of the body; they must, in addition, be attacked on their own ground and conquered by steady cultivation of the mental habits which oppose them; by universal benevolence; by the return of good for evil; by humility; by abstinence from evil thought; in short, by total renunciation of that self-assertion which is the essence of the cosmic process.

Doubtless, it is to these ethical qualities that Buddhism owes its marvellous success.[10] A system which knows no God in the western sense; which denies a soul to man; which counts the belief in immortality a blunder and t⊦ hope of it a sin; which refuses any efficacy to prayer and sacrifice; which bids men look to nothing but their own efforts for salvation; which, in its original purity, knew nothing of vows of obedience, abhorred intolerance, and never sought the aid of the secular arm; yet spread over a considerable moiety of the Old World with marvellous rapidity, and is still, with whatever base admixture of foreign superstitions, the dominant creed of a large fraction of mankind.

Let us now set our faces westwards, ⸗owards Asia Minor and Greece and Italy, to view the rise and progress of another philosophy, apparently independent, but no less pervaded by the conception of evolution.[11]

The sages of Miletus were pronounced evolutionists; and, however dark may be some of the sayings of Heracleitus of Ephesus, who was probably a contemporary of Gautama, no better expressions of the essence of the modern doctrine of evolution can be found than are presented by some of his pithy aphorisms and striking metaphors.[12] Indeed, many of my present auditors must have observed that, more than once, I have borrowed from him in the brief exposition of the theory of evolution with which this discourse commenced.

But when the focus of Greek intellectual activity shifted to Athens, the leading minds concentrated their attention upon ethical problems. Forsaking the study of the macrocosm for that of the microcosm, they lost the key to the thought of the great Ephesian, which, I imagine, is more intelligible to us than it was to Socrates, or to Plato. Socrates, more especially, set the fashion of a kind of inverse agnosticism, by teaching that the problems of physics lie beyond the reach of the human intellect; that the attempt to solve them is essentially vain; that the one worthy object of investigation is the problem of ethical life; and his example was followed by the Cynics and the later Stoics. Even the comprehensive knowledge and the penetrating intellect of Aristotle failed to suggest to him that in holding the eternity of the world, within its present range of mutation, he was making a retrogressive step. The scientific heritage of Heracleitus passed into the hands neither of Plato nor of Aristotle, but into those of Democritus. But the world was not yet ready to receive the great conceptions of the philosopher of Abdera. It was reserved for the Stoics to return to the track marked out by the earlier philosophers; and, professing themselves disciples of Heracleitus, to develop the idea of evolution systematically. In doing this, they not only omitted some characteristic features of their master's teaching but they made additions altogether foreign to it. One of the most influential of these importations was the transcendental theism which had come into vogue. The restless, fiery energy, operating according to law, out of which all things emerge and into which they return, in the endless successive cycles of the great year; which creates and destroys worlds as a wanton child builds up, and anon levels, sand castles on the seashore; was metamorphosed into a material world-soul and decked out with all the attributes of ideal Divinity; not merely with infinite power and transcendent wisdom, but with absolute goodness.

The consequences of this step were momentous. For if the cosmos is the effect of an immanent, omnipotent, and infinitely beneficent cause, the existence in it of real evil, still less of necessarily inherent evil, is plainly inadmissible.[13] Yet the universal experience of mankind testified then, as now, that, whether we look within us or without us, evil stares us in the face on all sides; that if anything is real, pain and sorrow and wrong are realities.

It would be a new thing in history if *a priori* philosophers were daunted by the factious opposition of experience; and the Stoics were the last men to allow themselves to be beaten by mere facts. 'Give me a doctrine and I will find the reasons for it', said Chrysippus. So they perfected, if they did not invent, that ingenious and plausible form of pleading, the Theodicy; for the purpose of showing firstly, that there is no such thing as evil; secondly, that if there is, it is the necessary correlate of good; and, moreover, that it is either due to our own fault, or inflicted for our benefit. Theodicies have been very popular in their time, and I believe that a numerous, though somewhat dwarfed, progeny of them still survives. So far as I know, they are all variations of the theme set forth in those famous six lines of the 'Essay on Man', in which Pope sums up Bolingbroke's reminiscences of stoical and other speculations of this kind—

> All nature is but art, unknown to thee;
> All chance, direction which thou canst not see;
> All discord, harmony not understood;
> All partial evil, universal good;
> And spite of pride, in erring reason's spite
> One truth is clear: whatever is, is right.

Yet, surely, if there are few more important truths than those enunciated in the first triad, the second is open to very grave objections. That there is a 'soul of good in things evil' is unquestionable; nor will any wise man deny the disciplinary value of pain and sorrow. But these considerations do not help us to see why the immense multitude of irresponsible sentient beings, which cannot profit by such discipline, should suffer; nor why, among the endless possibilities open to omnipotence—that of sinless, happy existence among the rest—the actuality in which sin and misery abound should be that selected. Surely it is mere cheap rhetoric to call arguments which have never yet been answered by even the meekest and the least rational of Optimists, suggestions of the pride of reason. As to the concluding aphorism, its fittest place would be as an inscription in letters of mud over the portal of some 'stye of Epicurus';[14] for that is where the logical application of it to practice would land men, with every aspiration stifled and every effort paralyzed. Why try to set right what is right already? Why strive to improve the best of all possible worlds? Let us eat and drink, for as to-day all is right, so to-morrow all will be.

But the attempt of the Stoics to blind themselves to the reality of evil, as a necessary concomitant of the cosmic process, had less success than that of the Indian philosophers to exclude the reality of good from their purview. Unfortunately, it is much easier to shut one's eyes to good than to evil. Pain and sorrow knock at our doors more loudly than pleasure and happiness; and the prints of their heavy footsteps are less easily effaced. Before the grim realities of practical life the pleasant fictions of optimism vanished. If this were the best of all possible worlds, it nevertheless proved itself a very inconvenient habitation for the ideal sage.

The stoical summary of the whole duty of man, 'Live according to nature', would seem to imply that the cosmic process is an exemplar for human conduct. Ethics would thus become applied Natural History. In fact, a confused employment of the maxim, in this sense, has done immeasurable mischief in later times. It has furnished an axiomatic foundation for the philosophy of philosophasters and for the moralizing of sentimentalists. But the Stoics were, at bottom, not merely noble, but sane, men; and if we look closely into what they really meant by this ill-used phrase, it will be found to present no justification for the mischievous conclusions that have been deduced from it.

In the language of the Stoa, 'Nature' was a word of many meanings. There was the 'Nature' of the cosmos and the 'Nature' of man. In the latter, the animal 'nature', which man shares with a moiety of the living part of the cosmos, was distinguished from a higher 'nature'. Even in this higher nature there were grades of rank. The logical faculty is an instrument which may be turned to account for any purpose. The passions and the emotions are so closely tied to the lower nature that they may be considered to be pathological, rather than normal, phenomena.

The one supreme, hegemonic, faculty, which constitutes the essential 'nature' of man, is most nearly represented by that which, in the language of a later philosophy, has been called the pure reason. It is this 'nature' which holds up the ideal of the supreme good and demands absolute submission of the will to its behests. It is this which commands all men to love one another, to return good for evil, to regard one another as fellow-citizens of one great state. Indeed, seeing that the progress towards perfection of a civilized state, or polity, depends on the obedience of its members to these commands, the Stoics sometimes termed the pure reason the 'political' nature. Unfortunately, the sense of the adjective has undergone so much modification, that the application of it to that which commands the sacrifice of self to the common good would now sound almost grotesque.[15]

But what part is played by the theory of evolution in this view of ethics? So far as I can discern, the ethical system of the Stoics, which is essentially intuitive, and reverences the categorical imperative as strongly as that of any later moralists, might have been just what it was if they had held any other theory; whether that of special creation, on the one side, or that of the eternal existence of the present order, on the other.[16] To the Stoic, the cosmos had no importance for the conscience, except in so far as he chose to think it a pedagogue to virtue. The pertinacious optimism of our philosophers hid from them the actual state of the case. It prevented them from seeing that cosmic nature is no school of virtue, but the headquarters of the enemy of ethical nature. The logic of facts was necessary to convince them that the cosmos works through the lower nature of man, not for righteousness, but against it. And it finally drove them to confess that the existence of their ideal 'wise man' was incompatible with the nature of things; that even a passable approximation to that ideal was to be attained only at the cost of renunciation of the world and mortification, not merely of the flesh, but of all human affections. The state of perfection was that 'apatheia'[17] in which desire, though it may still be felt, is powerless to move the will, reduced to the sole function of executing the commands of pure reason. Even this residuum of activity was to be regarded as a temporary loan, as an efflux of the divine world-pervading spirit, chafing at its imprisonment in the flesh, until such time as death enabled it to return to its source in the all-pervading logos.

I find it difficult to discover any very great difference between Apatheia and Nirvana, except that stoical speculation agrees with pre-Buddhistic philosophy, rather than with the teachings of Gautama, in so far as it postulates a permanent substance equivalent to 'Brahma' and 'Atman'; and that, in stoical practice, the adoption of the life of the mendicant cynic was held to be more a counsel of perfection than an indispensable condition of the higher life.

Thus the extremes touch. Greek thought and Indian thought set out from ground common to both, diverge widely, develop under very different physical and moral conditions, and finally converge to practically the same end.

The Vedas and the Homeric epos set before us a world of rich and vigorous life, full of joyous fighting men

> That ever with a frolic welcome took
> The thunder and the sunshine . . . .

and who were ready to brave the very Gods themselves when their blood was up. A few centuries pass away, and under the influence of civilization the descendants of these men are 'sicklied o'er with the pale cast of thought'—frank pessimists, or, at best, make-believe optimists. The courage of the warlike stock may be as hardly tried as before, perhaps more hardly, but the enemy is self. The hero has become a monk. The man of action is replaced by the quietist, whose highest aspiration is to be the passive instrument of the divine Reason. By the Tiber, as by the Ganges, ethical man admits that the cosmos is too strong for him; and, destroying every bond which ties him to it by ascetic discipline, he seeks salvation in absolute renunciation.[18]

Modern thought is making a fresh start from the base whence Indian and Greek philosophy set out; and, the human mind being very much what it was six-and-twenty centuries ago, there is no ground for wonder if it presents indications of a tendency to move along the old lines to the same results.

We are more than sufficiently familiar with modern pessimism, at least as a speculation; for I cannot call to mind that any of its present votaries have sealed their faith by assuming the rags and the bowl of the mendicant Bhikku, or the cloak and the wallet of the Cynic. The obstacles placed in the way of sturdy vagrancy by an unphilosophical police have, perhaps, proved, too formidable for philosophical consistency. We also know modern speculative optimism, with its perfectibility of the species, reign of peace, and lion and lamb transformation scenes; but one does not hear so much of it as one did forty years ago; indeed, I imagine it is to be met with more commonly at the tables of the healthy and wealthy, than in the congregations of the wise. The majority of us, I apprehend, profess neither pessimism nor optimism. We hold that the world is neither so good, nor so bad, as it conceivably might be; and, as most of us have reason, now and again, to discover that it can be. Those who have failed to experience the joys that make life worth living are, probably, in as small a minority as those who have never known the griefs that rob existence of its savour and turn its richest fruits into mere dust and ashes.

Further, I think I do not err in assuming that, however diverse their views on philosophical and religious matters, most men are agreed that the proportion of good and evil in life may be very sensibly affected by human action. I never heard anybody doubt that the evil may be thus increased, or diminished; and it would seem to follow that good must be similarly susceptible of addition or subtraction. Finally, to my knowledge, nobody professes to doubt that, so far forth as we possess a power of bettering things, it is our paramount duty to use it and to train all our intellect and energy to this supreme service of our kind.

Hence the pressing interest of the question, to what extent modern progress in natural knowledge, and, more especially, the general outcome of that progress in the doctrine of evolution, is competent to help us in the great work of helping one another?

The propounders of what are called the 'ethics of evolution', when the 'evolution of ethics' would usually better express the object of their speculations, adduce a number of more or less interesting facts and more or less sound arguments, in favour of the origin of the moral sentiments, in the same way as other natural phenomena, by a process of evolution. I have little doubt, for my own part, that they are on the right track; but as the immoral sentiments have no less been evolved, there is, so far, as much natural sanction for the one as the other. The thief and the murderer follow nature just as much as the philanthropist. Cosmic evolution may teach us how the good and the evil tendencies of man may have come about; but, in itself, it is incompetent to furnish any better reason why what we call good is preferable to what we call evil than we had before. Some day, I doubt not, we shall arrive at an understanding of the evolution of the æsthetic faculty; but all the understanding in the world will neither increase nor diminish the force of the intuition that this is beautiful and that is ugly.

There is another fallacy which appears to me to pervade the so-called 'ethics of evolution'. It is the notion that because, on the whole, animals and plants have advanced in perfection of organization by means of the struggle for existence and the consequent 'survival of the fittest'; therefore men in society, men as ethical beings, must look to the same process to help them towards perfection. I suspect that this fallacy has arisen out of the unfortunate ambiguity of the phrase 'survival of the fittest'. 'Fittest' has a connotation of 'best'; and about 'best' there hangs a moral flavour. In cosmic nature, however, what is 'fittest' depends upon the conditions. Long since,[19] I ventured to point out that if our hemisphere were to cool again, the survival of the fittest might bring about, in the vegetable kingdom, a population of more and more stunted and humbler and humbler organisms, until the 'fittest' that survived might be nothing but lichens, diatoms, and such microscopic organisms as those which give red snow its colour; while, if it became hotter, the pleasant valleys of the Thames and Isis might be uninhabitable by any animated beings save those that flourish in a tropical jungle. They, as the fittest, the best adapted to the changed conditions, would survive.

Men in society are undoubtedly subject to the cosmic process. As among other animals, multiplication goes on without cessation, and involves severe competition for the means of support. The struggle for existence tends to eliminate those less fitted to adapt themselves to the circumstances of their existence. The strongest, the most self-assertive, tend to tread down the weaker. But the influence of the cosmic process on the evolution of society is the greater the more rudimentary its civilization. Social progress means a checking of the cosmic process at every step and the substitution for it of another, which may be called the ethical process; the end of which is not the survival of those who may happen to be the fittest, in respect of the whole of the conditions which obtain, but of those who are ethically the best.[20]

As I have already urged, the practice of that which is ethically best—what we call goodness or virtue—involves a course of conduct which, in all respects, is opposed to that which leads to success in the cosmic struggle for existence. In place of ruthless self-assertion it demands self-restraint; in place of thrusting aside, or treading down, all competitors, it requires that the individual shall not merely respect, but shall help his fellows; its influence is directed, not so much to the survival of the fittest, as to the fitting of as many as possible to survive. It repudiates the gladiatorial theory of existence. It demands that each man who enters into the enjoyment of the advantages of a polity shall be mindful of his debt to those who have laboriously constructed it; and shall take heed that no act of his weakens the fabric in which he has been permitted to live. Laws and moral precepts are directed to the end of curbing the cosmic process and reminding the individual of his duty to the community, to the protection and influence of which he owes, if not existence itself, at least the life of something better than a brutal savage.

It is from neglect of these plain considerations that the fanatical individualism[21] of our time attempts to apply the analogy of cosmic nature to society. Once more we have a misapplication of the stoical injunction to follow nature; the duties of the individual to the State are forgotten, and his tendencies to self-assertion are dignified by the name of rights. It is seriously debated whether the members of a community are justified in using their combined strength to constrain one of their number to contribute his share to the maintenance of it; or even to prevent him from doing his best to destroy it. The struggle for existence, which has done such admirable work in cosmic nature, must, it appears, be equally beneficent in the ethical sphere. Yet if that which I have insisted upon is true; if the cosmic process has no sort of relation to moral ends; if the imitation of it by man is inconsistent with the first principles of ethics; what becomes of this surprising theory?

Let us understand, once for all, that the ethical progress of society depends, not on imitating the cosmic process, still less in running away from it, but in combating it. It may seem an audacious proposal thus to pit the microcosm against the macrocosm and to set man to subdue nature to his higher ends; but I venture to think that the great intellectual difference between the ancient times with which we have been occupied and our day, lies in the solid foundation we have acquired for the hope that such an enterprise may meet with a certain measure of success.

The history of civilization details the steps by which men have succeeded in building up an artificial world within the cosmos.

Fragile reed as he may be, man, as Pascal says, is a thinking reed:[22] there lies within him a fund of energy, operating intelligently and so far akin to that which pervades the universe, that it is competent to influence and modify the cosmic process. In virtue of his intelligence, the dwarf bends the Titan to his will. In every family, in every polity that has been established, the cosmic process in man has been restrained and otherwise modified by law and custom; in surrounding nature, it has been similarly influenced by the art of the shepherd, the agriculturist, the artisan. As civilization has advanced, so has the extent of this interference increased; until the organized and highly developed sciences and arts of the present day have endowed man with a command over the course of non-human nature greater than that once attributed to the magicians. The most impressive, I might say startling, of these changes have been brought about in the course of the last two centuries; while a right comprehension of the process of life and of the means of influencing its manifestations is only just dawning upon us. We do not yet see our way beyond generalities; and we are befogged by the obtrusion of false analogies and crude anticipations. But Astronomy, Physics, Chemistry, have all had to pass through similar phases, before they reached the stage at which their influence became an important factor in human affairs. Physiology, Psychology, Ethics, Political Science, must submit to the same ordeal. Yet it seems to me irrational to doubt that, at no distant period, they will work as great a revolution in the sphere of practice.

The theory of evolution encourages no millennial anticipations. If, for millions of years, our globe has taken the upward road, yet, some time, the summit will be reached and the downward route will be commenced. The most daring imagination will hardly venture upon the suggestion that the power and the intelligence of man can ever arrest the procession of the great year.

Moreover, the cosmic nature born with us and, to a large extent, necessary for our maintenance, is the outcome of millions of years of severe training, and it would be folly to imagine that a few centuries will suffice to subdue its masterfulness to purely ethical ends. Ethical nature may count upon having to reckon with a tenacious and powerful enemy as long as the world lasts. But, on the other hand, I see no limit to the extent to which intelligence and will, guided by sound principles of investigation, and organized in common effort, may modify the conditions of existence, for a period longer than that now covered by history. And much may be done to change the nature of man himself.[23] The intelligence which has converted the brother of the wolf into the faithful guardian of the flock ought to be able to do something towards curbing the instincts of savagery in civilized men.

But if we may permit ourselves a larger hope of abatement of the essential evil of the world than was possible to those who, in the infancy of exact knowledge, faced the problem of existence more than a score of centuries ago, I deem it as essential condition of the realization of that hope that we should cast aside the notion that the escape from pain and sorrow is the proper object of life.

We have long since emerged from the heroic childhood of our race, when good and evil could be met with the same 'frolic welcome'; the attempts to escape from evil, whether Indian or Greek, have ended in flight from the battle-field; it remains to us to throw aside the youthful over-confidence and the no less youthful discouragement of nonage. We are grown men, and must play the man

> strong in will
> To strive, to seek to find, and not to yield,

cherishing the good that falls in our way, and bearing the evil, in and around us, with stout hearts set on diminishing it. So far, we all may strive in one faith towards one hope:

> It may be that the gulfs will wash us down,
> It may be we shall touch the Happy Isles,
> . . . . but something ere the end,
> Some work of noble note may yet be done.    (24)

# (3) NOTES

*Note* 1,
*p.* 69. I have been careful to speak of the 'appearance' of cyclical
evolution presented by living things; for, on critical
examination, it will be found that the course of vegetable
and of animal life is not exactly represented by the figure
of a cycle which returns into itself. What actually happens,
in all but the lowest organisms, is that one part of the
growing germ ($A$) gives rise to tissues and organs; while
another part ($B$) remains in its primitive condition, or is
but slightly modified. The moiety $A$ becomes the body of
the adult and, sooner or later, perishes, while portions of
the moiety $B$ are detached and, as offspring, continue the
life of the species. Thus, if we trace back an organism
along the direct line of descent from its remotest ancestor,
$B$, as a whole, has never suffered death; portions of it,
only, have been cast off and died in each individual offspring.

Everybody is familiar with the way in which the 'suckers'
of a strawberry plant behave. A thin cylinder of living
tissue keeps on growing at its free end, until it attains a
considerable length. At successive intervals, it develops buds
which grow into strawberry plants; and these become independent by the death of the parts of the sucker which
connect them. The rest of the sucker, however, may go on
living and growing indefinitely, and, circumstances remaining favourable, there is no obvious reason why it should ever
die. The living substance $B$, in a manner, answers to the
sucker. If we could restore the continuity which was once
possessed by the portions of $B$, contained in all the individuals of a direct line of descent, they would form a sucker,
or *stolon*, on which these individuals would be strung, and
which would never have wholly died.

A species remains unchanged so long as the potentiality
of development resident in $B$ remains unaltered; so long,
*e.g.*, as the buds of the strawberry sucker tend to become
typical strawberry plants. In the case of the progressive
evolution of a species, the developmental potentiality of
$B$ becomes of a higher and higher order. In retrogressive
evolution, the contrary would be the case. The phenomena
of atavism seem to show that retrogressive evolution, that
is, the return of a species to one or other of its earlier
forms, is a possibility to be reckoned with. The simplifica-

tion of structure, which is so common in the parasitic members of a group, however, does not properly come under
this head. The worm-like, limbless *Lernæa has no re-*
*semblance to any of the stages of development of the many-*
*limbed active animals of the group to which it belongs.*

*Note 2,*   Heracleitus says, Ποταμῷ γὰρ οὐκ ἔστι δὶς ἐμβῆναι τῷ αὐτῷ
*p. 70.*   but, to be strictly accurate, the river remains, though the
water of which it is composed changes—just as a man
retains his identity though the whole substance of his body
is constantly shifting.

This is put very well by Seneca (Ep. lvii. i, 20, Ed.
Ruhkopf): 'Corpora nostra rapiuntur fluminum more,
quidquid vides currit cum tempore; nihil ex his quae vide-
mus manet. Ego ipse dum loquor mutari ista, mutatus sum.
Hoc est quod ait Heraclitus "In idem flumen bis non
descendimus". Manet idem fluminis nomen, aqua transmissa
est. Hoc in amne manifestius est quam in homine, sed nos
quoque non minus velox cursus prætervehit'.

*Note 3,*   'Multa bona nostra nobis nocent, timoris enim tormentum
*p. 74.*   memoria reducit, providentia anticipat. Nemo tantum
præsentibus miser est'. (Seneca, Ed. v. 7.)

Among the many wise and weighty aphorisms of the
Roman Bacon, few sound the realities of life more deeply
than 'Multa bona nostra nobis nocent'. If there is a soul
of good in things evil, it is at least equally true that there
is a soul of evil in things good: for things, like men, have
'les défauts de leurs qualités'. It is one of the last lessons
one learns from experience, but not the least important,
that a heavy tax is levied upon all forms of success; and
that failure is one of the commonest disguises assumed by
blessings.

*Note 4,*   'There is within the body of every man a soul which, at
*p. 77.*   the death of the body, flies away from it like a bird out
of a cage, and enters upon a new life . . . either in one
of the heavens or one of the hells or on this earth. The
only exception is the rare case of a man having in this life
acquired a true knowledge of God. According to the pre-
Buddhistic theory, the soul of such a man goes along the
path of the gods to God, and, being united with Him,
enters upon an immortal life in which his individuality
is not extinguished. In the latter theory, his soul is directly
absorbed into the Great Soul, is lost in it, and has no
longer any independent existence. The souls of all other
men enter, after the death of the body, upon a new existence

in one or other of the many different modes of being. If in heaven or hell, the soul itself becomes a god or demon without entering a body; all superhuman beings save the great gods, being looked upon as not eternal, but merely temporary creatures. If the soul returns to earth it may or may not enter a new body; and this either of a human being, an animal, a plant, or even a material object. For all these are possessed of souls, and there is no essential difference between these souls and the souls of men—all being alike mere sparks of the Great Spirit, who is the only real existence'. (Rhys Davids, *Hibbert Lectures*, 1881, p. 83.)

For what I have said about Indian Philosophy, I am particularly indebted to the luminous exposition of primitive Buddhism and its relations to earlier Hindu thought, which is given by Prof. Rhys Davids in his remarkable *Hibbert Lectures* for 1881, and *Buddhism* (1890). The only apology I can offer for the freedom with which I have borrowed from him in these notes, is my desire to leave no doubt as to my indebtedness. I have also found Dr. Oldenberg's *Buddha* (Ed. 2, 1890) very helpful. The origin of the theory of transmigration stated in the above extract is an unsolved problem. That it differs widely from the Egyptian metempsychosis is clear. In fact, since men usually people the other world with phantoms of this, the Egyptian doctrine would seem to presuppose the Indian as a more archaic belief.

Prof. Rhys Davids has fully insisted upon the ethical importance of the transmigration theory. 'One of the latest speculations now being put forward among ourselves would seek to explain each man's character, and even his outward condition in life, by the character he inherited from his ancestors, a character gradually formed during a practically endless series of past existences, modified only by the conditions into which he was born, those very conditions being also, in like manner, the last result of a practically endless series of past causes. Gautama's speculation might be stated in the same words. But it attempted also to explain, in a way different from that which would be adopted by the exponents of the modern theory, that strange problem which it is also the motive of the wonderful drama of the book of Job to explain—the fact that the actual distribution here of good fortune, or misery, is entirely independent of the moral qualities which men call good or bad. We cannot wonder that a teacher, whose whole system was so essentially an ethical reformation, should have felt it incumbent upon him to seek an explanation of this apparent injustice. And all the more so, since the belief he had inherited, the theory of the transmigration of souls, had provided a solution perfectly sufficient to any one who could accept that belief'. (*Hibbert Lectures*, p. 93.) I should venture to suggest the substitution of 'largely' for 'entirely' in the foregoing passage. Whether a ship makes a good or a bad voyage is largely independent of the conduct of the captain, but it is largely affected by that conduct. Though powerless before a hurricane he may weather many a bad gale.

*Note* 5, *p.* 77. The outward condition of the soul is, in each new birth determined by its actions in a previous birth; but by each action in succession, and not by the balance struck after the evil has been reckoned off against the good. A good man who has once uttered a slander may spend a hundred thousand years as a god, in consequence of his goodness, and when the power of his good actions is exhausted, may be born as a dumb man on account of his transgression; and a robber who has once done an act of mercy, may come to life in a king's body as the result of his virtue, and then suffer torments for ages in hell or as a ghost without a body, or be re-born many times as a slave or an outcast, in consequence of his evil life.

'There is no escape, according to this theory, from the result of any act; though it is only the consequences of its own acts that each soul has to endure. The force has been set in motion by itself and can never stop; and its effect can never be foretold. If evil, it can never be modified or prevented, for it depends on a cause already completed, that is now for ever beyond the soul's control. There is even no continuing consciousness, no memory of the past that could guide the soul to any knowledge of its fate. The only advantage open to it is to add in this life to the sum of its good actions, that it may bear fruit with the rest. And even this can only happen in some future life under essentially the same conditions as the present one: subject, like the present one, to old age, decay, and death; and affording opportunity, like the present one, for the commission of errors, ignorances, or sins, which in their turn must inevitably produce their due effect of sickness, disability, or woe. Thus is the soul tossed about from life to life, from billow to billow in the great ocean of transmigration. And there is no escape save for the very few, who, during their birth as men, attain to a right knowledge of the Great Spirit: and thus enter into immortality, or, as the later philosophers taught, are absorbed into the Divine Essence'. (Rhys Davids, *Hibbert Lectures*, pp. 85, 86.)

The state after death thus imagined by the Hindu philosophers has a certain analogy to the purgatory of the Roman Church; except that escape from it is dependent, not on a divine decree modified, it may be, by sacerdotal or saintly intercession, but by the acts of the individual himself; and that while ultimate emergence into heavenly bliss of the good, or well-prayed for, Catholic is professedly assured, the chances in favour of the attainment of absorption, or of Nirvana, by any individual Hindu are extremely small.

*Note* 6, 'That part of the then prevalent transmigration theory
*p.* 78. which could not be proved false seemed to meet a deeply felt necessity, seemed to supply a moral cause which would explain the unequal distribution here of happiness or woe, so utterly inconsistent with the present characters of men'. Gautama 'still therefore talked of men's previous existence, but by no means in the way that he is generally represented to have done'. What he taught was 'the transmigration of character'. He held that after the death of any being, whether human or not, there survived nothing at all but that being's 'Karma', the result, that is, of its mental and bodily actions. 'Every individual, whether human or divine, was the last inheritor and the last result of the Karma of a long series of past individuals—a series so long that its beginning is beyond the reach of calculation, and its end will be coincident with the destruction of the world'. (Rhys Davids, *Hibbert Lectures*, p. 92.)

In the theory of evolution, the tendency of a germ to develop according to a certain specific type, *e.g.*, of the kidney bean seed to grow into a plant having all the characters of *Phaseolus vulgaris*, is its 'Karma'. It is the 'last inheritor and the last result' of all the conditions that have affected a line of ancestry which goes back for many millions of years to the time when life first appeared on the earth. The moiety *B* of the substance of the bean plant (see *Note* 1) is the last link in a once continuous chain extending from the primitive living substance: and the characters of the successive species to which it has given rise are the manifestations of its gradually modified Karma. As Prof. Rhys Davids aptly says, the snowdrop 'is a snowdrop and not an oak, and just that kind of snowdrop, because it is the outcome of the Karma of an endless series of past existences'. (*Hibbert Lectures*, p. 114).

*Note* 7,
*p.* 79. 'It is interesting to notice that the very point which is the weakness of the theory—the supposed concentration of the effect of the Karma in one new being—presented itself to the early Buddhists themselves as a difficulty. They avoided it, partly by explaining that it was a particular thirst in the creature dying (a craving, Tanhā, which plays otherwise a great part in the Buddhist theory) which actually caused the birth of the new individual who was to inherit the Karma of the former one. But, how this took place, how the craving desire produced this effect, was acknowledged to be a mystery patent only to a Buddha'. (Rhys Davids, *Hibbert Lectures,* p. 95.)

Among the many parallelisms of Stoicism and Buddhism, it is curious to find one for this Tanhā, 'thirst', or 'craving desire' for life. Seneca writes (Epist. lxxvi, 18): 'Si enim ullum aliud est bonum quam honestum, sequetur nos *aviditas vitæ,* aviditas rerum vitam instruentium: quod est intolerabile, infinitum, vagum.'

*Note* 8,
*p.* 81. 'The distinguishing characteristic of Buddhism was that it started a new line, that it looked upon the deepest questions men have to solve from an entirely different standpoint. It swept away from the field of its vision the whole of the great soul-theory which had hitherto so completely filled and dominated the minds of the superstitious and the thoughtful alike. For the first time in the history of the world, it proclaimed a salvation which each man could gain for himself and by himself, in this world, during this life, without the least reference at all to God, or to Gods, either great or small. Like the Upanishads, it placed the first importance on knowledge; but it was no longer a knowledge of God, it was a clear perception of the real nature, as they supposed it to be, of men and things. And it added to the necessity of knowledge, the necessity of purity, of courtesy, of uprightness, of peace and of a universal love far reaching, grown great and beyond measure'. (Rhys Davids, *Hibbert Lectures*, p. 29.)

The contemporary Greek philosophy takes an analogous direction. According to Heracleitus, the universe was made neither by Gods nor men; but, from all eternity, has been, and to all eternity, will be, immortal fire, glowing and fading in due measure. (Mullach, *Heracliti Fragmenta,* 27.)

And the part assigned by his successors, the Stoics, to the knowledge and the volition of the 'wise man' made their Divinity (for logical thinkers) a subject for compliments, rather than a power to be reckoned with. In Hindu speculation the 'Arahat', still more the 'Buddha', becomes the superior of Brahma; the stoical 'wise man' is, at least, the equal of Zeus.

Berkeley affirms over and over again that no idea can be formed of a soul or spirit—'If any man shall doubt of the truth of what is here delivered, let him but reflect and try if he can form any idea of power or active being; and whether he hath ideas of two principal powers marked by the names of *will* and *understanding* distinct from each other, as well as from a third idea of substance or being in general, with a relative notion of its supporting or being the subject of the aforesaid power, which is signified by the name *soul* or *spirit*. This is what some hold: but, so far as I can see, the words *will*, *soul*, *spirit*, do not stand for different ideas or, in truth, for any idea at all, but for something which is very different from ideas, and which, being an agent, cannot be like unto or represented by any idea whatever [though it must be owned at the same time, that we have some notion of soul, spirit, and the operations of the mind, such as willing, loving, hating, inasmuch as we know or understand the meaning of these words]'. (*The Principles of Human Knowledge*, lxxvi. See also §§ lxxxix, cxxxv, cxlv.)

It is open to discussion, I think, whether it is possible to have 'some notion' of that of which we can form no 'idea'.

Berkeley attaches several predicates to the 'perceiving active being, mind, spirit, soul or myself' (Parts I, II). It is said, for example, to be 'indivisible, incorporeal, unextended, and incorruptible'. The predicate indivisible, though negative in form, has highly positive consequences. For, if 'perceiving active being' is strictly indivisible, man's soul must be one with the Divine spirit: which is good Hindu or Stoical doctrine, but hardly orthodox Christian philosophy. If, on the other hand, the 'substance' of active perceiving 'being' is actually divided into the one Divine and innumerable human entities, how can the predicate 'indivisible' be rigorously applicable to it?

Taking the words cited, as they stand, they amount to

the denial of the possibility of any knowledge of substance. 'Matter' having been resolved into mere affections of 'spirit', 'spirit' melts away into an admittedly inconceivable and unknowable hypostasis of thought and power—consequently the existence of anything in the universe beyond a flow of phenomena is a purely hypothetical assumption. Indeed a pyrrhonist might raise the objection that if 'esse' is 'percipi' spirit itself can have no existence except as a perception, hypostatized into a 'self', or as a perception of some other spirit. In the former case, objective reality vanishes; in the latter, there would seem to be the need of an infinite series of spirits each perceiving the others.

It is curious to observe how very closely the phraseology of Berkeley sometimes approaches that of the Stoics: thus (cxlviii). 'It seems to be a *general pretence of the unthinking* herd that *they cannot see God.* . . . But, alas, we need only open our eyes to see the Sovereign Lord of all things with a more full and clear view, than we do any of our fellow-creatures . . . we do at all times and in all places perceive manifest tokens of the Divinity: everything we see, hear, feel, or any wise perceive by sense, being a sign or effect of the power of God' . . . cxlix. 'It is therefore plain, that *nothing can be more evident* to any one that is capable of the least reflection, *that the existence of God*, or a spirit who is intimately present to our minds, producing in them all that variety of ideas or sensations which continually affect us, on whom we have an absolute and entire dependence, in short, *in whom we live and move and have our being.*' cl. '[But you will say hath Nature no share in the production of natural things, and must they be all ascribed to the immediate and sole operation of God? . . . if by *Nature* is meant some being distinct from God, as well as from the laws of nature and things perceived by sense, I must confess that word is to me an empty sound, without any intelligible meaning annexed to it.] Nature in this acceptation is a vain *Chimæra* introduced by those heathens, who had not just notions of the omnipresence and infinite perfection of God.'

Compare Seneca (*De Beneficiis*, iv, 7):

'Natura, inquit, hæc mihi præstat. Non intelligis te, quum hoc dicis, mutare Nomen Deo? Quid enim est aliud Natura quam Deus, et divina ratio, toti mundo et partibus ejus inserta? Quoties voles tibi licet aliter hunc auctorem rerum nostrarum compellare, et Jovem illum optimum et

maximum rite dices, et tonantem, et statorem: qui non, ut
historici tradiderunt, ex eo quod post votum susceptum acies
Romanorum fugientum stetit, sed quod stant beneficio ejus
omnia, stator, stabilitorque est: hunc eundem et fatum si
dixeris, non mentieris, nam quum fatum nihil aliud est,
quam series implexa causarum, ille est prima omnium causa,
ea qua cæteræ pendent.' It would appear, therefore, that the
good Bishop is somewhat hard upon the 'heathen', of whose
words his own might be a paraphrase.

There is yet another direction in which Berkeley's philosophy, I will not say agrees with Gautama's, but at any rate
helps to make a fundamental dogma of Buddhism intelligible.

'I find I can excite ideas in my mind at pleasure, and
vary and shift the scene as often as I think fit. It is no
more than willing, and straightway this or that idea arises
in my fancy: and by the same power, it is obliterated, and
makes way for another. This making and unmaking of
ideas doth very properly denominate the mind active. This
much is certain and grounded on experience. . . .' (*Principles*, xxviii.)

A good many of us, I fancy, have reason to think that
experience tells them very much the contrary; and are
painfully familiar with the obsession of the mind by ideas
which cannot be obliterated by any effort of the will and
steadily refuse to make way for others. But what I desire
to point out is that if Gautama was equally confident that
he could 'make and unmake' ideas—then, since he had
resolved self into a group of ideal phantoms—the possibility
of abolishing self by volition naturally followed.

*Note* 9,  According to Buddhism, the relation of one life to the next
*p.* 82.  is merely that borne by the flame of one lamp to the flame
of another lamp which is set alight by it. To the 'Arahat'
or adept 'no outward form, no compound thing, no creature,
no creator, no existence of any kind, must appear to be
other than a temporary collocation of its component parts,
fated inevitably to be dissolved'.—(Rhys Davids, *Hibbert
Lectures*, p. 211.)

The self is nothing but a group of phenomena held
together by the desire of life; when that desire shall have
ceased, 'the Karma of that particular chain of lives will
cease to influence any longer any distinct individual, and
there will be no more birth; for birth, decay, and death,

grief, lamentation, and despair will have come, so far as regards that chain of lives, for ever to an end'.

The state of mind of the Arahat in which the desire of life has ceased is Nirvana. Dr. Oldenberg has very acutely and patiently considered the various interpretations which have been attached to 'Nirvana' in the work to which I have referred (pp. 285 *et seq.*). The result of his and other discussions of the question may I think be briefly stated thus: 1. Logical deduction from the predicates attached to the term 'Nirvana' strips it of all reality, conceivability, or perceivability, whether by Gods or men. For all practical purposes, therefore, it comes to exactly the same thing as annihilation.

2. But it is not annihilation in the ordinary sense, inasmuch as it could take place in the living Arahat or Buddha.

3. And, since, for the faithful Buddhist, that which was abolished in the Arahat was the possibility of further pain, sorrow, or sin; and that which was attained was perfect peace; his mind directed itself exclusively to this joyful consummation, and personified the negation of all conceivable existence and of all pain into a positive bliss. This was all the more easy, as Gautama refused to give any dogmatic definition of Nirvana. There is something analogous in the way in which people commonly talk of the 'happy release' of a man who has been long suffering from mortal disease. According to their own views, it must always be extremely doubtful whether the man will be any happier after the 'release' than before. But they do not choose to look at the matter in this light.

The popular notion that, with practical, if not metaphysical, annihilation in view, Buddhism must needs be a sad and gloomy faith seems to be inconsistent with fact; on the contrary, the prospect of Nirvana fills the true believer, not merely with cheerfulness, but with an ecstatic desire to reach it.

*Note* 10, *p.* 82. The influence of the picture of the personal qualities of Gautama, afforded by the legendary anecdotes which rapidly grew into a biography of the Buddha; and by the birth stories, which coalesced with the current folk-lore, and were intelligible to all the world, doubtless played a great part. Further, although Gautama appears not to have meddled with the caste system, he refused to recognize any distinction, save that of perfection in the way of salvation, among his followers; and by such teaching, no less than by the inculcation of love and benevolence to all sentient beings, he practically levelled every social, political, and racial barrier. A third important condition was the organization of the Buddhists into monastic communities for the stricter professors, while the laity were permitted a wide indulgence in practice and were allowed to hope for accommodation in some of the temporary abodes of bliss. With a few hundred thousand years of immediate paradise in sight, the average man could be content to shut his eyes to what might follow.

*Note* 11, *p.* 83. In ancient times it was the fashion, even among the Greeks themselves, to derive all Greek wisdom from Eastern sources; not long ago it was as generally denied that Greek philosophy had any connection with Oriental speculation; it seems probable, however, that the truth lies between these extremes.

The Ionian intellectual movement does not stand alone. It is only one of several sporadic indications of the working of some powerful mental ferment over the whole of the area comprised between the Ægean and Northern Hindostan during the eighth, seventh, and sixth centuries before our era. In these three hundred years, prophetism attained its apogee among the Semites of Palestine; Zoroasterism grew and became the creed of a conquering race, the Iranic Aryans; Buddhism rose and spread with marvellous rapidity among the Aryans of Hindostan; while scientific naturalism took its rise among the Aryans of Ionia. It would be difficult to find another three centuries which have given birth to four events of equal importance. All the principal existing religions of mankind have grown out of the first three: while the fourth is the little spring, now swollen into the great stream of positive science. So far as physical possibilities go, the prophet Jeremiah and the oldest Ionian philosopher might have met and conversed. If they had done so, they would probably have disagreed a good deal; and it is interesting to reflect that their discussions might have embraced questions which, at the present day, are still hotly controverted.

The old Ionian philosophy, then, seems to be only one of many results of a stirring of the moral and intellectual life of the Aryan and the Semitic populations of Western Asia. The conditions of this general awakening were doubtless manifold; but there is one which modern research has brought into great prominence. This is the existence of extremely ancient and highly advanced societies in the valleys of the Euphrates and of the Nile.

It is now known that, more than a thousand—perhaps more than two thousand—years before the sixth century B.C., civilization had attained a relatively high pitch among the Babylonians and the Egyptians. Not only had painting, sculpture, architecture, and the industrial arts reached a remarkable development; but in Chaldæa, at any rate, a vast amount of knowledge had been accumulated and methodized, in the departments of grammar, mathematics, astronomy, and natural history. Where such traces of the scientific spirit are visible, naturalistic speculation is rarely far off, though, so far as I know, no remains of an Accadian, or Egyptian, philosophy, properly so called, have yet been recovered.

Geographically, Chaldæa occupied a central position among the oldest seats of civilization. Commerce, largely aided by the intervention of those colossal pedlars, the Phœnicians, had brought Chaldæa into connection with all of them, for a thousand years before the epoch at present under consideration. And in the ninth, eighth, and seventh centuries, the Assyrian, the depositary of Chaldæan civilization, as the Macedonian and the Roman, at a later date, were the depositaries of Greek culture, had added irresistible force to the other agencies for the wide distribution of Chaldæan literature, art, and science.

I confess that I find it difficult to imagine that the Greek immigrants—who stood in somewhat the same relation to the Babylonians and the Egyptians as the later Germanic barbarians to the Romans of the Empire—should not have been immensely influenced by the new life with which they became acquainted. But there is abundant direct evidence of the magnitude of this influence in certain spheres. I suppose it is not doubted that the Greek went to school with the Oriental for his primary instruction in reading, writing, and arithmetic; and that Semitic theology supplied him with some of his mythological lore. Nor does there now seem to be any question about the large indebtedness of Greek art to that of Chaldæa and that of Egypt.

But the manner of that indebtedness is very instructive. The obligation is clear, but its limits are no less definite. Nothing better exemplifies the indomitable originality of the Greeks than the relations of their art to that of the Orientals. Far from being subdued into mere imitators by the technical excellence of their teachers, they lost no time in bettering the instruction they received, using their models as mere stepping stones on the way to those unsurpassed and unsurpassable achievements which are all their own. The shibboleth of Art is the human figure. The ancient Chaldæans and Egyptians, like the modern Japanese, did wonders in the representation of birds and quadrupeds; they even attained to something more than respectability in human portraiture. But their utmost efforts never brought them within range of the best Greek embodiments of the grace of womanhood, or of the severer beauty of manhood.

It is worth while to consider the probable effect upon the acute and critical Greek mind of the conflict of ideas, social, political, and theological, which arose out of the conditions of life in the Asiatic colonies. The Ionian polities had passed through the whole gamut of social and political changes, from patriarchal and occasionally oppressive kingship to rowdy and still more burdensome mobship —no doubt with infinitely eloquent and copious argumentation, on both sides, at every stage of their progress towards that arbitrament of force which settles most political questions. The marvellous speculative faculty, latent in the Ionian, had come in contact with Mesopotamian, Egyptian, Phœnician theologies and cosmogonies; with the illuminati of Orphism and the fanatics and dreamers of the Mysteries; possibly with Buddhism and Zoroasterism; possibly even with Judaism. And it has been observed that the mutual contradictions of antagonistic supernaturalisms are apt to play a large part among the generative agencies of naturalism.

Thus, various external influences may have contributed to the rise of philosophy among the Ionian Greeks of the sixth century. But the assimilative capacity of the Greek mind—its power of Hellenizing whatever it touched—has here worked so effectually, that, so far as I can learn, no indubitable traces of such extraneous contributions are now allowed to exist by the most authoritative historians of Philosophy. Nevertheless, I think it must be admitted that the coincidences between the Heracleito-stoical doctrines and those of the older Hindu philosophy are extremely remarkable. In both, the cosmos pursues an eternal succession of cyclical changes. The great year, answering to the Kalpa, covers an entire cycle from the origin of the universe as a fluid to its dissolution in fire—'Humor initium, ignis exitus mundi', as Seneca has it. In both systems, there is immanent in the cosmos a source of energy, Brahma, or the Logos which works according to fixed laws. The individual soul is an efflux of this world-spirit and returns to it. Perfection is attainable only by individual effort, through ascetic discipline, and is rather a state of painlessness than of happiness; if indeed it can be said to be a state of anything, save the negation of perturbing emotion. The hatchment motto 'In Cœlo Quies' would serve both Hindu and Stoic; and absolute quiet is not easily distinguishable from annihilation.

Zoroasterism, which, geographically occupies a position intermediate between Hellenism and Hinduism, agrees with the latter in recognizing the essential evil of the cosmos; but differs from both in its intensely anthropomorphic personification of the two antagonistic principles, to the one of which it ascribes all the good; and, to the other, all the evil. In fact, it assumes the existence of two worlds, one good and one bad; the latter created by the evil power for the purpose of damaging the former. The existing cosmos is a mere mixture of the two, and the 'last judgment' is a root-and-branch extirpation of the work of Ahriman.

*Note* 12, *p.* 83. There is no snare in which the feet of a modern student of ancient lore are more easily entangled, than that which is spread by the similarity of the language of antiquity to modern modes of expression. I do not presume to interpret the obscurest of Greek philosophers; all I wish is to point out, that his words, in the sense accepted by competent interpreters, fit modern ideas singularly well.

So far as the general theory of evolution goes there is no difficulty. The aphorism about the river; the figure of the child playing on the shore; the kingship and fatherhood of strife, seem decisive. The ὁδός ἄνω κάτω μίη expresses, with singular aptness, the cyclical aspect of the one process of organic evolution in individual plants and animals: yet it may be a question whether the Heracleitean strife included any distinct conception of the struggle for existence. Again, it is tempting to compare the part played by the Heracleitean 'fire' with that ascribed by the moderns to heat, or rather to that cause of motion of which heat is one expression; and a little ingenuity might find a foreshadowing of the doctrine of the conservation of energy, in the saying that all things are changed into fire and fire into all things, as gold into goods and goods into gold.

Pope's lines in the *Essay on Man* (Ep. i, 267-8),

> All are but parts of one stupendous whole,
> Whose body Nature is, and God the soul,

*Note* 13, simply paraphrase Seneca's 'quem in hoc mundo locum
*p.* 84. deus obtinet, hunc in homine animus: quod est illic materia, id nobis corpus est'.—(Ep. lxv, 24); which again is a Latin version of the old Stoical doctrine, εἰς ἅπαν τοῦ κόσμου μέρος διήκει ὁ νοῦς, καθάπερ ἀφ ἡμῶν ἡ ψυχή.

So far as the testimony for the universality of what ordinary people call 'evil' goes, there is nothing better than the writings of the Stoics themselves. They might serve as a storehouse for the epigrams of the ultra-pessimists. Heracleitus (*circa* 500 B.C.) says just as hard things about ordinary humanity as his disciples centuries later; and there really seems no need to seek for the causes of this dark view of life in the circumstances of the time of Alexander's successors or of the early Emperors of Rome. To the man with an ethical ideal, the world, including himself, will always seem full of evil.

*Note* 14, I use the well-known phrase, but decline responsibility for
*p.* 85. the libel upon Epicurus, whose doctrines were far less compatible with existence in a stye than those of the Cynics. If it were steadily borne in mind that the conception of the 'flesh' as the source of evil, and the great saying 'Initium est salutis notitia peccati', are the property of Epicurus, fewer illusions about Epicureanism would pass muster for accepted truth.

*Note* 15, The Stoics said that man was a ζῷον λογικὸν πολιτικὸν
*p.* 87. φιλάλληλον, or a rational, a political, and an altruistic or philanthropic animal. In their view, his higher nature tended to develop in these three directions, as a plant tends to grow up into its typical form. Since, without the introduction of any consideration of pleasure or pain, whatever thwarted the realization of its type by the plant might be said to be bad, and whatever helped it good; so virtue, in the Stoical sense, as the conduct which tended to the attainment of the rational, political, and philanthropic ideal, was good in itself, and irrespectively of its emotional concomitants.

Man is an 'animal sociale communi bono genitum'. The safety of society depends upon practical recognition of the fact. 'Salva autem esse societas nisi custodia et amore partium non possit', says Seneca. (*De Ira*, ii, 31.)

*Note* 16,  The importance of the physical doctrine of the Stoics lies in
*p.* 87.  its clear recognition of the universality of the law of causation, with its corollary, the order of nature: the exact form
of that order is an altogether secondary consideration.

Many ingenious persons now appear to consider that the
incompatibility of pantheism, of materialism, and of any
doubt about the immortality of the soul, with religion and
morality, is to be held as an axiomatic truth. I confess
that I have a certain difficulty in accepting this dogma. For
the Stoics were notoriously materialists and pantheists of
the most extreme character; and while no strict Stoic
believed in the eternal duration of the individual soul,
some even denied its persistence after death. Yet it is
equally certain that of all gentile philosophies, Stoicism
exhibits the highest ethical development, is animated by
the most religious spirit, and has exerted the profoundest
influence upon the moral and religious development not
merely of the best men among the Romans, but among the
moderns down to our own day.

Seneca was claimed as a Christian and placed among the
saints by the fathers of the early Christian Church; and
the genuineness of a correspondence between him and the
apostle Paul has been hotly maintained in our own time,
by orthodox writers. That the letters, as we possess them,
are worthless forgeries is obvious; and writers as wide apart
as Baur and Lightfoot agree that the whole story is devoid
of foundation.

The dissertation of the late Bishop of Durham (*Epistle
to the Philippians*) is particularly worthy of study, apart
from this question, on account of the evidence which it
supplies of the numerous similarities of thought between
Seneca and the writer of the Pauline epistles. When it is
remembered that the writer of the Acts puts a quotation
from Aratus, or Cleanthes, into the mouth of the apostle;
and that Tarsus was a great seat of philosophical and
especially stoical learning (Chrysippus himself was a native
of the adjacent town of Sôli), there is no difficulty in
understanding the origin of these resemblances. See, on
this subject, Sir Alexander Grant's dissertation in his edition
of *The Ethics of Aristotle* (where there is an interesting
reference to the stoical character of Bishop Butler's ethics),
the concluding pages of Dr. Weygoldt's instructive little
work *Die Philosophie der Stoa*, and Aubertin's *Sénèque et
Saint Paul.*

It is surprising that a writer of Dr. Lightfoot's stamp should speak of Stoicism as a philosophy of 'despair'. Surely, rather, it was a philosophy of men who, having cast off all illusions, and the childishness of despair among them, were minded to endure in patience whatever con ditions the cosmic process might create, so long as those conditions were compatible with the progress towards virtue, which alone, for them, conferred a worthy object on existence. There is no note of despair in the stoical declaration that the perfected 'wise man' is the equal of Zeus in everything but the duration of his existence. And, in my judgment, there is as little pride about it, often as it serves for the text of discourses on stoical arrogance. Grant the stoical postulate that there is no good except virtue; grant that the perfected wise man is altogether virtuous, in consequence of being guided in all things by the reason, which is an effluence of Zeus, and there seems no escape from the stoical conclusion.

*Note* 17, Our 'Apathy' carries such a different set of connotations
*p.* 88. from its Greek original that I have ventured on using the latter as a technical term.

*Note* 18, Many of the stoical philosophers recommended their disci-
*p.* 89. ples to take an active share in public affairs; and in the Roman world, for several centuries, the best public men were strongly inclined to Stoicism. Nevertheless, the logical tendency of Stoicism seems to me to be fulfilled only in such men as Diogenes and Epictetus.

*Note* 19, 'Criticisms on the Origin of Species', 1864. *Collected Essays*,
*p.* 91. vol. ii, p. 91. [1894].

*Note* 20, Of course, strictly speaking, social life, and the ethical
*p.* 91. process in virtue of which it advances towards perfection, are part and parcel of the general process of evolution, just as the gregarious habit of innumerable plants and animals, which has been of immense advantage to them, is so. A hive of bees is an organic polity, a society in which the part played by each member is determined by organic necessities. Queens, workers, and drones are, so to speak, castes, divided from one another by marked physical barriers. Among birds and mammals, societies are formed, of which the bond in many cases seems to be purely psychological; that is to say, it appears to depend upon the liking of the individuals for one another's company. The tendency of individuals to over self-assertion is kept down by fighting.

Even in these rudimentary forms of society, love and fear come into play, and enforce a greater or less renunciation of self-will. To this extent the general cosmic process begins to be checked by a rudimentary ethical process, which is, strictly speaking, part of the former, just as the 'governor' in a steam-engine is part of the mechanism of the engine.

Note 21, p. 92. See 'Government: Anarchy or Regimentation', *Collected Essays,* vol. i, pp. 413-418. It is this form of political philosophy to which I conceive the epithet of 'reasoned savagery' to be strictly applicable. [1894.]

Note 22, p. 93. 'L'homme n'est qu'un roseau, le plus faible de la nature, mais c'est un roseau pensant. Il ne faut pas que l'univers entier s'arme pour l'écraser. Une vapeur, une goutte d'eau, suffit pour le tuer. Mais quand l'univers l'écraserait, l'homme serait encore plus noble que ce qui le tue, parce qu'il sait qu'il meurt; et l'avantage que l'univers a sur lui, l'univers n'en sait rien'.—*Pensées de Pascal.*

Note 23, p. 94. The use of the word 'Nature' here may be criticized. Yet the manifestation of the natural tendencies of men is so profoundly modified by training that it is hardly too strong. Consider the suppression of the sexual instinct between near relations.

Note 24, p. 94. A great proportion of poetry is addressed by the young to the young; only the great masters of the art are capable of divining, or think it worth while to enter into, the feelings of retrospective age. The two great poets whom we have so lately lost, Tennyson and Browning, have done this, each in his own inimitable way; the one in the *Ulysses,* from which I have borrowed; the other in that wonderful fragment 'Childe Roland to the dark Tower came .

## II

### *Julian Huxley*

# Evolutionary Ethics

[*The Romanes Lectures,* 1943]

I

T. H. HUXLEY'S ANTITHESIS BETWEEN ETHICS AND EVOLUTION

I HARDLY need to say how much I valued the invitation to deliver this lecture. To be asked to join the band of Romanes lecturers, which has included so many of our greatest men during the past half-century, is a valued honour. To be able, in that situation, to speak in and to my old university, which not only formed my mind but later provided both the opportunity and the stimulus for its most intensive exercise, is a cherished privilege.

That is already a great deal; but you have enhanced both the honour and the privilege by extending this invitation to me on the fiftieth anniversary of the Romanes lecture of my grandfather, Thomas Henry Huxley, and by suggesting that I might have something to contribute on the tremendous theme which he selected.

As I grew up, the example of T. H. Huxley was constantly before me. He was great not only as a scientist, but also as a man: the Romanes lecture on *Evolution and Ethics* which, two years before his death, he delivered from where I now stand, was one of his notable contributions to general thought.

But this honour carries its peculiar responsibilities. For one thing, it is almost an impertinence for anyone to embark upon a discussion of abstract ethical questions when all around us the straightforward practical ethics of performing one's immediate duty are leading millions uncomplainingly to new heights of heroism and sacrifice. On this, however, I am comforted by the reflection that some of the most abstract ethical problems have in recent times become intensely and increasingly practical. Fifty years ago T. H. Huxley could, it seems, consider what he called the ethical process as based on general principles which were both immutable and rationally self-evident. Since his time this conception of absolute and unquestioned ethical standards has steadily become less tenable, to be replaced by an even more thoroughgoing ethical relativism. But this process did not only manifest itself in the intellectual sphere. It has emerged into the domain of brutal and gigantic fact. Fascism, notably in its National-Socialist guise, has developed its own ethical principles, in which millions of our fellow-men firmly believe; and these are almost diametrically opposed to anything which Huxley considered as self-evident. We live under the grim material necessity of defeating the Nazi system, ethics and all, but no less under the spiritual and intellectual necessity not merely of feeling or believing but of *knowing* that Nazi ethics are not just different from ours, but wrong and false; or at least less right and less true.

Nazi Germany also demonstrates what strength a society can draw from its ethical beliefs, however distorted they may appear to us. Meanwhile for us in this country and the other united Nations, the fateful responsibilities of the peace loom daily larger. Split them up as you will, into their economic and political compartments, into devices for technical and administrative improvement, they *must* add up to make a better world. No jesting Pilate can escape the implications of that word *better*. To know that the new world at which we aim is better than the old, is to have some assurance of the adequacy of our own ethical beliefs to meet the new situation. Yet this is precisely what we lack. There has been a collapse of our traditional values, so that we live in a bewildering atmosphere of ethical relativity. Thus beyond the immediate duties concerned with waging the war there is the further duty of contributing anything one can to the urgent business of clarifying our general ethical principles: the relation between ethics and evolution may not be so abstract after all.

This is a daunting task, and a bewildering one. Yet a biologist may, I hope, make his contribution by showing how some of the knowledge slowly amassed by thousands of his fellow-scientists may be used as the outline of a map of these difficult and dangerous verges, and so help to bring them within the assured domain of human safety and order.

A map is not reality; it does not even attempt to reproduce or evoke reality, only to give a convenient representation of certain of its physical features. And a small-scale outline map must concentrate on major features, leaving the details to be filled in later. I am perfectly aware of the immense complexity of our moral lives, each of which, and every separate ethical problem within each life, is unique. But they are irrelevant to this business of map-drawing. Nor, in his brief hour, has a lecturer time for documentation or for technical discussion of the steps in his argument. If I make what appear sweeping pronouncements on biological or psychological matters, it is because I conceive it my business here to be merely to present the broad outlines of a map.

For T. H. Huxley, fifty years ago, there was a fundamental contradiction between the ethical process and the cosmic process. By the former, he meant the universalist ethics of the Victorian enlightenment, bred by nineteenth-century humanitarianism out of traditional Christian ethics, and in him personally tinged by a noble but stern puritanism and an almost fanatical devotion to scientific truth and its pursuit. And the cosmic process he restricted almost entirely to biological evolution and to the selective struggle for existence on which it depends. 'The ethical progress of society' —this was the main conclusion of his Romanes lecture—'consists, not in imitating the cosmic process, still less in running away from it, but in combating it'.

To-day, that contradiction can, I believe, be resolved—on the one hand by extending the concept of evolution both backward into the inorganic and forward into the human domain, and on the other by considering ethics not as a body of fixed principles, but as a product of evolution, and itself evolving. In both cases, the intellectual tool which has given us new insight is that of developmental analysis—the scientific study of change, of becoming, of the production of novelty, whether of life from not-life, of a baby from an ovum and a man from a baby, of ants and swallows and tigers out of ancestral protozoa, of civilized societies out of barbarism and barbarism out of the dim beginnings of social life.

II

INDIVIDUAL ETHICS: THE PROTO-ETHICAL MECHANISM

ETHICS is not an entity. It is the name we assign to the results of the workings of a particular psychological mechanism. This ethical mechanism is an agency for securing that certain of our actions and thoughts shall be consciously felt and judged to have the qualities of rightness or wrongness. It gives us what is popularly called our moral sense. This sense of rightness or wrongness is charged with the driving force of strong emotions, so that the ethical mechanism, once established, helps to determine both our actions and those potential actions that are included under the head of sentiments, beliefs, and principles. On the other hand, it provides no guarantee that the feelings it engenders are correct, or its judgments objectively valid.

Our ethics can be classified, like our backbone, among our supporting mechanisms. The backbone, together with the rest of the bony skeleton, the cartilages, tendons, and all the connective tissues, serves as a supporting physical framework. Our ethical mechanism, together with our conditioned reflexes, skills, habits, likes, and dislikes, serves as a supporting psychological framework. Its peculiarity is that it charges all that passes through its mill with the special emotive qualities of rightness or wrongness.

We cannot make a map of the strange world of ethics until we study the embryology and later development of the ethical mechanism. The development of the mind has this in common with that of the body, that we have no recollection at all of its earlier stages, and that even later the most important changes take place below the surface, to be unravelled only by painstaking scientific investigation. Mental embryology to-day is still a very young science, no further advanced than physical embryology perhaps a century ago. The map we can derive from it is still crude and full of blanks, mistakes, and distortions, like the maps of the world produced by the early explorers.

The ovum has no ethics, any more than it has a backbone. Ethics, like backbones, come out of non-existence into existence *de novo* in each individual development. Somewhat as the physical stiffening of the backbone is later built round an embryological forerunner in the shape of the notochord, so the normal infant develops a forerunner for the moral stiffening of adult ethics. The Freudians call it the primitive super-ego. I will venture to coin a more non-committal term—the proto-ethical mechanism.

This spiritual notochord appears to be formed early in the infant's second year of post-natal life. It arises as the result of a special kind of conflict among the chaos of unregulated impulses with which the infant is originally endowed.

As the baby begins to draw a distinction between itself and outer reality, it is the mother[1] who comes to represent the external world, and to mediate its impacts on the child. But she dawns upon its growing consciousness under two opposite aspects. She is the child's chief object of love, and its fountainhead of satisfaction, security, and peace. But she is also Authority, the chief

---

[1] And/or any efficient mother-substitute, such as a nurse who takes over the care of the baby, or a large part of it.

source of power mysteriously set over the child and arbitrarily thwarting some of the impulses along whose paths its new life quests outwards.

The frustration of infantile impulse generates anger, hate, and destructive wishes—what the psychologists generally style aggression—directed against the thwarting authority. But this hated authority is also the loved mother. The infant is thus faced with the primal conflict. Two irreconcilable sets of impulses are directed towards the same object, and that object is the centre of its surrounding universe.

The conflict is normally won by love. The anger and the aggression, the accompanying magic fantasies of death-wishes and the like, become branded and tinged with the quality of guilt—in other words wrongness—and more or less completely banished. They emerge occasionally into action in the form of rages and tempers, but for the most part are either suppressed into the background of consciousness, or wholly repressed into the unconscious. If repressed, part of their charge of guilt (to borrow a metaphor from electricity) accompanies them into the unconscious; and in the unconscious they continue to exist, refused conscious recognition, but constantly demanding an outlet in some disguised form.

The proto-ethical mechanism may be considered as a special adaptation to the peculiar conditions of human infancy. Owing to the plastic and decompartmentalized nature of human mind, man is faced with all kinds of conflicts to which other animal species are not subject. When adult, he can generally arrive at their resolution in action, with the aid of reason and experience. But the infant is unable to solve them rationally or even consciously for lack of a requisite basis of experience. How then shall action be secured?

The same general type of problem has had to be solved by life on many occasions, and has been met by the evolution of nervous machinery whereby one of the conflicting impulses is inhibited when the other comes into action. This occurs on the muscular level: when the flexors of our arm are thrown into action and contracted, the antagonistic extensors are automatically thrown out of action and relaxed. It occurs on the reflex level: the throwing into activity of one reflex inhibits other reflexes, especially those which demand the use of the same muscles. It seems also to occur on the instinctual level: the student of animal behaviour is constantly struck by the way in which instincts which compete, if one may use the phrase, for the possession of the animal's activity, alternate in an all-or-nothing way. And finally in man, especially in infancy, the same sort of mechanism operates on the highest level of thought and behaviour, by repression, or later by suppression. In repression particularly, the mechanism is somewhat different from what is found in lower forms: instead of an alternating all-or-nothing activity of two rival tendencies, one of the competitors is permanently inhibited.[1] In suppression, the same type of inhibitory mechanism is at work, but not with the same automaticity and completeness.

From the biological point of view, the proto-ethical mechanism is in part an adaptation for securing action instead of indecision in the face of conflict. But it is something more—it is an adaptation for weighting the scales between the conflicting impulses, by attaching a load of guilt to one of them, and thus securing the complete or partial ascendancy of the other. It is not merely an adaptation for securing action instead of indecision, but also one for securing one kind of action rather than another.

Almost certainly there is always some true repression involved in the formation of the proto-ethical mechanism; but the amount will vary immensely from one child to another, both according to inherited temperament and still more to its relations with its mother.

These discoveries of modern psychology concerning the proto-

[1] In dual personality, there is alternating repression of two conflicting partial systems. Alternation of conflicting moods occurs in manic-depressives; and in suppression there is an occasional emergence of what is suppressed.

ethical mechanism and its function have finally put out of court all purely intuitive theories of ethics. All that the child inherits is a capacity for building up what we have called a proto-ethical mechanism; and even that will not take place in all circumstances. Its 'intuitions' as to what constitutes right or wrong are derived from its environment, largely mediated through its mother.

Our modern knowledge also helps us to understand the absolute, categorical, and other-worldly quality of moral obligation, on which moral philosophers lay such stress. It is due in the first instance to the compulsive all-or-nothing mechanism by which the primitive super-ego operates. It is also due to the fact that, as Waddington points out, the external world first intrudes itself into the baby's magic solipsism in the form of the parents' demands for control over primitive impulses, so that infantile ethics embody the shock of the child's discovery of a world outside itself and unamenable to its wishes.

This quality of absoluteness is later reinforced by the natural human desire for certitude, as well as by certain peculiarities of our language mechanism, which I shall discuss later. Thus the absoluteness of moral obligation turns out on analysis to be no true absolute, but a result of the nature of our infantile mental machinery, combined with later rationalization and wish-fulfilment.

And there may be other complications. The impulses whose thwarting generated the guilty hate may themselves become coloured with guilt, or be repressed. Or if the impulses of love alone are too weak to ensure obedience, the repressed aggression may be turned against the original offending impulse and employed as it were as a policeman or gaoler. These and other variations on the main theme must be studied in the text-books and the case-histories. But the central fact remains that out of this primal conflict there grows the beginning of ethics. Primitive love conquers primitive hate by saddling it with the burden of primal guilt: and with this the polarity of right and wrong becomes attached to our thoughts and actions.

We none of us normally remember this first stage in our moral development. Part of it may sometimes be recovered by special psychological procedures; but in the main the proto-ethical mechanism is an intellectual construction, deduced on scientific grounds, like the atom or the gene.

That this is so is particularly evidenced by recent studies of so-called 'moral defectives'—children who lack any normally operative moral sense. In the majority this is due not to any hereditary defect of mental make-up, but to the absence in the infant's life of a mother or effective mother-substitute during the crucial period from about one to three years old. Without a mother, no strong love focused on a personal object; without such love, no conflict of irreconcilable impulses; without such conflict, no guilt; and without such guilt, no effective moral sense.

Neither is the moral sense a mere affair of conditioned reflexes. It develops only when the child's mind is able to grasp the mother as a separate person, not merely as a set of stimuli or sensory cues setting off or conditioning this or that reaction. During its first twelve months the child acquires many habits and may be conditioned in various ways, for instance in regard to cleanliness. But unless this conditioning is brought into relation with the dynamic structure of focused impulse which develops in the second year, it will wear out or break down.

Once the moral sense is developed, the developing human being can continue to tilt the balance of action and thought by means of the ethical forces now at its disposal—the moral load of guilt or felt wrongness, the moral wings of felt rightness. These can be attached to any conflict, but always in relation to some person or thing for whom we feel love or respect, either alone or blended into awe or other ambivalent feeling—parents, teachers, public opinion, God, one's own self-respect, a country or a cause.

But our central problem remains to haunt us as insistently as ever. How can we be sure that the objects or aims to which our moral sense affixes the labels of felt rightness and wrongness are in fact right or wrong? What external standards have we for the validity of our moral sense? We must leave this problem until we have been brought back to it by another route; for the moment we must continue our brief outline of individual ethical development.

III

### INDIVIDUAL ETHICS: THE PASSAGE TO MATURITY

AFTER the embryonic mental structure has been thus laid down, the main development of the mind has still to unfold itself. It must undertake what Walter Lippmann has called the passage to maturity. The infant, endowed by nature with unlimited desires, must grow up in a world where they can be satisfied only to a limited extent. His earliest thought, unbacked by experience and unfortified by reason, is a form of magic operating almost wholly by non-rational phantasy; it must be adjusted to external reality, and must learn to incorporate experience with the aid of reason. He is beset by conflicts, both external and internal, which must in some measure be resolved before he can think clearly or act decisively.

His primitive and absolutist ethics, based on non-rational and unconscious mental processes, inevitably tend to an undue restriction of his human activities, by locking up conflicting psychological 'energies' in the repressive mechanism of the unconscious. To arrive at a constructive and truly humanistic ethics, he needs to liberate these forces from their unconscious grappling.

But mental development differs from physical in being far less standardized. It can be varied to an enormous extent at any stage, including the earliest; and early variations exert a lasting effect, so that adult character is to a large extent determined by the form given to the mind in infancy and childhood, through processes which we have irrevocably forgotten.

There is one kind of variation in our mental development that particularly concerns us—the degree to which our ethical mechanism is itself unrealistic, to use the neutral term which psychologists prefer, though *untrue* or *irrational* might often be more descriptive. It is unrealistic when unjust or merely stupid treatment of the child superposes on the normal and healthy guilt evoked by hate for those whom we must at all costs love, an excess load which does not correspond with any reality, and so is too great to be discharged in the simple happy business of living. This may lead to an unbearable and quite irrational sense of unworthiness and even self-hatred—'Hell under the skull bones, Death under the breast-bones', as Walt Whitman wrote.

This excess load of unrealistic guilt leads on to further distortions, as when authority is injected into the growing mind as an over-harsh super-ego, or reprojected outwards in the form of a jealous and vengeful God; or when, unable to bear the condemnation of his super-ego, the persecution maniac projects this into society, thus removing his own feeling of guilt, while at the same time being able to accuse the world of cruelty or oppression.

Again, our ethics will be unrealistic if, after dividing our impulses into sheep and goats, we then with the aid of a form of magic thinking transform the goats into scapegoats, by projecting into others the evil which we cannot bear to acknowledge in ourselves. Most Nazis genuinely believe that Jews are a major source of evil; they can do so because they have projected the beastliness in their own souls into them. The terrible feature of such projection is that it can turn one's vices into virtues: thus, granted the Nazi believes the Jews are evil, it is his moral duty to indulge his repressed aggression in cruelty and violence towards them. It is an ethical mechanism, but a grossly unrealistic one.

Thus conscience itself, and also our beliefs concerning it, can become distorted or unrealistic. I will give three illustrations of this. A modern English theologian writes that 'conscience is a special exercise or activity of the faculty of reason . . . conscience is the mind of man when it is passing moral or ethical judgments'.

This is unrealistic in leaving out all the irrational and compulsive elements in conscience, and in failing to consider its developmental origin.

Mark Twain's Huckleberry Finn at least faces the facts—'It don't make no difference whether you do right or wrong, a person's conscience ain't got no sense and just goes for him anyway. If I had a yaller dog that didn't know more than a person's conscience does, I'd pizon him. It takes up more room than all the rest of a person's insides, and yet ain't no good nohow. Tom Sawyer says the same'. We may hazard the guess that Huck Finn was burdened with a moderate excess of unrealistic guilt.

Finally Jonathan Swift—'Is not conscience a pair of breeches, which, though a cover for lewdness as well as nastiness, is easily slipt down for the service of both'. The gloomiest Dean of all was only too well aware of the gross distortions to which our ethical mechanism may be subjected, though he doubtless never realized the extent of his own deformation.

This is not, of course, to deny the importance of conscience. Conscience develops directly out of the proto-ethical mechanism, which as we saw is a necessary adaptation in our early years for securing action backed by a sense of rightness. And in so far as the proto-ethical mechanism is itself undistorted and its feeling of rightness reflects, albeit in embryonic form, a morality that is objectively right, it can then be developed by reason and aspiration into a conscience which will be an indispensable moral guide. What psychologists and sociologists demonstrate is that conscience can set up no claims to absolute authority. They can point out further that such claims are peculiarly dangerous, since those who make them are likely to be victims of a distorted and hyperactive conscience, charged with aggression which seeks an outlet in attacking in others all those tendencies of which itself bears the unconscious guilty burden.

However, in favourable circumstances human beings *are* able to develop without these overdoses of untruth and unreality in their moral system. It is perfectly realistic to feel some guilt about hating one's beloved mother. But the load need not be too heavy and can be dissipated in acts of obedience, love, and co-operation. True repression into the unconscious may be so small in extent as not to disturb later development at all dangerously. The unrealistic mists of magic phantasy-thinking can be in large measure dispersed. Reason and reasonableness can be brought in to aid the development of the mind; the internal judgments of ethics can be checked against the external facts of experience; conflicts can achieve some sort of resolution in the realistic business of earning a living and bringing up a family; and the individual, if not grossly frustrated or oppressed, can adjust himself without too much unreality to the ethical standards of his society.

It is thus a fact that human beings can, in certain circumstances, achieve an internal ethical realism. And it is I think self-evident that it must be *better* to be realistic in one's ethics than unrealistic. Thus here, in the proper adjustment of the sense of guilt to reality, we find one element in the validation of our ethics.

However, ethics can be looked at from the angle of society as well as from that of the individual; and once we consider social ethics, we perceive that there must be an external as well as an internal realism. A man may be well and realistically adjusted to the ethical standards of his society, but these may themselves be unrealistic. When this is so, the primary reason is lack of knowledge. In many primitive societies every death or disaster is ascribed to witchcraft or some other form of magic. For a tribal African the ethical duty of smelling out and killing or punishing a guilty witch is realistic: for us, with the knowledge at our disposal, it is wholly unrealistic.

Similarly it has become ethically unrealistic for us to make expiation in face of volcanic eruptions or other natural catastrophes, to treat disease as a divine punishment or the insane as possessed by evil spirits, or to propitiate God by human sacrifice. We are beginning to think it ethically unrealistic for any human group to regard itself as a Chosen People or in any way inherently superior to others, or to believe that we alone are in receipt of the Divine Will as regards our morality. Some time in the future we can be sure that much that to-day is ethically quite realistic will prove wholly unrealistic—for instance, if I am to hazard a personal guess, in the fields of our sexual morality and our current attitude towards the Deity.

It will not, of course, become unrealistic until the entire social scene has become transformed—its state of knowledge, its intellectual and moral climate, its social and economic structure, the very quality of the human beings living in it. But we are apt to forget that this has been happening to man for hundreds of thousands of years. Human societies and the effective character of the human beings composing them have radically changed: evolution has been at work and has produced a series of new results.

IV

THE RELATIVITY OF SOCIAL ETHICS

THIS at once implies a relativity of ethics. Individual ethics develop, social ethics evolve. And the evolution of ethical systems and standards shows a broad correlation with that of the societies in which they flourish. I shall not attempt to document this thesis, on which there is a whole library of learned works available, but shall confine myself to a few generalizations, which I am quite aware are over-sweeping.

First, however, I must clear a stumbling-block out of the way. Much recent anthropological work seems at first sight not to confirm this concept of ethical relativity, but to point rather towards an ethical chaos. Thus a recent study on thirteen primitive societies from all over the world in most instances failed to find any correlation between the degree of competitiveness or co-operation enjoined by the ethical system in vogue, and the mode of life imposed upon the society by nature. The same lack of social correlation has been shown to apply elsewhere to other ethical qualities, such as those on the scale from peaceable to aggressive. In other words, the distinctive characters of an ethical system may have no detectable significance for the particular group in which it is found.

On further analysis, however, this disconcerting fact is found to apply only as between societies on the same general level of social evolution, and indeed to be confined in the main to primitive groups which are small and fairly well isolated culturally. It is doubtless analogous to the similar fact seen in biological evolution, that small and well-isolated populations develop non-adaptive variations. In both cases the circumstances permit chance to exert an abnormally large effect—in fixing random hereditary variations in the one case, random cultural variations in the other.

But as between societies at different cultural levels, or between advanced societies on quite different lines of cultural and economic development, chaotic ethical variability becomes negligible and ethical relatedness the rule.

Broadly speaking, and allowing for much overlap and blurring, one can distinguish certain main stages in the evolution of our ethics. In savage pre-agricultural communities, ethics grade over into the prescriptions of totem and tabu; it is largely concerned with propitiation and group solidarity, and its form is conditioned by magic. In post-agricultural barbarism, and especially in the early phases of civilization, the ethics of class domination and of group rivalry come to the front; the form of ethics begins to be affected by theology, and particular moral codes are laid down as the will of God.

The most important ethical change during the historical period was the appearance of universalist ethics, which seems to have been initiated towards the middle of the first millennium B.C. In some cases this accompanied the emergence of the idea of a single Deity from the rivality of hostile tribal gods; while elsewhere, as in Greece, it was associated with the rise of free intellectual inquiry, and involved the recognition of some standard beyond and above that of polytheist divinities.

By universalist ethics I mean, of course, the conception that ethical principles apply to all humanity, irrespective of race, language, creed, or station. In the earlier ethics of small closed groups, a different treatment of those outside the group is normally implied and often expressly enjoined.

Even within a universalist framework, many social adjustments of ethical outlook and emphasis have occurred. One of the most striking examples of such ethical relativity was the change in moral beliefs and attitude associated with the emergence of modern capitalism, which has been fully analysed by Weber and Tawney. The removal of the ethical ban on lending money at interest; the emphasis on the moral value of thrift and of individual independence and initiative—these and many other changes in ethical judgment were at one and the same time products of the economic revolution and agencies accelerating its accomplishment. The net result was to clothe individualist capitalism with the respectability and the driving force of morality.

Another example was the investment of nineteenth-century *laisser-faire* with an ethical halo, in the doctrine that the freest play of individualist competition would automatically secure the most rapid and extensive progress. It was largely this rationalization which enabled the bulk of the Victorians to acquiesce in slums and sweated labour.

In general, however, universalist ethics have been conceived of statically, in terms of a fixed standard. In this, the imperfections of our language mechanism have materially aided. Uncritically used, an abstract noun like 'the good' becomes a fictitious entity, bristling with fictitious properties, instead of a convenient pigeonhole for a variety of qualities which have in common only a certain emotive quality. A good baby gives little trouble; a good God is beneficent and moral; a good beef-steak satisfies our palate and our appetite; a good law—but why continue?

As various critical minds, from Bacon onwards, have pointed out, such fictitious entities facilitate the slipping of false certitudes into reality. In the field which we are considering, they make it easier to conceive of universalist ethics in terms of a fixed Absolute or ideal Good, or of the eternally valid injunctions of a God.

But this, we are beginning to perceive, does not hold water. For all practical purposes the Absolute is some particular philosopher's idea of the Absolute, and God is some particular person's or church's idea of God. It would be extremely salutary for the progress of clear thinking if every one invoking the support of the Deity for his beliefs would substitute for the word *God* the phrase *my idea* or *our idea of God*.[1]

The so-called immutable laws and will of God, which are invoked to guarantee the principles of ethics, turn out on examination to have been extremely changeable; and the principles of ethics have changed with them. So here too, in the fields where ethical certainty seems at first sight most authoritarian and most static, it is being undermined, until we are now in the midst of the complete transposition of ethics into dynamic or evolutionary terms.

To this crucial point I will shortly return. Meanwhile let us remember that in all the advanced civilizations known to history there have always been several more or less separate sets of ethics, in part competing, in part merely overlapping.

There have been the official ethics imposed by the ruling class, usually to secure stability. There has been the working moral code of ordinary citizens, and the ethics of simple everyday goodness.

[1] Lord Halifax, in a war-time speech (*The Times*, 31 May, 1943), came halfway towards this view when he said that 'wherever we found a false idea about men its origin lay in a false idea of God'. Most modern psychologists would go further back and say that the ideas we have about God originate mainly or wholly in projections from our own ideas. Advanced theologians have, of course, for some time been concerning themselves with the facts and implications of the evolution of our ideas of God. It remains for them, however, to draw the necessary conclusion that the time has come to coin a new term which shall have the dynamic meaning of *evolving idea of God* in place of the inevitably static term *God*.

There have been the ethics of oppressed classes and minorities, concerned either with escape or with revolution. There have been the ethics that conduce to a sense of personal salvation, serving to escape from a too heavy load of guilt or from the squalor, violence, or wickedness of current existence. There have been the true ethics of perfection, those of disciplined and developed goodness and of sainthood. There have also been what I may call the ethics of impossible perfection, which arise in part from men's realization that there are infinite possibilities beyond the imperfect compromises of the present, in part from their need for what modern psychologies variously call an ego-ideal or a *persona*—an idealized ethical mask, strangely compounded of moral aspiration, spiritual conceit, and hypocrisy, in which we can disguise ourselves from ourselves, or which we can present to the world to enhance our self-respect and our apparent moral stature.

The actual variety is immense. The relevant fact is that all existing societies manifest considerable ethical disunity, and that this is an expression of the conflicts and contradictions inherent in the situation—conflicts between classes and groups, between long-term and short-term good, conflicts within the individual between his needs for conformity and practical action and his needs for salvation, escape, or fullness of perfection. Once more, ethics is not an entity, but a loose covering term for a large number of quite different kinds of individual and social adaptations which have this alone in common—that they are concerned with the labels of rightness and wrongness. And, in all historical societies, these different kinds of adaptations may be of very various degrees of efficiency, and are always to some extent in conflict.

V

#### EVOLUTIONARY LEVELS AND DIRECTIONS

UP TO this point, increase of knowledge has produced only increase of doubt. We know more than we used to about the mechanism which affixes the labels of right and wrong: but we are as far as ever from knowing whether the labels are correctly attached. We know more about the adaptation of particular systems of ethics to particular kinds of societies; but what right have we to say that one adaptation, or one kind of society, is better than another?

However, ethics do not merely vary at random: they also evolve. That fact provides our clue. Our ethics evolve because they are themselves part of the evolutionary process. And any standards of rightness or wrongness must in some way be related to the movement of that process through time.

Now that the moment has arrived when we are able to perceive evolution as an all-comprehensive process of which human existence forms a part, it is impossible any longer to rely on any static guarantees for ethics. Our fuller knowledge discloses not a set of absolute or fixed standards, but a direction of change. This is no more available to casual inspection than any other of the discoveries of science. It is one of those 'secrets of excellent use, laid up in the womb of time', as Bacon called them, which are to be elicited only by the slow accumulation and distillation of tested fact.

Evolution, from cosmic star-dust to human society, is a comprehensive and continuous process. It transforms the world-stuff, if I may use a term which includes the potentialities of mind as well as those of matter. It is creative, in the sense that during the process new and more complex levels of organization are progressively attained, and new possibilities are thus opened up to the universal world-stuff.

Increase in organization is for the most part gradual, but now and again there is a sudden rapid passage to a totally new and more comprehensive type or order of organization, with quite new emergent properties, and involving quite new methods of further evolution. The two major breaks which concern us here are that between inorganic matter and life, and, more particularly, that between pre-human life and man.

Evolution on the inorganic level operates over an appalling vastness of space and on an equally appalling slowness of time-scale. In this phase, there is continuity of bodies such as stars and nebulæ, which are largely mere aggregations with a very low degree of organization. It is chiefly they which show the combination of persistence with change which constitutes evolution. Here and there, however, matter was able to attain the molecular type of organization; and finally on our earth (and possibly on a few other specks within the cosmos) the world-stuff arrived at the new type of organization that we call life. This is characterized by very great material complexity and by the capacity for self-reproduction, or better self-reproductive evolution, since it includes both persistence and self-reproducing change. On this new level, the evolutionary process was much accelerated in time, though immensely restricted in extent.

This speeding up was due to the emergence of a new method or agency of evolution—natural selection between competing variants. Natural selection automatically produces change in living matter, including change towards higher degrees of organization. The efficiency of natural selection was after a time much increased by the biological inventions of sexual fusion and mendelian re-combination. Previously to this, new mutations had to compete individually; subsequently, they could be combined, so that favourable variations could be pooled, and the speed of evolutionary change much increased.

Below the organizational level of life the world is one of mere interaction. But organizations of matter which are alive, though still interacting in what we call the balance of nature, are introduced to a new possibility—a measure of *de facto* control: they utilize other matter, both living and non-living, in securing their own continuance and spread. Through their capacity for self-reproduction and internal adjustment they also acquire a certain independence of changes in their environment.

During the thousand million years of organic evolution, the degree of organization attained by the highest forms of life increased enormously. And with this there increased also the possibilities of control, of independence, of inner harmony and self-regulation, of experience. Compared with what a protozoan or a polyp can show, the complexity of later forms of life, like bee or swallow or antelope, is stupendous, their capacity for self-regulation almost miraculous, their experience so much richer and more varied as to be different in kind.

And finally there is, in certain types of animals, an increase in consciousness or mind. Whether mind be a sudden emergent or, as biologists prefer to think, a gradual development of some universal property of the world-stuff, mind of the same general nature as ours is clearly present on the higher organizational levels of life, and at least in the birds and mammals we can trace its steady evolution towards greater capacities for feeling, knowing, willing, and understanding.

There is thus one direction within the multifariousness of evolution which we can legitimately call progress. It consists in the capacity to attain a higher degree of organization, but without closing the door to further advance. In the organic phase of evolution, this depends on all-round improvement as opposed to the limited improvement or one-sided specialization which, it can be demonstrated, automatically leads sooner or later to a dead end, after which no true advance is possible, but only minor variations on an already existent theme. Insects appear to have reached an evolutionary dead end over 30 million years ago; birds a little later; and all the main lines of higher mammals except the primates—carnivores, ungulates, whales, bats, rodents, and so forth—at least no later than the early Pliocene. Most evolutionary lines or trends are specializations which either thus come to a stop or are extinguished; true progress or the unlimited capacity for advance is rare.

However, the details of biological evolution need not concern us overmuch, since during the last half-million years or so a new and more comprehensive type of order of organization has arisen; and on this new level, the world-stuff is once more introduced to altogether new possibilities, and has quite new methods of evolutionary operation at its disposal. Biological or organic evolution has at its upper end been merged into and largely succeeded by conscious or social evolution.

Just as biological evolution was rendered both possible and inevitable when material organization became self-reproducing, so conscious evolution was rendered both possible and inevitable when social organization became self-reproducing. This occurred when the evolving world-stuff, in the form of ancestral man, became capable of true speech and conceptual thought. For just as animal organization, however elaborate, had been transmissible across the generation by the vehicle of the chromosomes and genes, so from then on conscious experience could be transmitted down the stream of time on the vehicle of words and other symbols and representations. And somewhat as sexual fusion made possible the pooling of individual mutations, so reason made possible the pooling of individual experiences. For the first time in evolution, tradition and education became continuous and cumulative processes.

With this, a new type of organization came into being—that of self-reproducing society. So long as man survives as a species (and there is no reason for thinking he will not) there seems no possibility for any other form of life to push up to this new organizational level. Indeed there are grounds for suspecting that biological evolution has come to an end, so far as any sort of major advance is concerned. Thus further large-scale evolution has once again been immensely restricted in extent, being now it would seem confined to the single species man; but at the same time again immensely accelerated in its speed, through the operation of the new mechanisms now available.

In any case, it is only through social evolution that the world-stuff can now realize radically new possibilities. Mechanical interaction and natural selection still operate, but have become of secondary importance. For good or evil, the mechanism of evolution has in the main been transferred onto the social or conscious level. Part of the blind struggle for existence between separate individuals or groups is transposed into conflict in consciousness, either within the individual mind or within the tradition which is the vehicle of pooled social consciousness. The slow methods of variation and heredity are outstripped by the speedier processes of acquiring and transmitting experience. New tools of living originated *ex post facto* as biological adaptations or unconscious adjustments become increasingly unimportant compared with the tools deliberately produced by human design. Physical trial and error can be more and more transposed to the sphere of thought.

And in so far as the mechanism of evolution ceases to be blind and automatic and becomes conscious, ethics can be injected into the evolutionary process. Before man that process was merely amoral. After his emergence onto life's stage it became possible to introduce faith, courage, love of truth, goodness—in a word moral purpose—into evolution. It became possible, but the possibility has been and is too often unrealized. It is the business of an enlightened ethics to help in its realization.

The attainment of the social type of organization opens a new and apparently indefinite range of possibilities to the evolving world-stuff. It can now proceed to some understanding of the cosmos which gave it birth, and of the conflicts which it must endure; it can for the first time consciously both appreciate and create beauty, truth, and other values; it becomes aware of good and evil; it becomes capable of new emotional states like love, reverence, or mystical contemplation and peace; it can inject some of its own purpose into events; finally and most significantly, many of the new experiences that are being made available have inherent value.

Even in the brief space that man has been in existence, there has been considerable evolutionary advance in the degree of social organization, considerable realization of new possibilities previously unavailable to life. What is more, the general rate of advance, in spite of periodic setbacks, has been growing progressively quicker. There is every reason to believe that through the attainment of this new level of conscious and social organization, the evolutionary process has taken on a new and apparently indefinite lease of life.

VI

### EVOLUTION AND GENERAL ETHICAL STANDARDS

What guidance does all this give us in our search for independent ethical standards? There are, it seems to me, three rather separate areas in which such guidance may be found—that of nature as a whole, that of human society, and that of the human individual. All three must be considered from the dynamic angle of evolution or development; and when thus considered, all three are interlocked.

In the broadest possible terms evolutionary ethics must be based on a combination of a few main principles: that it is right to realize ever new possibilities in evolution, notably those which are valued for their own sake; that it is right both to respect human individuality and to encourage its fullest development; that it is right to construct a mechanism for further social evolution which shall satisfy these prior conditions as fully, efficiently, and as rapidly as possible.

To translate these arid-sounding generalities into concrete terms and satisfying forms is beyond the scope of a lecture; it is a task for an entire generation. But I must attempt a certain expansion, and some development of their implications.

When we look at evolution as a whole, we find, among the many directions which it has taken, one which is characterized by introducing the evolving world-stuff to progressively higher levels of organization and so to new possibilities of being, action, and experience. This direction has culminated in the attainment of a state where the world-stuff (now moulded into human shape) finds that it experiences some of the new possibilities as having value in or for themselves; and further that among these it assigns higher and lower degrees of value, the higher values being those which are more intrinsically or more pemanently satisfying, or involve a greater degree of perfection.

The teleologically-minded would say that this trend embodies evolution's purpose. I do not feel that we should use the word purpose save where we know that a conscious aim is involved; but we can say that this is the *most desirable* direction of evolution, and accordingly that our ethical standards must fit into its dynamic framework. In other words, it is ethically right to aim at whatever will promote the increasingly full realization of increasingly higher values.[1]

In this aim we must reconcile the claims of the present and the future. The minimum claim of the future is that our direction of evolution (which on the human level means the direction of social change) should leave the door open for further advance in the same desirable direction—towards still higher levels of organization and as yet unrealized possibilities; its maximum claim is that future possibility should take complete precedence over present realization. The course of greatest moral rightness lies somewhere between these two extremes, at an optimum, varying according to circumstances.

If desirable direction of evolution provides the most comprehensive (though also the least specific) external standard for our ethics, then one very important corollary at once follows: namely

[1] A mistake often made by devotees of genetic and evolutionary methods is to think that complex phenomena can be in any real sense explained in terms of their development. In point of fact, such a procedure merely explains away some of their most important characteristics. A study of the less developed will often help us to understand the more developed; but the most important subject for the evolutionist is the nature and direction of the developmental process itself, and here the more developed gives the significant clue, both to the actualities of the past and the possibilities of the future.

that social organization should be planned, not to prevent change, nor merely to permit it, but to encourage it. Thus a static stability is undesirable, and a complete or static certitude of ethical belief itself becomes unethical.

In the sphere of the intellect, the last three hundred years have witnessed the reconciliation of the demands of certainty and change, through the growth of the scientific attitude and method. We have the certainty that our knowledge is increasing, but we are aware that it is incomplete and imperfect. The result is not the possession of absolute Truth but a progressive advance towards more truth. We need the same kind of reconciliation, the same facilitation of progressive change, in the sphere of religion and ethics. The theologian and the moralist will be doing wrong so long as they cling to any absolute or unyielding certitude. Let any such recall Cromwell's appeal to the Scottish Church Assembly: 'I beseech you, in the bowels of Christ, think it possible you may be mistaken.'

Furthermore, the rate as well as the direction of change is important. Theoretically, there must be an optimum rate of change, above which stability is endangered and the sacrifices of the present are excessive, below which advance is so slow that the welfare of future generations is needlessly impaired. Thus anything which retards advance below this optimum, even if it be moving in the same right direction, is wrong.

Next we have the guidance derived from an understanding of the workings of human societies. In the first place, it is clear on evolutionary grounds that the individual is in a real sense higher than the State or the social organism. The possibilities which are of value for their own sake, and whose realization must be one of our primary aims, are not experienced by society as a unit, but by some or all of the human beings which compose it.

All claims that the State has an intrinsically higher value than the individual are false. They turn out, on closer scrutiny, to be rationalizations or myths aimed at securing greater power or privilege for a limited group which controls the machinery of the State.

On the other hand the individual is meaningless in isolation, and the possibilities of development and self-realization open to him are conditioned and limited by the nature of the social organization. The individual thus has duties and responsibilities as well as rights and privileges, or if you prefer it, finds certain outlets and satisfactions (such as devotion to a cause, or participation in a joint enterprise) only in relation to the type of society in which he lives.

In any case, the mechanism by which evolutionary advance can be produced on the human or conscious level is that of the social organization, and this operates by the pooling of experience and co-operative action in a cumulative tradition. On the biological level intra-specific competition is often not merely useless but harmful to the species as a whole. Somewhat similarly, on the social level it is clearly of evolutionary advantage that there should be a single universal pool of experience and action, not a number of isolated or even competing and hostile ones. For then evolutionary advance can be more continuous, more rapid, and better consolidated.

But if unity as against multiplicity is of advantage for evolutionary advance and is therefore desirable in respect of groups, so is equality of opportunity in respect of individuals. The more individuals there exist whose desirable potentialities are fully developed, the more health, vigour, knowledge, wisdom, happiness, beauty, and the rest can go into the common pool, and the better that common pool will work. That is one of the evolutionary bases for universalism in ethics.

By the unification of separate groups with their competing pools of tradition, desirable evolution can become a single joint enterprise of the human species as a whole; and the efficiency of the enterprise will rise with the degree and universality of individual development and welfare.

Unification and universality will in many minds raise the spectre of regimented compulsion and uniformity; but this again is contradicted by our evolutionary standards. For one thing, the pooling of effort and experience will be more efficient if there is voluntary participation in what is felt to be a common enterprise, a plan accepted by all, less efficient if the plan is carried out under compulsion.

For another, it will be more efficient the greater the variety of skills and experiences that are unified in the pool. It is not uniformity which our evolutionary analysis shows to be right, but the maximum of variety-in-unity. As with the animal body, the common pool of our species becomes more efficient as it achieves greater differentiation combined with more integrated harmony of organization. This holds both for groups and for individuals. We should not aim at the spread of one uniform type of culture over the entire globe, but at what has been well described as a world orchestration of cultures. Man probably also has the highest genetic variability of any species, so that within a single group, national or cultural, there will always be an immense innate variety of temperament, capacity, and talent. The more this variability can be not merely permitted but encouraged within the confines of a common pool, and the more it is integrated within those confines, the more efficient will the pool become as an agency of desirable evolution. Again it is not uniformity that is demanded, but a variety of which the components are compatible with each other and, if possible, integrated into some sort of a whole.

With this we are brought into the area of the individual. The human individual is not merely inherently higher than the State, but the rightly-developed individual is, and will continue to be, the highest product of evolution, even though he needs the proper organization of society to achieve his welfare and realize his development.

The phrase *rightly-developed* begs a question. I would suggest that it includes not only the full, all-round development of potentialities, but also the one-sided development of particular possibilities or special talents, provided always that these restrict the development or interfere with the welfare of other individuals or groups as little as possible. For instance, the new possibilities of experience that have become available on the human level include the enjoyment of great wealth or privilege built upon exploitation or oppression; such are obviously not desirable, any more than distortions like the sadistic enjoyment of torture of others.

The case is less clear when there is a conflict between the full development of a special talent, such as artistic genius or saintly and ascetic devotion to a good cause, on the one hand, and on the other the more ordinary but no less real duties we have to our friends or dependents. For instance, was Gauguin morally right in leaving his wife and family to devote himself to painting? There is always a price to be paid, both by oneself and by others, for bringing a talent to fruition. We must face that fact; but who is to decide if it is a just price? Some would say that the proof of the pudding is in the eating, and that the rightness of such a decision can only be judged by the quality of the results produced. Personally, I would not go so far as this, but would feel that wherever there is a genuine and informed sense of vocation, this will be a sufficient ethical sanction.

Many moralists will doubtless disagree; however, we must remember that moralists are almost certainly not a random sample of the population, but that most of them have become moralists because of an excessive load of infantile guilt. They are consequently over-preoccupied with that limited sphere of morality to which the term is often inaccurately restricted, namely actions and beliefs which are concerned with lightening the load of guilt or escaping from the sense of sin. And through this preoccupation they are apt to attach less value to other types of achievement—artistic, intellectual, or practical—and indeed often fail to realize that they enter the moral sphere at all. However, our evolutionary standards here provide definite ethical guidance; they socialize morality and enlarge the scope of its values. Thus art and science, music and philosophy, all have their ethical aspect, since they provide new possibilities of experience of value in and for themselves, and this is a desirable evolutionary outcome. Again, these activities, or their results, are capable of being shared and can go into the common pool, enhancing its efficiency by adding to its extent and variety.

Although morality thus includes a duty of the individual to himself, or rather towards the development of that self to include as many as possible of those qualities wherein, as Wordsworth wrote, 'we are greater than we know', of those potentialities that can so easily remain unrealized, it must assuredly be in the main concerned with our behaviour towards others—in a word, with social relations.

If the right development of the individual is an evolutionary end in itself, then it is right that there should be universal equality of opportunity for development, and to the fullest degree. The reciprocal of this is the rightness of unselfishness and kindness, as the necessary means for realizing general well-being. Thus individual ethics will always in large measure be concerned with the conflict between the claims of self-expression and self-sacrifice, and their best reconciliation through love.

The Golden Rule, as various philosophers have pointed out, is an impossible ideal; it cannot ever be put into practice, not merely because of the imperfections of human nature, but also because it does not provide a real basis on which to make practical ethical decisions. However, it is the hyperbole beyond a perfectly practical ideal—the extension of more opportunity of fuller life to more human beings. Psychologically, this can be promoted by extending the child's love and sympathy to an ever-widening circle, and linking the idea of any and all avoidable suffering and stunting of development with his personal sense of wrong. And it can be promoted institutionally by the rational acceptance of certain moral principles, and then by laws and practical measures designed to give effect to those principles.

To accept this view is to give a new content to that sector of ethics concerned with justice. Justice is an abstract term, and therefore of itself empty of meaning beyond the fact of being applied to acts which we happen to think just: its content varies from age to age with the social context. There is retributive justice, and there is distributive justice; there is justice concerned with fairness in administering existing codes of law, and justice concerned with some unrealized abstract standard. To give it the particular content implied by evolutionary ethics is to erect a new ideal of distributive justice, and to assert that our laws should be modified to give effect to this ideal.

An important negative consequence of accepting the welfare, development, and dignity of the human individual as a yardstick by which to measure evolutionary advance on the social level, is the confirmation of Kant's insistence that it is always morally wrong to treat other human beings merely as means, since they are the embodiment of the highest ends we know. All men are of course to some extent means—for producing goods, for winning battles, for administering social functions, for creating art, or knowledge, or entertainment. But they should all be treated as also ends, never wholly as the tools or instruments of the ends of other individuals.[1]

Honesty and truthfulness are further implications of evolutionary ethics, since they are the intellectual lubricants of free and equal co-operation, and the basis for collective knowledge, as well as an expression of respect for one's own and others' individual integrity. Faith finds its place within the evolutionary scheme once we manage to turn society into a continuing enterprise in which ordinary men and women can believe; and self-sacrifice remains

[1] That most men like to feel that they are serving as means to ideal and corporate ends is another matter. In such activities men find a new freedom and a further self-realization. What is immoral is the exploitation of one individual as means to another's ends.

a primary virtue, though with slightly different content and connotations.

VII

### THE SPECIAL CHARACTER OF EVOLUTIONARY ETHICS

IT WILL perhaps be objected that this elaborate detour through the realms of evolution has been quite unnecessary, as it has merely brought us back to the blend of Christian and humanist universalism characteristic of the ethics of Western civilization. The intrinsic worth of the human individual, the brotherhood of man, the universal duty of kindness and unselfishness—is not the evolutionist merely dressing up in new terminology what we have accepted for centuries?

The objection is not valid. It is of course true that the intuition and the spiritual logic of the religious moralists perceived the necessity for a universalist ethics grounded in a belief in the ultimate and intrinsic value of human personality, centuries before the evolutionists were able to provide the inductive basis for this conclusion. But with this common insistence on universalism and on the value of the individual, together with their various direct consequences, the resemblance ends. For one thing the evolutionist is able to provide new general standards or criteria for ethics, when the older universalist standards, grounded in Authority, Absolute, or Revelation, were proving to be no standards at all, and to provide no guarantees against moral inflation or the debasement of ethical currency. For another, the standards are dynamic instead of static; and this fundamental fact produces many important differences in the details and indeed the principles of the resultant ethical system.

The evolutionist is not the only begetter of a dynamic ethics. Sociologists and social historians, psycho-analysts and other proponents of a dynamic or a genetic psychology, certain liberal theologians, philosophic Marxists, have all made their contribution

towards the transformation of static into dynamic ethics. But the contributions from these various fields have been either incomplete (as in theology) or limited in extent. It is only in relation to the evolutionary process as a whole that our ethical standards can be fully generalized, and the new system be rounded out to completion.

Let me now briefly enumerate some of the main differences to our thinking which arise from acceptance of an evolutionary ethics. The most obvious is that our ethical yardstick is itself dynamic, and must be used for making long-term social measurements as well as immediate individual ones. The individual can and should continue to make ethical progress, whether in bringing a greater range of experience into an internal harmony, or in achieving a greater degree of such harmony; whether in the reconciliation of self and not-self, or the synthesis of suffering and joy in a single deeper reality; whether in a further extension of love and good works, or in a more perfect fruition of some special quality or talent. But around and beyond individual ethics lie social ethics, which must be judged by the direction and the rate of change in human society.

To one immediate implication of this I have already referred, namely the ethical obligation to plan for the encouragement of social change. A further consequence is the higher ethical value set upon knowledge. Knowledge is not merely an end in itself, but the only satisfactory means for controlling our future evolution. Social morality is seen to include the duty of providing an immense extension of research, and its integrated planning to provide the basis for desirable change.

If science is allotted a higher place in an evolutionary system of ethics, so too are art and certain aspects of personal religion. I have already touched on the subject of the arts. Their ethical value lies in introducing man to new possibilities of desirable experience, as well as in providing the chief means of communicating and pooling experience in the emotional as opposed to the

intellectual sphere. And personal religion, in the form of a disciplined mysticism, a trained reverence aimed at enlarging and harmonizing the microcosm of the individual personality, provides the chief road to certain types of satisfying experience and desirable being.

This has its negative implications—namely that what I may call salvationist ethics, aimed at achieving salvation in a supernatural other life, become redundant; indeed, if overemphasized they may themselves become unethical by our evolutionary standards, by retarding or opposing right social change. The desirable sense of 'salvation' can, in part, be achieved through right discipline of the soul, in part through devotion to some common continuing enterprise.

That a considerable section of the Churches is aware of this latter fact is shown by the recent rapid growth of their interest in economic and political affairs; we may prophesy that as the evolutionary concept of ethics spreads, organized Christianity will devote less attention to salvation and the life hereafter, more attention to realizing the Kingdom of God on earth.

The age-old opposition between faith and works finds a new expression in the transvaluation of values imposed by the evolutionary outlook. The aim of evolutionary 'faith' consists partly in a belief in the high possibilities of man's evolutionary future, partly in achieving states of being that are of positive value in their own right, in free and satisfying activities enjoyed for their own sake, in transcendent self-dedication or sacrifice.

In place of 'works' we now have the practical achievements of human society, as measured by the same criteria by which progress was measured on the biological level—greater control, greater independence or self-regulation, greater but at the same time more harmonious complexity of organization, greater range of knowledge or available experience. These trends are still desirable on the social level, but here become increasingly secondary—not ends in themselves, but means to the realization of experiences valued as ends.

This is not to say that such evolutionary works may not become temporary ethical ends. The more efficient organization of production, distribution, and other physical functions of society, the abolition of insecurity, oppression, ill-health, physical under-development, or illiteracy—these in the long run merely provide the means by which higher or more intrinsic values may be realized, the practical foundation for a fuller and more satisfying life; but meanwhile they can provide temporary ends for our intense ethical striving. The implications of this for immediate practice will be discussed in the following section.

As regards the individual and his inescapable passage to maturity, we have already seen that degree of development, whether of a single talent, of all-round richness and fulness, or of that internal harmony which is the self-regulation of the soul, is itself a positive end, and morally right, provided it is not achieved by the exploitation or to the detriment of other human beings and their development.

Acceptance of our evolutionary ethical principles has a particular implication of some present importance: it affords a complete condemnation and refutation of Nazi ethical principles. In providing an external sanction for universalist ethics it at once condemns any system which repudiates universalism and reverts to group ethics. The prime postulate of Nazi ethics is the rightness of all which exalts the organized German group, preferably at the expense of any competing group. In this the Nazis merely translate into modern terms the ethics of tribes or peoples in an early barbarous phase of the world's history, such as the ancient Hebrews before the prophetic period.

Nazi ethics put the State above the individual. Being postulated on the success of a particular group, they cannot help being rooted in naked power and the use of force as a primary instrument. On the inter-group level, this results in forcible and often cruel domination and in persecution and oppression, to the denial of co-operation. It also results in the perversion of truth and the suppression of free speech and inquiry, since a naked power-system cannot tolerate tolerance or face even intellectual opposition. It is unrealistic and perverted, as in its attitude to the Jews. It expressly denies the principles of the equality of opportunity and the universality of justice, and is opposed to the establishment of a single common but varied pool of human experience and effort.

There have been good features in the Nazi system, but these are all short-term details, quite outweighed by its general and basic wrongness. Indeed, in the long run, any such system is in all probability self-defeating, however much of disaster it may bring on the world in the meantime. Its methods run counter to those which, on grounds of efficiency alone, the evolutionist demonstrates to be desirable. Furthermore, its principles run counter to those guaranteed by universalist evolutionary ethics, and their application in practice provokes immense moral indignation, which in turn provides much of the driving force that will inevitably encompass its downfall.

But to be certain that Nazi ethics are wrong does not imply that ours are right; they may merely be less wrong. There is indeed a widespread belief in the democracies that our ethics need reformulating. And to-day this can only be done in relation to general evolutionary standards.

VIII

### GENERAL STANDARDS AND IMMEDIATE PRINCIPLES

HOWEVER, this task must also be related to the needs and principles of the times. We may look forward to an eventual future in which the organization of society will be good by our evolutionary standards of goodness. But meanwhile the world in which we live is hatefully imperfect. In a rudimentary and makeshift stage of social evolution like ours, such general ethical principles as I have been sketching can only be counsels of perfection, largely inapplicable in current practice. Unless we are careful they will tend to float off and become irrelevant or even opposed to the effective social ethics of the time.

Our practical problem is thus to build a bridge of faith between the practical and the ideal, by constructing an effective ethical system which shall be adapted concretely to our age and translatable into action to meet its needs, but shall also be compatible with the general ethical standards we have been able to distil out of evolutionary fact. Here history provides us with another general conclusion. General ethical principles can be brought down to earth out of their ideal empyrean when it is possible to apply them in large-scale practice: and when it is also expedient to do so. This involves no crude materialist theory of history; on the contrary, moral principles, once conditions call for their practical application, may be powerful agencies in changing those conditions.

Slavery provides an obvious example. The universalist principle of respect for the individual is inherently opposed to slavery. But, over much of history, slave labour was a necessary element in production. It was no good being an abolitionist in ancient Rome: all that the most clear-sighted moralist could *do* was to demand humane treatment for slaves. But by the early nineteenth century, technical advance had made it possible to put much of the mechanical drudgery of existence off the shoulders of men to where it belonged—on to machines. Further, in the new conditions free workers were on the whole becoming more efficient than slave labour. For the first time it became both possible and expedient to apply the general moral principle of human equality to the particular moral problem of abolishing slavery. And history bears witness to the practical effectiveness of the resultant moral forces in overcoming the violent resistance of the vested interests opposed to the change.

What are the special conditions of the present and immediate future which will canalize particular applications of our general ethical principles? I will instance three. For one thing, recent scientific and technical advances have, for the first time since civilization began, made it theoretically possible for every human individual, within a limited future, to be properly fed, reasonably clothed and housed, freed from the major burden of ill-health and insecurity, and provided with some opportunities for education and leisure. In the second place, communications have improved so that events everywhere are entangled: the separate regions of the world have shrunk into a single unit, though so far not an orderly but a chaotic one. And thirdly, the breakdown of the *laisser-faire* system has introduced the possibility of large-scale planning.

Thus the general moral principle of equality can now come down to earth in the concrete task of achieving what I may call minimum equality: it can and should now be regarded as immoral to leave any human being below certain standards of physical and mental welfare and development.[1] The general moral principle of human unity and pooling of effort can come down to earth in the concrete task of achieving a minimum co-operative organization for the world-unit: it can and should now be regarded as immoral to let anything stand in the way of producing that degree of international order which will free the world from its major burdens of disunity, both as regards war and economic competition. And finally the general moral principle of evolutionary purpose can come down to earth in the concrete task of achieving minimum planning: it can and should now be regarded as immoral for society not to be at least one move ahead of events.

The tasks of increasing the amount of goodness in the world and of deciding on the rightness or wrongness of particular actions must be related to some such concrete but limited applica-

---

[1] This implies an ethical revaluation of charity. So long as intense poverty was abundant and apparently irremediable, charitable benevolence was the only outlet for the consciences of the more fortunate, and ranked high in the moral scale of virtues. In the latter half of the last century, it began to be realized that indiscriminate or even extensive charity might do more harm than good, and that to aim at social amelioration was a higher duty. To-day we realize that it is not necessary that the poor shall be always with us: poverty can perfectly well be abolished. With this realization, the ethical value of charity in the traditional sense falls below that of measures for the abolition of poverty, and it will become progressively less of a virtue as its scope is restricted.

tions of general ethical principles. It is of no avail merely saying or believing that one must be as unselfish, or kind, or pure, or merciful as possible. Does unselfishness extend to providing milk for Hottentots? What does kindness mean in respect of Germans after the war? What are the ethics of birth-control? Or of private profit? Or of the ownership of colonies? There are perhaps no correct solutions to such questions as there are to arithmetical problems in an examination paper; but there are some answers which are more right, others which are more wrong. And to work them out we need both our general principles and their special applications to present conditions.

But we must beware of over-optimism. All attempts at setting up any general principles of ethics, and at working out their immediate applications, will be useless or worse than useless if ethics is to be a mere façade, or even a superficial justification for basic evil. We must face the question whether human nature is not fundamentally wicked. If so, are our moral principles merely a convenient cloak for conscious immorality, as with Molière's *Tartuffe*; or an unconscious screen for powerful inner tendencies whose non-moral or anti-moral nature we are afraid to face; or at best a salve for an uneasy conscience? Even if we are not so pessimistic as that, must we believe that, in present conditions, the evil in us is bound to gain the upper hand over the good? There are at present a number of adherents of this relativistic Manicheism, who point to the fact that man's command of material power has outrun his capacity for its wise control. As Lord Acton said, power corrupts, and absolute power corrupts absolutely. And the power made available by the modern science is for various purposes approximating to the absolute. Is man thus entering upon a period where his immoral qualities will inevitably have the preponderance?

I recognize the possibility, but not its inevitability. Nor do I believe that man's nature is fundamentally evil or that his immorality is bound to prevail over his morality. All our evidence goes to show that our ethics, and our conscience, which is at the base of our ethics, are the product of conflict between what is desired or loved and what is feared or hated; and this issues in the inevitable polarity of right and wrong. Many theologians and moral philosophers have endeavoured to soften the fact of evil by arguing that without the existence of evil we could not appreciate good, or even that objective good could not exist without objective evil, any more than light could exist without shadow. (In passing, this last analogy is, of course, fallacious. In the natural conditions of this planet light does involve shadow; but in other conditions, including artificial situations which we could readily create, a shadowless illumination would be possible.) I do not consider that the fact of evil is softened, or the burden of its existence lightened, by such considerations; nor do I consider that the existence of objective good is dependent on or conditioned by that of objective evil. What is true is that our subjective conception of good is dependent on a simultaneous conception of evil, our feeling of wrongness a necessary prerequisite of our feeling of rightness. In later life we, or those few of us to whom it is given to achieve saintliness or high moral status, can educate our moral natures and extend our sense of goodness and righteousness, can relegate our sense of wrong and evil to the background, and in some rare instances can attain to an existence which is wholly or at least essentially good. But this does not contradict the fact that in its origin our moral sense is as inevitably and automatically polarized in regard to the categories of right and wrong, of good and evil, as is a magnetized iron bar in regard to the 'North' and 'South' properties of magnetic attraction or repulsion.

Neither good nor evil is by its nature preponderant, though either may gain the upper hand through circumstances, through self-discipline or the reverse, or through education. As to man's corruption through power we should remember that Lord Acton was using the word power in the political and social sense, of the power which a man, or a group of men, can exert over the lives of his fellows, not in the more objective sense of available energy. There is no necessary reason why power of this sort should corrupt man—always provided that the social organization controlling it operates for the general good. This is an important proviso: and a merely quantitative increase in the amount of power available does constitute a real danger so long as it can be used by privileged firms or groups for one-sided economic exploitation, or by privileged nations or groups of nations for militaristic aggrandizement. This fact further sharpens the urgency of the need for right political and economic world organization.

Another moral duty of our times is that of extending and applying our new psychological knowledge so as to prevent mental and especially moral distortion and under-development. If we could see minds as we see bodies, we should be astonished at their variety. But in the present state of the world we should also be horror-struck at their deformations and their dwarfish failures to develop. And there is the frightening fact that the imperfections and distortions so often manage to attach the label of goodness or rightness to themselves. Stunted spiritual growth masquerades as humility or acceptance of the decrees of Providence, sadistic projection as a crusade against evil, the excessive asceticism or moral rigour which springs from an unrealistic sense of sin and from failure to face one's own nature, as a badge of special righteousness.

According to Dr. Ernest Jones, our leading British psychoanalyst, man is 'a creature blindly resisting, with all the means at his command, the forces that are making for a higher and fuller consciousness'. This cannot perhaps be maintained as a general and permanent statement; but it is undoubtedly true that resistances to mental or spiritual advance are all but universal, and that in the majority of people they are powerful. The reluctance to admit new knowledge, the refusal to acknowledge some of our own impulses, the clinging to non-rational and non-realistic methods of thought, the tendency to put off the burdens of our conflicts and the responsibility of our choices on to the shoulders of some external authority, or to retreat within the shelter of some ivory tower—all these constitute formidable drags on our passage towards true maturity, as well as often piling up dangerous stores of guilt and pent-up aggression within the social organism.

There are several specific problems to be tackled. The most obvious is the prevention of the warping of the whole structure of personality, with accompanying primary ethical distortion, in infancy and early childhood. Another is the provision during education of outlets for repressed impulses, and of creative activities which shall be either what William James would have called the moral equivalents of anti-social action, or the moral substitutes for inhibition and further distortion. This implies a greater attention to the education of the emotions, for instance through the arts, and also to the desire of growing boys and girls to feel of use, to make sacrifices, to participate in some exciting or valuable enterprise. A more limited yet equally important problem is that of the sensitive adolescent. Too often under our present system he (or she) shrinks away from the rough school of practice, and so leaves the control of affairs increasingly to the thick-skinned, or the blatant, or the ambitious seeker after power. In existing conditions, the sensitive aware-ness, the unselfishness, the desire for self-dedication, which should be available to society's common pool, and are needed in the highest and most responsible positions, tend to be self-defeating, by causing their owner to withdraw from the struggle.

A related subject is that of innate variations in temperament or temperamental tendencies. Our knowledge in this field is only beginning to take shape, but it appears more than probable that, for instance, certain psycho-physical types are predisposed to callous and tireless aggressiveness. Here we have the reciprocal of the problem of the sensitive adolescent—how can we either prevent the innately aggressive from seizing power, or, prefer-ably, provide creative instead of anti-social outlets for him?

It is our duty to set psychologists to work studying the variations and imperfections in man's mental machinery and the obstacles to its proper development, so as eventually to overcome these resistances to his mental and spiritual growth, to provide him with understanding and the means for a rational and fruitful self-discipline, and to improve the social mechanism underlying his further evolutionary advance. For here as elsewhere it is only knowledge that will set us free. To the evolutionist, knowledge and faith are not opposites, but complements. Faith inspires the quest for more knowledge, knowledge provides the foundation for new faith.

But in our grossly imperfect world the individual will continue to suffer painful conflict. He must reflect that this is one of the means by which we as a species have emerged into a new and more hopeful phase of evolution. It is part of the price we pay for being men.

And society will long be faced with the conflict between the general affirmation and the particular denial of principles that we know to be right. Our ethical principles assure us that war is a general wrong: yet to urge it may still be a particular right. Tolerance and kindness are general virtues: yet ruthless suppression of opponents may be a particular duty. It is the eternal conflict between means and ends. There is a slight comfort in the reflection that fuller understanding of general principles will give us more assurance of what ends are right.

Nor will clearer ethical vision prevent us from suffering what we feel as injustice at the hands of the cosmos—congenital deformity, unmerited suffering, physical disaster, the early death of loved ones. Such cosmic injustice represents the persistence of chance and its amorality into human life: we may gradually reduce its amount but we assuredly shall never abolish it. Man is the heir of evolution: but he is also its martyr. All living species provide their evolutionary sacrifice: only man knows that he is a victim.

But man is not only the heir of the past and the victim of

the present: he is also the agent through whom evolution may unfold its further possibilities. Here, it seems, is the solution of our riddle of ethical relativity: the ultimate guarantees for the correctness of our labels of rightness and wrongness are to be sought for among the facts of evolutionary direction. Here, too, is to be found the reconciliation of T. H. Huxley's antithesis between the ethical and the cosmic process: for the cosmic process, we now perceive, is continued into human affairs. Thus man can impose moral principles upon ever-widening areas of the cosmic process, in whose further slow unfolding he is now the protagonist. He can inject his ethics into the heart of evolution.

In attempting to deal with so vast a subject, or rather range of subjects, within the space of an hour's lecture, I found myself driven to a compression of statements which I fear may have been excessive. This is especially likely to have been so in the passages dealing with recent developments in psychological and evolutionary theory, which are still inevitably unfamiliar to most people. I am therefore appending a few notes and references: this brief and partial documentation may render acceptable some of my statements that as they stand are over-compressed or over-sweeping, and will enable interested readers to pursue the subject further should they so desire.

*Note* 1,  T. H. Huxley's Romanes lecture is available, together with *Section* 1,  a Preface and the lengthy *Prolegomena*, in vol. ix, 'Evolu-
*p.* 113.  tion and Ethics', of his *Collected Essays* (London: Macmillan, 1894 and 1906).

*Note* 2,  The most comprehensive recent attempt to bring ethics *p.* 115 ff.  into relation with the scientific outlook, notably by way of psycho-analysis and evolutionary biology, is the symposium on *Science and Ethics*, by C. H. Waddington and others (London: Allen and Unwin, 1942). Philosophers and theologians, as well as psychologists, physicists, and biologists, here exchange views on the subject. Dr. Waddington's challenging thesis gave me the first impetus towards a radical treatment of the subject, which I followed up with an essay entitled 'Philosophy and a World at War' (*Fortune,* December, 1942; *Hibbert Journal,* April, 1943). I had, however, already made an approach to the problem in the title-essay of my *Uniqueness of Man* (London: Chatto and Windus, 1941), and in particular to the adaptive nature of the mechanism of repression in infancy, and to the nature of biological progress. Among other biologists who have recently treated the subject I may mention R. W. Gerard of Chicago, with his essay on 'A Biological Basis for Ethics' (*Philos. of Sci.* 9: 92; 1942).

*Note* 3,  A lecturer may assume some general familiarity with the *Section* 2,  principles of psycho-analysis and other modern dynamic *p.* 116,  theories of psychology. Thus the work of psycho-analysts *et seq.* like Melanie Klein, in *The Psycho-analysis of Children* (London, 1932), is modifying to a considerable extent the original Freudian views as to the nature and mode of formation of the super-ego. (See also Melanie Klein's later papers in *Internat. J. Psychoan.* 16 (1935) and 21 (1940), M. Brierley's 'Present Tendencies in Psycho-Analysis', *Brit. J. Med. Psychol.* 14: 211; 1934, and G. Zilboorg's *Mind, Medicine and Man*, New York, 1943.)

*Note 4,*   For inhibition, see Sherrington's *Integrative Action of the*
*p.* 118. *Nervous System* (1906).

*Note 5,*   For a recent study of 'moral defectives' see J. Bowlby,
*p.* 120. 'The Influence of Early Environment in the Development of Neurosis and Neurotic Character' (*Internat. J. Psychoan.,* 21 (2): 1940). In general, the view is coming to prevail that there is great variability in the amount of guilt and repression between different individuals, so that the average degree of repression is not so intense nor the extent of distortion so widespread as was originally supposed. The early psychoanalysts were perhaps predisposed to an interest in the abnormal by their own psychological make-up, and in any case were dealing with a non-random sample of the population. For a recent comprehensive survey see C. W. Valentine, *The Psychology of Early Childhood* (London, 1943).

G. Lowes Dickinson's *The Meaning of Good* is a delightful symposium on ethics, which, though written in 1901, comes to a conclusion very similar to that of the neo-Freudians. They derive ethics from the guilt produced by the conflict of love and hate, and believe that a sound universalist ethics can be reached only by extending the love and the sense of duty experienced towards parents to an ever-widening circle. Lowes Dickinson's principal character has a vision of the world of souls in which 'the energy of love was constantly striving to annihilate distance and unite in a single sphere the scattered units that were only kept apart by the energy of hate'. And he concludes (p. 231) that:

whatever Reality may ultimately be, it is in the life of the affections, with all its confused tangle of loves and hates, attractions, repulsions, and, worst of all, indifferences, it is in this intricate commerce of souls that we may come nearest to apprehending what perhaps we shall never wholly apprehend but the quest of which alone, as I believe, gives any significance to life, and makes it a thing which a wise and brave man will be able to persuade himself it is right to endure.'

*Note 6,* Walter Lippmann's book, *A Preface to Morals* (New York,
*Section* 3, 1929), is an admirably sane statement by a general thinker
  *p.* 122. uncommitted to any particular philosophical or psychological doctrines.

For an account of various unrealistic distortions of the
developing personality, the reader may consult such books
as J. A. Hadfield, *Psychology and Morals* (London, 1923);
R. H. Thouless, *An Introduction to the Psychology of
Religion* (Cambridge, 1924); P. Nathan, *The Psychology
of Fascism* (London, 1943); E. F. M. Durbin and J.
Bowlby, *Personal Aggressiveness and War* (London, 1939);
etc. Wilfred Trotter's *Instincts of the Herd in Peace and
War* (London, 1916) can still be read with much profit,
though many of its detailed points would now be presented
in a different framework.

*Note 7,* The three quotations on conscience are from K. E. Kirk,
*p.* 123 ff. *The Threshold of Ethics* (London, 1933); Mark Twain,
*Huckleberry Finn*; and Jonathan Swift, *The Tale of a Tub.*
As studies of 'realistic' or normal development, in addition
to Valentine's previously cited book, we have works such
as J. Piaget, *The Moral Judgment of the Child* (London,
1932), which points out how reason and experience normally cause the child's idea of justice to pass through a
series of progressively less irrational phases; and G. All-
port's recent valuable general study, *Personality, a Psychological Interpretation* (London, 1938), which stresses the
way in which the psychological structures of childhood may
become more radically transformed in the course of development than is admitted by traditional genetic psychology.
Thus in place of regarding adult personality-structure as
'explained' by its origins or as a mere extension of infantile
instincts or primitive emotional structures, we are given
the concept of the functional autonomy of adult motives.
In this, what I have called mental embryology is following
the path already trodden by physical embryology. This,
while admitting that a study of origins is necessary for an
understanding of adult structure, concludes that it is not
sufficient; for totally new constructions arise during individual development.

*Note 8,* On the pitfalls created for the thinker by the uncritical
*Section* 4, use of an imperfect language mechanism, see C. K. Ogden
  *p.* 126, and I. A. Richards, *The Meaning of Meaning* (London,
  *et seq.* 1930); C. K. Ogden, 'The Magic of Words, I-III' (*Psyche,*

14: 9-87; 1934); and Stuart Chase's popular book *The Tyranny of Words.*

On whether the authority of revelation is needed as a basis for ethics, see the *New Statesman* for 3 April, 1943, and subsequent issues. Here Kingsley Martin makes a strong case for the view that our concepts of right and wrong are 'composed of valuable truths discovered by man through many aeons of human experience. They arise from the nature of human Society' (and also, we may add, directly out of new social circumstances).

The view that theology, with any ethical beliefs based on theology, evolves owing to an evolution of man's idea of God is now a commonplace both among liberal theologians and rationalist critics of theology. See, *e.g.*, F. B. Jevons, *The Idea of God in Early Religions* (Cambridge, 1910); R. Otto, *The Idea of the Holy* (Oxford, 1923); J. S. Huxley, *Religion without Revelation* (London, 1927; abridged version, London, 1941).

For the non-adaptive nature of much in the ethical systems of primitive peoples see, *e.g.*, Ruth Benedict, *Patterns of Culture* (London, 1935); Margaret Mead, *Sex and Temperament in Three Primitive Societies* (New York and London, 1935); Margaret Mead (Ed.), *Co-operation and Competition among Primitive Peoples* (New York and London, 1937); Margaret Mead and Gregory Bateson, *The Balinese Character* (New York Academy of Sciences, New York, 1942).

Non-adaptive variation in isolated small biological populations is discussed in my *Evolution: the Modern Synthesis* (London, 1942), pp. 199-202, 242.

For ethics as a social adaptation see M. A. Alihan, *Social Ecology* (New York: Columbia University Press). On the relativity of ethics to social structure there are many studies. Among these a few may be mentioned, *e.g.*, the pioneer work of A. E. Taylor, *The Problem of Conduct* (London, 1901), L. T. Hobhouse's *Morals in Evolution* (London, 1906), and E. Westermarck's *Ethical Relativity* (London, 1932), which distilled the vast body of facts contained in his *Origin and Development of the Moral Ideas* (London, 1908). Sumner's *Folkways* also contains numerous examples. For a primitive society, K. Birkett Smith, *The Eskimos*; for the ethical adaptations to the impact of civilization on the tribal native, I. Hogbin, *Experiments in Civilization*, or Lucy Mair, *An African People in the Twentieth*

*Century*; for the ethics of early Christianity, E. Wester-marck, *Christianity and Morals* (London, 1939); for the adjustment of ethics to the emergence of capitalism, R. H. Tawney's *Religion and the Rise of Capitalism* (London, 1926).

Sections of Lewis Mumford's *Faith for Living* (New York and London, 1941) are well worth reading on the subject of the limitations of the ethics of *laisser-faire* capitalism, though the book as a whole suffers from having been hastily written in response to the crisis produced by the Nazi successes of the spring and summer of 1940. Thus (p. 20):

'The sort of life that is made possible in the tropical isles of the Pacific through the bounties of nature, through an almost playful round of labour—this sort of life was from the standpoint of pure capitalism little less than sacrilege. It involved too little effort, and, above all, it promised no profit, despite the fact that the natives, thanks to nature, were in the position of the favoured leisure classes of capitalistic civilization.'

This brings home the degree of the ethical adjustment we shall have to make in adapting our ideas to a system of plenty (cf. my § 8). Again (p. 52):

'Because of this overwhelming concern for the external environment as a field of interest, as a centre of organized activities, as a subject for scientific description, the pragmatic liberals lost their early tie with the human personality. Though the scientific exploration of the personality went farther than it had ever gone in the past, in the great progress made from Charcot and Janet to Freud and Jung, the arts of personal development remained on a relatively primitive level. For pragmatic liberalism avoided the normative disciplines, those dealing with purposes and values, rather than abstract matters of fact. Hence a steady neglect of the fields of aesthetics, ethics, and religion, fields which early modern liberals like Rousseau had duly cultivated.'

and (p. 56):

'Though the theologian's view of the external world might be weak as science, though he might be lazy in combining personal salvation and social aims, he at least knew that the internal world had dimensions of its own.'

—which Mumford's 'pragmatic liberal' did not.

For the relativity of Nazi ethics see Erich Fromm, 'Problems of German Characterology' (*Trans. N.Y. Acad. Sci.*, 1943, p. 79); and for that of Japanese ethics, Geoffrey Gorer, 'Themes in Japanese Culture' (ibid., 1943, p. 106).

Gorer points out that in Japan the concept of sin, as distinct from that of uncleanness, has never been differentiated; and draws the interesting conclusion that this has given rise to the Japanese emphasis on 'correct' or 'suitable' behaviour, as opposed to the abstract ethics and moral absolutes of traditional Western culture. Another peculiarity of Japanese ethics is the encouragement of aggressiveness in boy children towards their mothers and other female relations, coupled by its discouragement towards his male relatives and later his teachers and superiors. On the basis of these and other facts he is able to give a reasonable explanation 'for the striking contrast between the all-pervasive gentleness of life in Japan, which has charmed nearly every visitor, and the overwhelming brutality and sadism of the Japanese at war, which has horrified almost every observer and journalist and shocked the conscience of the democratic world'.

An acute and critical study of the difficulties and dangers resulting from applying ethical principles derived from one type of civilization to another at a quite different level, is given by A. T. Culwick in his pamphlet *Good out of Africa: a Study in the Relativity of Morals* (Rhodes-Livingstone Institute, Livingstone, Northern Rhodesia, 1942, pp. 1-42). Such factors as the attempt to inculcate a sense of sin, the 'anti-tribal bias' of much missionary teaching, and the 'battle between a number of conflicting and often irreconcilable points of view' over marriage and sexual morality, are having a disastrous and disintegrative effect on the African emerging into the modern world.

*Note* 9, *Section* v, *p.* 130, *et seq.* In the past, so-called evolutionary theories of ethics, such as Herbert Spencer's, Leslie Stephen's, or Nietzsche's, have been vitiated through their attempting to apply conclusions derived solely from the biological level of evolution to subjects like ethics which only come into existence on the social level.

Comte based his system on an evolutionary view of society, but had no theory of biological evolution available with which to link up his 'social dynamics'.

Indeed, we may say that it is only during the present century that sufficient data have been amassed in the fields of astronomy, physics, psychology, anthropology, and sociology to permit the attempt being made to advance any comprehensive theory of evolution covering all levels.

On the subject of evolutionary levels, see the important

analysis by Joseph Needham in *Time the Refreshing River* (London, 1943; notably the last two essays, which are fully documented); also R. W. Gerard, 'Higher Levels of Integration' (*Biol. Symposia*, 8: 67; 1942).

For an analysis of biological progress, see the last chapter of my *Evolution: the Modern Synthesis* (London, 1942) and the first essay in my *Essays of a Biologist* (London, 1924). The articles signed 'Archimedes' which appeared in *Horizon* for 1942 (vol. 6, nos. 31 ff.) contain a valuable analysis of the prerequisites for advance on the social level, though they do not relate this to advance on the biological level.

*Note* 10, *Sections* vi, vii, *p.* 136, *et seq.* These sections have, I fear, suffered most from the compression which was needful. For this and other reasons they are the most likely to be misunderstood. In them, I have been concerned only with the task of discovering what guarantees of ethical standards exist which are more comprehensive and more permanent than those provided by our own feelings and by the current ethical beliefs of the society to which we belong. Attempts have repeatedly been made to provide such guarantees both on a philosophical and on a religious basis; but I think I can claim the support of the great majority of my fellow-scientists in rejecting the validity of these claims. We reject those of the metaphysicians because we do not believe in the capacity of human reason to grasp the Absolute, and consider that the only method of attaining more truth and fuller knowledge is by means of the scientific method; and we reject those of the theological moralists because we are unable to take seriously the claims of revelation, and because even the most inspired moral pronouncements by the greatest religious leaders turn out on examination to be limited by the psychological peculiarities of their proponents and by the social conditions of the period, and thus to be not absolute but relative. We thus arrive at the apparent paradox that a process of change provides the only certainty to which man can hope to attain.

Most branches of science have begun by stating, analysing, and comparing the static qualities and characteristics of objects and phenomena. With the passage of time, however, the apparently static turns out to be a phase in a process, and scientific workers are forced to proceed on a dynamic basis, directing their efforts primarily to discovering the type, direction, and velocity of processes of change. This is obvious in such branches as physical geography, geology, astronomy, physical chemistry, or atomic physics; in biology it is equally obvious in palæontology and embryology, and is beginning to apply in psychology and genetics. In the social sciences the dynamic point of view has always been represented, and is now becoming dominant. Within a short period it should be possible to arrive at a generalized evolution theory which will provide a dynamic framework for all natural phenomena. Furthermore, the very nature of scientific method imposes a relativist or dynamic theory of knowledge.

But this process has scarcely begun to affect either popular or professional thinking in regard to such subjects as religion and morality; only when change instead of fixity is regarded as the goal, and the desirable is defined in terms of the direction and rate of change, not of the nature and properties of a static Absolute, will these branches of human activity fall into place within a general system of thought.

*Note* 11,   For a discussion of the evil effects of intra-specific com-
*p.* 139.   petition see J. B. S. Haldane, *The Causes of Evolution* (London, 1932), or a brief summary in my *Evolution: the Modern Synthesis* (London, 1942), pp. 483 ff.

*Note* 12,   For the changing content of Justice, see the paper by
*p.* 143.   Ginsberg discussed in the notes of § 8.

*Note* 13,   For the intrinsic value of certain types of mystical experi-
*p.* 146.   ence, see, *e.g.,* Evelyn Underhill, *Mysticism* (London, 12th Revision, 1930), Geraldine Coster, *Yoga and Western Psychology* (London, 1934), and Aldous Huxley, *Grey Eminence* (London, 1941).

*Note* 14,   For the morality of power see Bertrand Russell, *Power, a*
*p.* 147.   *New Social Analysis* (London, 1938).

*Note* 15,   After this lecture was delivered my attention was drawn
*Section*   to Professor Morris Ginsberg's interesting presidential
   viii.   address to the Aristotelian Society (*Proc. Aristot. Soc.,*
 p. 148,   1942-3 (N.S. 43) on 'The Individualist Basis of Inter-
*et seq.*   national Law and Morals', in which, in the particular sphere of international relations, he adopts a standpoint very similar to the general argument of this section. Thus, for instance, he writes:

'to give positive content to the notion of liberty it is necessary to define the *liberties* of the state or to mark out the spheres of activity within which the state should in the interests of humanity as a whole be given autonomy. The questions involved would require different

answers in different historical circumstances. It is being gradually
recognized, for example, that in future states ought not to have the
right to change their economic legislation. . . , without regard to
the effect of these changes on other states',

and so on. In general, his conclusion is that in the conditions of the modern world, international morality is
inevitably changing, so that, for instance, 'there is growing
acceptance of the view . . . that justice does not consist
in mere non-interference, but involves positive effort of
collaboration for common ends'.

E. A. Hoebel ('Primitive Law and Modern', *Trans. N.Y.
Acad. Sci.*, Dec., 1942) approaches the problem in a similar
way, and comes to the same general conclusions.

As regards the effects on morality of the economic effects
of science and its applications in transforming a régime of
permanent scarcity into one of potential plenty, E. J. D.
Radclyffe over ten years ago could write in his *Magic and
Mind* (London, 1932) 'we shall look back and be amazed
to see that we thought it common sense to be ungenerous.
. . . The attitude to debt will alter; at present the debtor is
ashamed. In the future the creditor will be ashamed to think
he had a debtor'. To-day, Lend-Lease and the Relief and
Rehabilitation proposals of the U.S.A. are the international
results of the beginning of such a changed economic
morality. Recent books like E. H. Carr's *The Foundations of
Peace* and Peter Drucker's *The End of Economic Man*
demonstrate the way in which the economic and social
foundations of morality are changing, while others, such as
Herbert Agar's *A Time for Greatness* and Michael Straight's
*Make This the Last War* more explicitly link up the material
revolution with a revolution in moral outlook and duties.

L. K. Frank ('World Order and Cultural Diversity', *Free
World*, 3, June, 1942) has some interesting remarks on the
relations between ethics and culture. At present, 'each culture
is asymmetrical, biased, and incomplete, making a virtue of
its deficiencies and its anesthesias'. Now that the world is
shrinking we must 'accept the cultural diversity of mankind
as the fundamental, inescapable basis of order', and aim at
what the same writer has elsewhere termed 'a world orchestration of cultures'.

With regard to the relations between innate qualities of
body-build and of temperamental predispositions, with their
implications for morality (p. 68), W. H. Sheldon's recent
book *The Varieties of Temperament* may be consulted. This

leads on to the more general topic of the need for safeguarding a planned society against undue concentrations and abuses of power. Bertrand Russell, in his previously cited book, has a valuable discussion of this point. On the problem of the sensitive adolescent (p. 67) see J. S. Huxley, 'The County Badge Scheme', *Spectator*, 13 Nov., 1942.

The ethics of birth-control have been discussed from every possible angle in the last quarter of a century. Those of colonial possession have recently begun to loom large. The newer attitude, rendered both possible and expedient by the changed political and economic conditions, has crystallized out in the replacement of *trusteeship* by *partnership* as the underlying basis for the relation between a colonial Power and its colonies, as forcibly expressed by Lord Hailey in recent pronouncements; and in the demand for a Colonial Charter as voiced by the recent Labour Party Conference and by independent organizations such as P.E.P. (*The Future of the Colonies*, Broadsheet No. 184, 20 Jan., 1942).

P.E.P. in its Broadsheet on *The New Pattern* (No. 178, 30 Sept., 1941) also has some interesting comments on the changing ethical valuation of charity and other virtues.

Indeed, one can hardly turn to any general discussion of present-day problems without coming across a reference to the way in which the social and economic revolution of our times implies also an ethical revolution; and this involves a revaluation of various traditional virtues, like chastity, charity, or faith, and the assignment of a new content to all general ethical concepts, such as rights and duties, social benevolence, and justice.

## III

### *Julian Huxley*

# The Vindication of Darwinism

DARWIN'S *essential* achievement was the demonstration that the almost incredible variety of life, with all its complex and puzzling relations to its environment, was explicable in scientific terms. It is for this reason that he has with justice been described as the Newton of Biology. Newton was able to account for a vast mass of apparently heterogeneous physical facts—the trajectory of cannon-balls, the movement of the planets, the fall of apples, the ebb and flow of the tides, the swing of pendulums, the orbits of moons and comets, and much besides—on the basis of a few simple general principles. With the aid of a few equally simple principles, Darwin was able to account for an equally vast mass of apparently heterogeneous biological facts—adaptations of every kind; the origin of the million and more separate species of animals and plants; the existence of fossils differing from existing species; the *raison d'être* of special masculine adornment and weapons; the puzzles of geographical distribution, such as the restriction of tapirs to South America and Malaya, of kangaroos to Australia, of elephants to the Indian and African regions; the development in embryos of structures found in adults of quite other type; the paucity of types, but the abundance of species within each type, to be found in the fauna and flora of oceanic archipelagoes; the elaborate mechanisms for ensuring cross-fertilization; the facts of parasitism; the resemblance of man to monkeys, and, more generally, the existence of structural plans common to large groups; and many others.

Again, Newton's work enabled him and his successors to make innumerable deductions and prophecies, from the return of comets to the time of eclipses, from the compilation of tide-tables to the formation of double stars and solar systems. The same is true of Darwin and those who came after him. He was able to prophesy a detail such as the future discovery of a moth with a proboscis longer than any previously known, and to deduce a general principle such as that no species would ever be found with any characters which were solely or primarily useful to some other species. Darwinian prophecies that palæontology would unearth fossils showing gradual modification of divergent types have been verified, and also that 'missing links' between various distinct types, including those between man and ape-like forms, would be discovered.

The kernel of Darwin's work was the principle of Natural Selection. The idea of evolution had been in the minds of many previous thinkers, but no one had suggested any plausible or reasonable method by which it could have taken place. My grandfather, T. H. Huxley, records the effect of Darwin's great idea upon the biological world of 1859:—'the effect . . . of a flash of light which, to a man who has lost himself on a dark night, suddenly reveals a road which, whether it takes him straight home or not, certainly goes a long way. That which we were looking for, and could not find, was a hypothesis respecting the origin of known organic forms which assumed the operation of no causes but such as could be proved to be actually at work. . . . The *Origin* provided us with the working hypothesis we sought. . . . My reflection, when I first made myself master of the central idea of the *Origin*, was, "How extremely stupid not to have thought of that!" I suppose that Columbus' companions said much the same when he made the egg stand on end'.

In parenthesis, I would like to add a word about the share of Alfred Russel Wallace in this great discovery. As is well known, the principle of Natural Selection was first published in a joint communication by Darwin and Wallace to the Linnæan Society. This resulted from Wallace, then in the Malay Archipelago, having sent Darwin an essay setting forth the idea of Natural Selection as the missing agency which would result in the transmutation of species and in evolution in general. But whereas Wallace's essay was the product of an idea which had flashed upon him a bare four months before his essay reached England, Darwin had hit upon the principle of Natural Selection no less than sixteen years earlier. As Darwin himself wrote to Lyell immediately after receiving Wallace's essay, 'I never saw a more striking coincidence; if Wallace had had my MS sketch written out in 1842, he could not have made a better short abstract'.

Thus, though Wallace deserves full credit for his brilliant intuition, Darwin had a long priority, as well as having thoroughly worked out the implications of the idea, and supported it with an immense body of facts.

The concept of Natural Selection is a remarkable blend of induction and deduction. As I have written elsewhere:[1] 'It is as well to remember the strong deductive element in Darwinism. Darwin based his theory of Natural Selection on three observable facts of nature and two deductions from them. The first fact is the tendency of all organisms to increase in a geometrical ratio. This tendency of all organisms to increase is due to offspring, in the early stages of their existence, always being more numerous than their parents. . . . The second fact is that, in spite of this tendency to progressive increase, the numbers of a given species remain more or less constant.

'The first deduction follows. From these two facts he deduced the struggle for existence. For since more young are produced than can survive, there must be competition for survival. In amplifying his theory, he extended the concept of the struggle

---

[1] *Evolution: the Modern Synthesis* (Allen and Unwin, 1942), p. 14.

for existence to cover reproduction. The struggle is in point of fact for survival of the stock. . . .

'Darwin's third fact of nature was variation: all organisms vary appreciably. And the second and final deduction, which he deduced from the first deduction and the third fact, was Natural Selection. Since there is a struggle for existence among individuals, and since these individuals are not all alike, some of the variations among them will be advantageous in the struggle for survival, others unfavourable. Consequently, a higher proportion of individuals with favourable variations will on the average survive; a higher proportion of those with unfavourable variations will die or fail to reproduce themselves. And since a great deal of variation is transmitted by heredity, these effects of differential survival will in large measure accumulate from generation to generation. Thus natural selection will act constantly to improve and to maintain the adjustment of animals and plants to their surroundings and their way of life'.

Darwinism may thus be broadly defined in the two-fold sense of a scientifically-grounded belief in the process of organic evolution, operating through the mechanism of Natural Selection. After the publication of the *Origin* in 1859, Darwinism had a rapid and striking success. Within a few years all but a handful of biologists had accepted Natural Selection as at least a reasonable working hypothesis, and, provisionally taking it for granted, had concentrated chiefly on demonstrating the reality of evolution as a historical and present fact. Within a quarter-century the concept of evolution had taken its place as one of the great ideas of the world, destined to colour man's thinking permanently in every department of life.

Then, however, a retrogression set in. It was not that the broad fact of evolution was doubted. The evidences which made it clear that evolution had occurred, continued to pile up: innumerable facts were accumulated by biology which fitted immediately into an evolutionary scheme of things and interlocked to form an ever-strengthening support for the idea of evolution, but were incapable of scientific interpretation, and indeed simply refused to make sense, on any alternative hypothesis. These facts included the striking discoveries of American paleontologists, which demonstrated by the concrete evidence of fossils that gradual evolution towards a fully specialized type had actually occurred during geological time in the horses, the titanotheres, and many other groups—facts which were unknown when Darwin wrote his great book, but confirmed his general contention in the most unequivocal way.

No, the 'decline of Darwinism', as it has sometimes been styled, which took place from about 1890 to about 1915, was mainly concerned with its second aspect—the principle of Natural Selection, the detailed evidences for it, and the modes of its operation. General biology, having accomplished the more urgent task of establishing the fact of evolution on an impregnable footing, turned to consider the working hypothesis of Natural Selection, on the basis of which the possibility of evolution was presumed. Now scientists cannot long continue to be satisfied with the merely possible, in the way of a working hypothesis. Inevitably they want a tested theory, based on factual (and wherever practicable, experimental) evidence, and operating through clear-cut (and wherever possible, quantitative) scientific laws which can serve as the basis for further predictions and verifications.

Objections began to pour in from the more cautious and the more critically-minded. One widespread criticism was that the theory of Natural Selection was a matter of arm-chair speculation. A certain section among the Darwinians would argue roughly as follows: this or that character appears *prima facie* to be of biological use to its possessor; it is therefore an adaptation; it has therefore been produced during evolution by Natural Selection. The paper demonstration (so the critics maintained, not without some justification) of presumptive adaptation was taken as evidence for the reality of Natural Selection; and vice versa the paper theory of Natural Selection was taken as evidence for the reality and value of biological adaptation. The anti-Darwinians concentrated their attack especially on the alleged adaptations of mimicry and of sexual selection. More positively, they criticized the absence of experimental work aimed at demonstrating the concrete biological value of the adaptations, and the reality and intensity of the process of selection in nature.

A parallel criticism was directed against the other pillar of the selection theory—the nature and amount of the variability which selection has at its disposal. Darwin himself was emphatic in repudiating the suggestion (whose absurdity did not prevent his critics from asserting it to be a part of his theory) that selection in some way produced its own raw material. Thus in Chapter IV of the *Origin* he writes that some writers 'have even imagined that natural selection induces variability, whereas it implies only the preservation of such variations as occur and are beneficial to the being under its conditions of life'. And he had previously defined Natural Selection as 'the preservation of favourable variations, and the destruction of injurious variations', the variations being taken (on the basis of his extensive survey of the facts) as previously provided by the operation of some natural process.

But, owing to the state of science in the mid-nineteenth century, he was unable to go much beyond these extremely broad generalities. The biologists of 1859 did not know which variations were inherited and which were not (a point of capital importance, since the latter could obviously not contribute to evolutionary change); they did not know how inherited variations were transmitted; they did not know how they originated; and they did not know whether the effects of environment or of use and disuse could be transmitted to subsequent generations.

There was a general assumption that such transmission (the inheritance of acquired characters, or lamarckian inheritance, as later generations called it) could and did occur to a certain rather small extent, and this historical fact doubtless influenced

Darwin in his belief in the importance of what he called 'the conditions of life' in producing evolutionary change. But conversely he was driven to acceptance of this belief by what he regarded as a fundamental difficulty—the difficulty of explaining how new advantageous variations, even if fully hereditary, would escape being swamped by subsequent crossing.

As R. A. Fisher has shown in the first chapter of his important book, *The Genetical Basis of Natural Selection* (1930), Darwin set out with the preconception that heredity was of the blending, not the particulate type—that is to say, that whatever material substratum it was which determined inherited characters, its parts blended with each other when two distinct stocks were crossed, like drops of differently-coloured inks, instead of remaining in some way discrete and distinct, like differently-coloured marbles.

Although this preconception was explicitly stated in the early essays (of 1842 and to a lesser extent of 1844) in which he set forth his first ideas about Natural Selection, by the time he came to write the *Origin* he was merely taking blending inheritance for granted. However, its implications still coloured his general thought and the details of his argument, and continued to do so throughout his life.

The immediate consequence of any theory of blending inheritance is that, as Darwin wrote in his notebook in 1842 of what we would call new variants, 'if varieties (are) allowed freely to cross, except by the *chance* of two characterized by (the) same peculiarity happening to many, such varieties will be constantly demolished'. In modern terms, the variance (or less technically, the variability) of the species or breeding population will decrease very rapidly. With random crossing it will be approximately halved in each generation, so that less than one-thousandth of the observed variance of such a species could be more than ten generations old. And even if the freedom of crossing were interfered with by a very high degree of assortative mating, the rate of decay of the variance would at best be little more than halved.

This means that to explain the existence of any reasonable amount of variability, such as is in point of fact to be found in many wild and domestic populations, we must either presuppose what would now be called a normal mutation-rate enormously much higher than any yet discovered, or else we must imagine, as Darwin did, not merely that changes in conditions can provoke variability—increase the mutation-rate—but that such a variability-provoking event had occurred in the very recent past of the population in question. In any case, as Fisher says, 'If variation is to be used by the human breeder, or by natural selection, it must be snapped up at once, soon after the mutation has appeared, and before it has had time to die away'.

It was considerations such as these which induced Darwin to ascribe such importance to 'the conditions of life'—changes in climate, general environment, amount and kind of food available, and so forth. And these changes in conditions, both in domesticated and wild species, he was driven to believe, caused the outburst of variability needed for artificial or natural selection to work on. In addition, it was these considerations which made Darwin assign a subordinate but considerable rôle in the production of evolutionary change to the main lamarckian idea of the inheritance of the effects of use and disuse, and a further but smaller rôle to Lamarck's subsidiary principle of the inheritance of the direct effects of 'the conditions of life'.

Immense difficulties remained. How was it, on these assumptions, that the variability of the longest-established domestic animals and plants was not merely as high as that of more recently domesticated forms, but usually higher? How was it that, according to the eminent Swiss-French botanist de Candolle, the variability of cultivated plants was usually highest in the country where they had been longest cultivated, instead of in the new countries with new climates to which they had been later introduced? Can we really suppose that the conditions of life or the abundance of food have undergone large changes sufficiently often to produce the torrents of variation required for evolution operating by Natural Selection? How is it possible on any such scheme to understand the frequent occurrence of variations which are reversions to ancestral types, be they near or remote?

The difficulties were, in point of fact, insurmountable—so long as the fundamental postulate, of blending inheritance, was accepted. It is Fisher's merit to have first shown that they all disappear once the principle of particulate inheritance is recognized. Indeed, the acceptance of neo-Mendelism, which happens to be the method by which particulate inheritance actually works, makes the process of evolution through Natural Selection very much easier to understand than it was for Darwin himself, or for his most ardent supporters up to 1920 or 1925.[1]

Thus, on a neo-mendelian basis, there is no longer any need to postulate the impossibly high mutation-rates required if Natural Selection is to operate with blending inheritance. The reason is that with mendelian inheritance the variance of a species or population is conserved. The variant particles, or mutant genes as we now call them, can remain in storage indefinitely until they are required. The only qualifications are that genes with deleterious effects will diminish in frequency and tend to disappear as a result of adverse selection, and that others may be lost to the stock through purely accidental elimination—owing to the few gametes or adults which contain them chancing not to be successful in reproduction. But this latter effect will play only a very minor part (except in very small populations), and both together will

[1] Fisher further pointed out as a remarkable fact that 'had any thinker in the middle of the nineteenth century undertaken, as a piece of abstract and theoretical analysis, the task of constructing a particulate theory of inheritance, he would have been led, on the basis of a few very simple [and we may add, necessary or at least natural] assumptions, to produce a system identical with the modern scheme of Mendelism or factorial inheritance'—a thesis which he develops in some detail, concluding 'it thus appears that, apart from dominance and linkage, including sex-linkage, all the main characteristics of the Mendelian system . . . could have been deduced a priori *had any one conceived it possible that the laws of inheritance could really be simple and definite*' (italics mine).

cause only a slight diminution of variance, which can readily be replenished by mutation at the sort of rates which have been found actually to occur.

This conservation of new variants is further aided by the fact of dominance. Many, probably most, mutant genes are recessive—*i.e.*, do not exert their effects when present together with the 'normal' gene as their partner. Thus even deleterious recessive genes will not become the subject of adverse selection unless present in double dose; and this, in the case of at all infrequent genes, will be a very rare event: for instance, a recessive gene present in the unusually high ratio of 1 individual per 1,000 will on the average exist in pure form (double dose) only in one in more than a million individuals—a total larger than the entire population of a number of species in nature.

Again, Mendelism at once explains the facts of reversion, which were at once so familiar and so puzzling to Darwin. If, as often happens, particularly in domesticated forms, one stock or variety has lost one gene which is necessary for the development of a given character such as colour or pattern, while a second has lost another contributor to the same character, then a cross between the two will restore the original or ancestral character or type. This fact is unintelligible on the assumption of blending inheritance, but follows immediately from elementary Mendelism.

Mendelism also accounts for the fact—so familiar that the need to explain it is often forgotten—that brothers and sisters (sibs), in human as well as animal and plant families, often differ markedly from one another—much more markedly than could possibly be accounted for by postulating an effect of differing 'conditions of life' either upon them or their parents.

This is one result of the more general fact of recombination—the most important single consequence of the conservation of variance through mendelian heredity. By recombination we mean the possibility, after a cross, of recombining the gene-differences between two stocks in all kinds of ways. In Mendel's classical experiments with peas, after crossing a variety with smooth yellow seeds with one having wrinkled green seeds, he found in the second generation ($F_2$) not merely the two original seed-types, but also the other two possible combinations—smooth green and yellow wrinkled. The number of combinations goes up rapidly with the number of genes involved, being $2^n$ for $n$ different genes, so that from a cross involving only ten independent gene-differences, there may be bred 1,024 combinations, all but two of which are new recombinations.

This fact is of the utmost importance. In the first place, it provides organisms with a second source of genetic variation. While in the really long run evolution must depend on the occurrence of mutations producing genes of new type, yet for many purposes it can draw on the short-term novelties provided by recombination. In the second place, it affords a biological rationale for the existence of sex. Sex, paradoxically at first sight, is in its essence not so much a matter of difference between male and female as a mechanism for recombining mutations. Without sex, mutations would remain confined to the lines in which they had originated; with sex they can be combined with other mutations originating in other lines. Ten mutations in a sexless species will provide only ten different variant types on which selection can get to work; in a species with sex the number jumps to over a thousand. Sex plus Mendelism makes possible a much greater rapidity and variety of evolution.

Finally, with the acceptance of neo-Mendelism the fact that the variability is greatest in the most anciently domesticated strains of plants and animals at once became explicable and indeed to be expected, instead of the stumbling-block it was for Darwin.

Neo-mendelian discovery and analysis have also resolved another major conflict—that between the mutationists and the Darwinian gradualists. Around the turn of the century, many critics of the theory of Natural Selection felt that the slow and gradual type of change postulated by Darwin could not or would not account for the immense results which had actually been achieved during evolution.

Since then, this criticism has, of course, in part fallen to the ground with the change in our views on the age of the earth and the period of its tenancy by living organisms, which has resulted from the discovery of radio-activity. This discovery has not merely enormously extended the time-scale of organic evolution; it has also provided a new and accurate method of dating its events. Not long after the general acceptance of evolution as a fact, Lord Kelvin, the eminent physicist, gave the earth a total age of between twenty and forty million years; which my grandfather immediately asserted to be impossibly short for evolution. The general impressions of the biologist proved to be more correct than the accurate calculations of physical science. The age of the earth has now been extended to about 2,000 million years, the age of life upon the earth to at least 1,100 million years, and the first appearance of even the most modern types, such as the horses, has been dated back to some 50 million years ago.

However, this is only half the story. The upholders of mutation also maintained that the slight and imperceptible changes of classical Darwinism *could* not by their nature produce large-scale evolutionary results. How was it possible, they asked, for selection to select so effectively as between such slight differences? If Natural Selection depended for its working on the survival of the fittest, how could one conceive that a small variation towards, let us say, a more protective coloration or pattern could make the crucial difference between survival and extinction?

To the fallacy I will return. Meanwhile the believers in short cuts to evolution were strengthened by two events—one, the promulgation of the Mutation Theory by the distinguished Dutch botanist de Vries in 1901; the other, the independent rediscovery of Mendel's Laws by de Vries, Correns, and Tschermak in 1900, and their further working-out, notably by Bateson in England.

De Vries, on the basis of striking inherited 'jumps' in character which he discovered and investigated in the Evening Primrose *Oenothera*, put forward the view that such 'jumps' or mutations, many of them already adapted and capable of maintaining themselves *ab initio*, were to be regarded as the main type of variation to play a part in evolutionary change, and therefore not merely the raw material of evolution (as would be the small variations postulated by Darwin), but its cause.

However, it soon appeared that the 'mutations' observed in Oenothera were something exceptional and in any case not to be regarded as a major factor in evolution. And later it turned out that they were not mutations at all, in the proper sense of that word as denoting the appearance of new genetic variations. In certain plants, including Oenothera, a peculiar condition has arisen whereby most or all of the chromosome-pairs exist normally in a markedly dissimilar or heterozygous state. The genetic mechanism by which this has originated and is maintained is too complex to discuss here. What concerns us is the fact that in Oenothera it permits occasional crossing-over; and it was the large-scale recombinations thus produced which were not unnaturally taken by de Vries for true mutations.

Bateson, followed by other early Mendelians such as Morgan in the first stages of his genetic career, also embraced the theory of large mutations. In Bateson's case this was a natural continuation of his valuable earlier work, embodied in his *Materials for the Study of Variation* in 1894. In this volume he had assembled a large body of evidence proving the existence of markedly discontinuous variation in nature, as opposed to (or at least in addition to) the continuous or fluctuating variation postulated by Darwin and his selectionist followers. After 1900, he extended this notion to mendelizing mutations. If not inevitable, this was at least natural. In the early 1900's the Mendelians were above all anxious to validate and generalize Mendel's two fundamental laws of segregation and recombination—a task clearly of the highest importance for biology. To achieve this, they naturally preferred to work with obvious and clear-cut differences—tall versus dwarf plants, seeds of different colours, pigmented versus albino rodents, the presence or absence of horns in cattle, markedly different comb-shapes in fowls, and so on. From the discovery that those clear-cut differences mendelized to the assumption that all mendelizing characters must depend on clear-cut differences was but a step.

It proved, however, to be a false step. In the first place, later research revealed that many variations whose demarcation and inheritance was not clear-cut, in reality obeyed mendelian laws—it was merely that with them mendelian dominance was not complete; or that the real but small genetic differences involved could be obscured by equally real but non-inherited differences, or modifications due to environment; or that their inheritance was complex, involving several genes with interacting effects, or one main gene together with a number of minor 'modifiers'. We now know that the inheritance of all mutations, except for a few rare cases of cytoplasmic variation, fits into the neo-mendelian scheme.

Further, it became progressively clearer that it is the mutations of small extent and often apparently trivial nature which form the great bulk of the raw material with which evolution actually operates, while large mutations with striking effects are but rarely serviceable.

Certain critics of Darwinism, such as Hogbin, at one time maintained that the discovery of mutation and of mendelian inheritance had put out of court the Darwinian idea of evolution as 'an essentially continuous process'. This, however, proved wholly erroneous. In any case, evolution, as revealed in fossil trends, *is* an essentially continuous process. Further (if I may again cite my own previous writings)[1] 'the building-blocks of evolution, in the shape of mutations, are, to be sure, discrete quanta of change. But, firstly, the majority of them (and the very great majority of

[1] *Evolution: the Modern Synthesis* (Allen and Unwin, 1942), p. 27.

those which survive to become incorporated in the genetic constitution of living things) appear to be of small extent; secondly, the effect of a given mutation will be different according to the combination of modifying genes present; and thirdly, its effect may be masked or modified by environmental modifications. The net result will be that, for all practical purposes, most of the variability of a species at any given moment will be continuous, however accurate the measurements made; and that most evolutionary change will be gradual, to be detected by a progressive shifting of a mean value from generation to generation'.

Bateson also developed the paradoxical and essentially antidarwinian thesis that evolution proceeds not by the addition of new characters but by the dropping out of old ones. This was based on the observed fact that many mutations, like many of the characters by which domestic breeds differ from the wild type, are recessive in their inheritance, and show the absence or the diminution of some wild-type character or property ('loss mutations'). Bateson concluded that recessiveness of inheritance, with its loss of visible character, corresponded to the loss of something material from the hereditary constitution; and put forward the so-called Presence-and-Absence theory, whereby the recessive character depended on the absence of the normal gene. Further, from the frequency of such loss, he jumped to a general law of evolution by loss.

These generalizations, however, were ill-founded. Some domestic breed-characters are not recessive to the wild type, but dominant, like rose and pea comb in fowls, or hornlessness in cattle; and many new mutations have since been discovered which are wholly or partly dominant.

Most significant, however, is the fact that modern mendelian theory has been able to explain the origin of recessivity itself. There was this important element of truth in Bateson's Presence-and-Absence theory—that most recessive characters seem to depend on the diminution or the absence of some process involved in producing the corresponding dominant. Thus albinism in verte-brates depends on the absence of the enzyme which is needed to produce melanin pigment; and there are various grades of partial albinism corresponding to a reduced or delayed action of the enzyme. Again, the recessive character 'vestigial' in Drosophila results from an incomplete development of the wing.

In addition, it soon appeared that most new mutations were not only recessive but were to a greater or lesser extent deleterious, either through the inadequacy of the visible character produced, or through a lowering of general vigour or variability. We should indeed *expect* most mutations to be deleterious: in a delicately adjusted system of interacting parts such as the hereditary con-stitution, most changes are likely to be for the worse unless com-pensated. Further, it was discovered that the majority of mutations recur repeatedly.

On the basis of these facts, R. A. Fisher from 1928 onwards developed his theory that dominance is usually not given in the nature of things, but has been evolved (through the selection of modifying genes) as an adaptation. It is an adaptation with a double function, the short-term one of shielding the species against the immediate harmful effects of most mutations, and the long-term one of enabling it to keep in its constitution a store of recessives, some of which may later be made useful through adjustment by modifying genes. Since then, conclusive evidence has accumulated from many quarters in favour of this general thesis that most dominance is 'made, not born', and has been evolved as an adaptation, though other mechanisms besides that suggested by Fisher may be operative. Thus facts which were originally cited as evidence against the selectionist position now turn out to be themselves the result of Natural Selection.

Of recent years, Goldschmidt has revived the essentials of de Vries' mutation theory in a new form. He divides evolution into two categories. The first he calls micro-evolution, involving small changes only and resulting in no more than subspecific novelty—the production of what Darwin called varieties. The formation of new species, and *a fortiori* all major evolutionary changes such as the origination of some radically new type (*e.g.*, flat fishes from ordinary fish), he styles macro-evolution, a process which, he considers, operates by a different mechanism. The small changes of micro-evolution he ascribes to the ordinary point-mutations or alterations in single genes, while the large changes of macro-evolution are put down to what he calls systemic mutations—radical rearrangements of the general pattern of the hereditary constitution, resulting in a quite new type of reaction-system.

It is true that recent work has shown that many apparent mutations are not the result of alterations within a single gene, but of rearrangements of bits of the chromosomes after breakage —inversions, when a piece is reversed end-to-end within one chromosome; translocations, when bits of two chromosomes change places; and so on. As a result, the genes adjacent to the breaks come to have new neighbours, and their interaction with these new neighbours may alter their own mode of action and the characters they produce. Such results are summed up under the term 'position-effect'.

These position-effects, however, are normally indistinguishable in type and scale from the effects of single-gene mutations; further, there is no evidence for the existence of radical rearrangements with the large effects such as Goldschmidt assumes; finally, there is plenty of evidence that small genetic changes (including position-effects as well as point-mutations) can actually be accumulated to produce new species.

But while the great majority of biologists have rejected Goldschmidt's views on the necessity of large 'systemic' mutations for macro-evolution, one category of large-scale 'jumps' in evolution remains (though it occurs almost exclusively in plants). This depends on the addition or subtraction of whole chromosomes, or of whole *genomes* or unit outfits of chromosomes. The simplest type of such large-scale mutation is known as autopolyploidy—the addition of one or more whole genomes to the normal set, which may take place by a number of different methods. The two commonest results are, firstly, the formation of triploid plants with three single sets or packs of chromosomes instead of the two normal for ordinary diploids, (in genetic shorthand, $3n$ instead of $2n$ chromosomes); and secondly, that of tetraploids with $4n$, or double the normal complement. Such polyploids may be not merely viable, but often larger and more resistant to extremes of temperature or drought than the original $2n$ types. When so, they have often given rise to new forms in nature, which have spread much more widely than their ancestral diploids. The process may be repeated, so that $6n$, $8n$, $12n$, and higher polyploids may arise.

Triploids are inevitably sterile, but can maintain themselves if the plant is capable of asexual reproduction. Since tetraploids initially always show some reduction of fertility, some degree of asexual reproduction is almost necessary for them also; but this applies only to the early stages of their evolutionary existence. Their reproduction can be adjusted later, by natural selection of the most fertile individuals, which will result in a new complex of genes concerned with promoting fertility.

A more spectacular form of tetraploidy is that known as allotetraploidy, in which two different parent species are involved. In plants, crosses between 'good' species are not infrequent, and the hybrid is often vigorous—sometimes more so than both parents—and also pre-adapted to slightly different conditions from those of either parent species. But it is invariably either sterile or else quite inconstant in type.

Sometimes, however, owing to accidents in the process of nuclear division, the entire hybrid complement of chromosomes is doubled, and tetraploid plants are produced. These $4n$ types now have two sets of chromosomes from each of the parent species, and these can then pair with each other before the formation of pollen and ova, so that viable gametes and fertile reproduction are now assured.

In this way, new species may be produced at a single bound, although minor adjustments, especially of reproductive mechanism, may remain to be made later by selection. Among the numerous examples known in nature, we may mention the rice-grass *Spartina townsendii*, a recent hybrid, which is pre-adapted to a new habitat, being able to colonize bare tidal mud below the level to which its parents can penetrate; and also the hemp-nettle *Galeopsis tetrahit*, which has been artificially re-synthesized by crossing two other wild species.

Space does not permit discussion of the cases where single chromosomes or small groups of chromosomes have been added or subtracted. Suffice it to say that the former are not infrequent in already polyploid forms; while the latter method seems to have been employed in the origin of certain quite large groups, such as the whole *Pomoideae* section of the order *Rosaceae*—the apples, pears, medlars, and their relatives.

Although such large and sudden effects (which would have distressed the pure gradualists of the Weismann school!) have thus played a definite part in evolution, that part is almost wholly confined to plants, and even in them is a minor one and one which also requires adjustment and polish through subsequent selection. The great bulk of the raw material for evolution consists of small mutations, and the great bulk of actual evolutionary change is gradual.

Furthermore, the major agency of evolutionary change is selection. The concept of Lamarckism, or the inheritance of the effects of use and disuse and of the direct effects of the conditions of life, appears now to be definitely exploded. For one thing, all the experiments claiming to prove its existence have been either disproved, or failed to be confirmed, or alternative explanations have been shown to be preferable. For another, there is a great bulk of evidence, both indirect and circumstantial, and direct and experimental, showing that Lamarckism does not operate in a very large number of cases. And finally there is a theoretical objection based on the recent development of mathematical genetics. Mathematical analysis demonstrates that a new variation giving even 0.1 per cent. of biological advantage—in other words, securing that on an average a thousand and one of its possessors should survive as against a thousand without it—would spread quite rapidly through a population; and one with an advantage of 1 per cent. would spread very rapidly. Now, some believers in the inheritance of acquired characters, in order to explain the non-appearance of lamarckian effects in the course of laboratory experiments, claim that these effects are so small that they require to accumulate for many generations before they can be detected.

However, it can now be asserted with certainty that, even if such small effects did occur, then if they were biologically advantageous, mutation and selection would be more efficacious and would produce a similar result but by non-lamarckian methods; whereas if they were even slightly deleterious, counter-selection would completely override them. Thus, even if lamarckian inheritance were a fact, evolution would still be non-lamarckian.

Similar reasoning applies to the theory of orthogenesis. Orthogenesis, in the strict sense of the term, denotes a mysterious 'inherent tendency' to vary and evolve steadily in one direction. This has been often invoked to explain the observed fact that evolution, as revealed by fossils, frequently pursues a straight course for tens of millions of years. However, first of all there is no evidence of mutation which is restricted to one or a few main directions in preference to others. Secondly, unless mutation were to occur simultaneously in all individuals of a species, which is contrary to all our knowledge, it would not have an orthogenetic effect; for otherwise, as can readily be calculated mathematically, the speed of favourable mutations would still be due to selection, not to the frequency of mutation; and unfavourable mutations would be prevented from spreading by counter-selection, except in cases of mutation-rates far higher than any yet observed in nature.

To which we may add that (apart from a few puzzling but isolated cases) straight-line evolution, as actually revealed by fossils in most groups, can.be perfectly well interpreted on the basis of mutation and selection. Further, such straight-line evolution is not universal, but there are cases where evolution changes its direction; these obviously cannot be explained by the theory of orthogenesis, but fit perfectly well into a darwinian scheme. For example, the elephant stock began by an elongation of the jaws: later, however, the direction of evolution changed and the jaws were exceedingly shortened, while the trunk became elongated.

Thus, while all the alternative methods of evolution—by large mutation, by lamarckian change, or by orthogenesis—have been either disproved or shown to be of quite subsidiary importance, the darwinian principle of Natural Selection of some among a random supply of small inherited variations has not merely been confirmed, but has been much strengthened by the development of neo-mendelian fact and theory.

It remains to discuss a few fallacies which, though repeatedly exposed, continue to be advanced as objections to Darwinism. Let us take first the assertion that selection is essentially destructive, and not creative. This, though it has been made in the fairly recent past by such eminent biologists as Morgan and Hogbin, is simply untrue. Selection is destructive in the sense that it eliminates the unfavourable; but equally it is creative in that it preserves the favourable. Without selection, evolutionary novelty could not be produced, and neither elaborate adaptation nor long-continued straight-line evolution towards higher specialization could occur.

Another version of the same argument is that selection can preserve and stabilize, but cannot produce 'adaptive' novelty. This again is simply untrue. Certainly there does exist what Schmal-hausen calls 'stabilizing selection', but it will operate only in certain conditions: in other conditions selection will operate against stability. Natural Selection is thus an extremely flexible mechanism, capable within limits of producing either stability or change according to which is biologically desirable.

Again, as R. A. Fisher has paradoxically but pithily said, selection provides a mechanism for generating a high degree of improbability. This fact does away with another anti-darwinian argument—that the random and automatic processes of mutation and selection could never produce complex adaptive results such as the human eye, the wing of birds, or the mimicry of various butterflies. Indeed we can now retort that the more complex and apparently 'incredible' the adaptation, the more it demonstrates the efficacy of selection.

Then there is the objection that selection cannot be operative because in many animals and plants the great bulk of the mortality is non-selective—the seeds that fail to germinate, the marine larvae that are gulped down in millions by fish—or non-selective with reference to the adults, as in butterflies, where most elimination takes place during the caterpillar stage. However, this does not mean that the characters of the adults cannot be adaptive. Even if 99 per cent. die young, whether selectively or not, selection still cannot help acting on the 1 per cent. of adults. If a certain coloration or other character enables its possessors to reproduce slightly more often than those without it, there we have an effect of Natural Selection. The whole argument is illogical: the fact that some mortality is non-selective does not prevent the rest from being selective.

There is also an old fallacy which asserts that because animals are not all the time fighting or actively preventing each other from obtaining food or mates, therefore Darwin's 'struggle for existence' does not itself exist. This is a purely verbal objection: those who advance it have forgotten that the term 'struggle' is used in a purely metaphorical sense. All that is implied by the phrase 'success in the struggle for existence' is differential survival of one or other type over the generations. Indeed, Darwin himself once wrote that it might have been preferable if he had used the term *struggle for reproduction* instead of *struggle for existence.*

If a hundred animals or plants of one type survive as against ninety-nine of another, then the selective struggle is still operative, whether the extra survival result from active struggle between individuals of the same species, from success in preying on other species, from extra vigour, protective coloration, or special reproductive success. What matters is merely that more of one type survive.

Of recent years there have been numerous experimental confirmations of the operation of selection, besides a still larger number of natural examples which illustrate selective effects; and they, together with modern mathematical analysis, have finally given us, not merely the proof of the overriding importance of natural selection, but a highly developed theory of Darwinism. With this, Darwinism has in the space of two or three decades risen from a non-quantitative working hypothesis to become the most advanced scientific discipline in general biology, one where, as in physics, high quantitative accuracy is possible, where calculation can predict results to be later verified by experiment, and where pure theory can suggest profitable lines of practical advance. Once more, but now on a higher level of scientific precision, we can employ the mixture of induction and deduction so successfully used by Darwin himself.

To-day, we have come to realize the universality and the immense power of Natural Selection. Selection may be temporarily relaxed, as in favourable periods which allow excessive over-multiplication of rodents and other animals; and when this is so variability is increased, and abnormalities often appear which could not maintain themselves under normal intensities of selection. But apart from such occasional relaxations, selection is omnipresent. And if not omnipotent it is immensely powerful. It provides both the driving force and the directive guidance for evolutionary change.

Selection is also flexible in its operation and varied in its nature. There are various kinds of selection—selection by the inorganic environment, extra-specific selection involving competition between species, intra-specific selection between competitors of the same species, intra-sexual selection between competitors of the same species and sex, pre-natal intra-uterine selection between individuals of the same litter. Intra-specific selection may produce immense prodigality, as in the vast amount of pollen in wind-pollinated trees like pines; further, many of its results may be useless to the species as a whole in its struggle for existence, like the incredible cryptic resemblance of the butterfly Kallima to a dead leaf.

I will give two examples of the great difference between the results of different kinds of selection. It is not for nothing that intra-sexual selection has given the world the most beautiful as well as the most bizarre manifestations of life. In this acute form of intra-specific selection, competition between rival males may achieve results which are of great advantage to one individual male as against another, in securing its successful reproduction, but are of no significance for the species as a whole. Indeed, this type of selection may even produce characters which are somewhat harmful to the species in the struggle for existence, for instance, the enormous tail of the male peacock, or the hypertrophied wings of the Argus Pheasant, which make their flight extremely clumsy.

As a second example we may take what has been called intra-uterine selection. In such mammals as produce many young at a time, there is a pre-natal selection between members of each litter, those which are less vigorous and develop more slowly usually dying before birth. In this way, a higher speed of pre-natal development is evolved, and this normally extends also into growth after birth.

Now one of the chief characters by which man differs from lower mammals, and to which he owes his biological success, is his extreme slowness of post-natal development, permitting a long period of education and the acquisition of necessary experience before he is launched into the full struggle for success. It is interesting to reflect that this very slow development could not have been evolved except in a group like the monkeys, in which only one young is produced at a time. Mental powers like those of man could never have evolved in a group like the rodents or the carnivores, where pre-natal competition produces very rapid development.

Natural Selection is a mechanism for introducing apparent purpose into evolution. After Darwin, it was no longer necessary to deduce the existence of divine purpose from the facts of biological adaptation. Instead of *conscious purpose* we can now say *adaptive function*, and the old theological teleology can be replaced by a scientific pseudo-teleology.

Perhaps most remarkable of all, Natural Selection is able to accomplish simultaneously two apparently contradictory results— it can both discourage and encourage change. It can and does preserve simple and primitive groups, while also producing evolutionary novelty in the shape of more complex and more varied types, according to the conditions.

In new types, selection will promote specialization. Once a type has arisen with an incipient adaptation to a particular mode of life, selection will normally continue to push this adaptation further. Thus the original members of the horse family showed slight adaptations to quicker running and better chewing of vegetable food. Further selection led to specialization of this tendency—to increase of size, longer legs with fewer toes, hoofs, and more complicated grinding teeth. Finally, however, it was impossible to go further—greater size would be clumsy; one cannot reduce the number of toes below one per foot; greater complexity of tooth-pattern would decrease their efficiency as grindstones. The straight-line evolution then comes to an end, and from now on selection acts to stabilize the perfected type.

Further, while most evolutionary novelties will thus be merely one-sided specializations, destined inevitably to come to an evolutionary dead end, selection can also produce true progress, which comprises not only all-round advance but also the possibility of still further advance in the future.

In conclusion, we have the glorious paradox that this purposeless mechanism, after a thousand million years of its blind and automatic operations, has finally generated purpose—as one of the attributes of our own species. And in so doing it has superseded itself. Natural Selection still operates in human affairs, but to a subsidiary and a decreasing extent. With the advent of man, major evolutionary change is and will continue to be mediated mainly through a social, not through a biological mechanism.

Thus Darwin's idea, in the short space of under a century, has become the central principle of general biology and the main key for unlocking the detailed secrets and the major problem of life—its evolution. We may well speak of the Vindication of Darwinism.

# Conclusion

## ETHICAL MECHANISMS, INDIVIDUAL AND SOCIAL

IN THE light of my historical introduction (pp. 3 to 37), brief and incomplete as it is, and of the inner adjustment of thought which always follows on any first attempt at formulation, in what follows I will attempt to restate the problem as I see it to-day.

Like every other human characteristic, our ethics, and its concrete manifestation in the shape of our morality, has its inner and outer components. The first main internal component is the capacity to experience acts or ideas as right or wrong, good or evil—to *feel* the sense of rightness or wrongness. And the second is the craving for certitude in respect of such feelings. These are given from within, by the nature of the human mind. But even so, they are not completely determined by genetics, like the colour of our hair. In particular, the development of an adequately intense capacity to feel rightness and wrongness—what is traditionally called a healthy conscience—seems to depend on the existence in the child, during a critical period of its early years, of an intimate and profound ambivalent emotion towards its mother or some other human being. Without this primordial conflict between love and hate, the feeling of guilt which is at the basis of the moral sense will not reach the threshold-value needed for the formation of the crude forerunner of the adult conscience, the proto-ethical mechanism, any more than a plant can form chlorophyll in the absence of light.

In addition to this general capacity to produce a primitive moral sense, the internal components help to confer variability upon human ethics. This is because inherited mental and emotional predispositions differ from one individual to another. Some human beings are extroverted, concerned primarily with concrete actions and relations with other human beings; others introverted, obsessed by the need to construct a coherent inner system of thought and feeling. Some are prone to pile up an excessive charge of infantile guilt, while in others the load tends to be inadequate to activate the moral machinery properly. And different external conditions will give greater scope for one or other of these different moral types.

Equally important are the external components of morality and ethics. Certain of these are given in the facts of nature, such as storm and earthquake, famine and disease, birth, sex, and death. The effects of these upon morality, however, will vary with the stage and type of human civilization. Thus epidemics and other diseases and disorders are to-day considered as preventable accidents. But in pre-scientific ages they were looked on as a divine scourge for human wickedness.[1] In regard to them ethics has shifted its focus from an emphasis on the general moral duty of righteous living to the specific moral duty of seeing that they do not occur. Again, sexual morality cannot but be affected by such external factors as the knowledge of effective birth-control or the existence of widespread venereal disease.

Another external component of ethics is provided by the current moral standards and practice of the society into which the individual is born. Indeed, many writers assert or imply that these are the essentials of ethics. In thus neglecting the share of

[1] Cf. Deuteronomy 28: 'But it shall come to pass, if thou wilt not hearken unto the voice of the Lord thy God, to observe to do his commandments and his statutes . . . that all these curses shall come upon thee. . . . The Lord shall smite thee with a consumption and with a fever, and with an extreme burning, and with the sword, and with blasting, and with mildew; and they shall pursue thee until they perish. And thy heaven that is over thy head shall be brass, and the earth that is under thee shall be iron. . . . The Lord will smite thee with the botch of Egypt, and with the emerods, and with the scab, and with the itch, whereof thou canst not be healed. The Lord shall smite thee with madness, and blindness, and astonishment of heart' . . . etcetera.

the internal components, they rob ethics of its specific character—the emotive force of felt rightness and wrongness—which springs directly from the nature of that main internal factor, the psychological organ developed in the early life of each human being, in the shape of the proto-ethical mechanism.

What is more, they deny, either explicitly or by implication, the possibility of finding any more comprehensive external component for ethics than that of a particular society, and therefore any universal or general ethical standards.

However, before discussing this last point, we must pursue a little further this subject of the moral framework of society by which the developing boy or girl finds himself surrounded and, if he wishes it, supported. For there is, of course, no question but that current moral codes and systems do have a decisive effect on individual ethics. In the majority of cases the individual merely accepts the circumambient social ethics. But it should be noted that if he does so without much question, he will almost inevitably regard any deviation from it as evil, mistaken, or foolish—in any case, as somehow bad; this is a consequence of the way our ethical mechanism works. An enquiring minority will question the validity of current ethical assumptions. Some will find their validity confirmed, and will become vigorous champions of the established moral order against any alteration. Others will fail to do so; if they do not lapse into a moral cynicism, they will for the most part react against the established order by crusading for some 'new morality', whose liberties and restraints will in general be found to be diametrically opposed to those of the old.

The most important point for us here, however, is the realization that moral systems are bound to change with change in social systems. The most obvious example of this concerns slavery. I have touched on this in my lecture, as illustrating the way in which general ethical principles can be fruitfully applied in practice only when material and social conditions permit. Here it may be further pointed out that in the absence of the appropriate material and social conditions, the relevant general ethical principles may even remain unformulated, or at least unformulated in such a way as to bear on the problems at issue. Thus nowhere in the New Testament do we find either Jesus or Paul or anyone else denouncing slavery as such. Slavery is taken for granted as an inevitable fact of human existence, and the general ethical principle of respect for the individual is stated in such a way that it applies only in the religious sphere. 'There is neither Jew nor Greek, there is neither bond nor free, there is neither male nor female; for ye are all one in Christ Jesus'—a magnificent formulation of the universalist principle of the intrinsic spiritual importance of human beings as such, and of their equality before God, but with no relevance in the social sphere, where the inequality of their treatment is accepted. Indeed, in the Epistle to the Ephesians Paul goes further in his adjuration to 'servants' (which here implies slaves, being indeed a mistranslation of δοῦλοι) and to their masters:—'Servants, be obedient to them that are your masters according to the flesh, with fear and trembling, in singleness of heart, as unto Christ. . . . And ye, masters, do the same things unto them, forbearing threatening: knowing that your Master also is in heaven; neither is there respect of persons with him.'

For the early Christian moralist, the evils of slavery were to be mitigated in the sphere of personal behaviour as between slave and master, and in the spiritual relationship between both and God; as a social institution, it was to be not merely accepted but supported.[1]

Another example confronts us today. The dropping of the two atomic bombs on Japan has initiated a drastic change in our ethical systems. The secret of atomic energy has suddenly been

---

[1] Cf. also the Epistle to Philemon, in which Paul asks a Christian convert to take back a runaway slave, also a convert, and offers to reimburse the slave-owner for any loss he has incurred through the slave's action.

put into our human hands; and this fact has forced upon us a hasty revaluation of many of our ethical principles and their concrete application. The ultimate effect may be that man shall embark on a new industrial revolution, compared to which the old was a mere flea-bite. This will bring its own ethical problems, many of them unpredictable, but some doubtless concerned with the value and the utilization of the world's new leisure, others with the provision of a firmer ethical assurance of the ends for which the overpowering new means are employed. But the immediate result of the discovery is that civilization, for the first time in its history, has the possibility of destroying itself, root and branch, thoroughly—or of pursuing its course over-shadowed and distorted by fear.

The atomic bomb has thus brought to a head the trend towards the contraction of our world. Communications have been improving so that events everywhere, even in the economic sphere, are interlocked with each other, though up till now the interlocking has resulted in more of entanglement and dislocation than in co-ordinated improvement or joint action for the general good: the separate regions of the world have, for the first time in history, shrunk politically into a single unit, though so far not an orderly but a chaotic one: and now the atomic bomb hangs with equal grimness over all parts of this infant commonwealth of man.

Human civilization has already been given a moral precept: nations must combine if man wishes truly to achieve the good. Today, that moral precept is reinforced by a moral threat, as the precepts of Christianity were reinforced by the moral threat of eternal damnation. The threat of the atomic bomb is simple— unite or perish.

So far I have spoken almost wholly of such external components of an ethics as change with the changing times. But there are others which are more lasting and may indeed be considered permanent. I say permanent and not eternal, for there appears to be no ground for believing that there exists any abstract good or eternal moral standard, apart from particular human beings and human societies. But some standards are permanent, in the sense that they will remain for as long as we can foresee, provided that human individuals and human societies continue to be of the same general type. I introduce this last caveat, for if humanity should ever embark on a eugenic policy designed to produce a specialized caste society as in social insects, then, as my brother Aldous set forth in his *Brave New World*, general moral standards of quite a new sort would inevitably be required. However, as we shall see later, to do so would violate other, still more general, external moral standards.

These permanent standards deriving from the nature of human society as we know it are those which proclaim the primacy of the individual over the State or any other social organization, and assert that, since the developed human individual is the highest product of evolution, therefore there must be equality of opportunity for human development. I have dealt with this subject in the body of my lecture, and need not return to it here in any detail. I will only emphasize that the primacy of the individual over the State, far from implying selfish development or development at the expense of others, has as its corollaries tolerance, the duty not to use others only or primarily as means, and the equality of all individuals in respect of certain important opportunities. These corollaries have been formulated as the so-called Rights of Man. If we use the word Rights as denoting what it is right for man to strive for, there is no quarrel with it; unfortunately it is usually employed to mean something that men have a mysterious prescriptive right to claim.

The specific content of these Rights of Man has varied in the brief space of time (brief by evolutionary measurements) during which attempts have been made to formulate them. It is likely to continue to vary somewhat in the future with changes in social and economic structure; but the variation will tend to be restricted to points which are essentially details, however important, while the general principles will become clearer and more assured as we come to understand more adequately the nature of the social process.

I say social process, not society; for we are beginning to grasp that societies, like the individuals which compose them, and like life in general, have a time-dimension. They are processes, and their direction in time is as important a part of their nature as their organization at any particular time.

This brings me to my last, most general and permanent, and most external of all the external components of ethics—those derived from biological and social evolution. This thesis, too, I have developed at length in my lecture. Here I will only touch on a couple of points. The most important is that biological progress exists as a fact of nature external to man, and that it consists basically of three factors—increase in control over the environment, increase in independence of the environment, and the capacity to continue further evolution in the same progressive direction. A further factor is an increase in capacity to experience reality—both outer and inner reality, in the shape of both knowledge and emotion: and this is not merely a steady increase, like those in control and independence, but an increasing increase or acceleration; and finally is not merely a quantitative process but in some sense a qualitative one, since it leads to the emergence of consciousness as a major factor both in individual life and in evolution. Whatever mental (or 'mentoid'—mind-like) processes may exist in plants and lower animals, they are assuredly not a major factor there; but equally assuredly they have become a major factor in higher vertebrates, and in man *the* major factor.

The paradox then arises that, with the fuller development of man's mental faculties, certain experiences come to have high intrinsic value—such as intellectual insight, falling in love, high æsthetic pleasure, mystical fulfilment, and so on. These become ends in themselves, apparently irrespective of the continuing cosmic process of evolution. I have already touched on the apparent contradictions between these two types of ends, those involved in a temporal process and those that are essentially 'out of time'—the Marthas and the Marys among our ends. Here I will only add that the reconciliation of these opposites can be effected in practice, and if it is not effected, the personality becomes one-sided and either consciously or unwittingly inferior to one in which the two are balanced. From another angle, the man who devotes himself too exclusively to the pursuit of these satisfying experiences is guilty of a selfishness which is no less blameworthy for operating on a higher plane than usual; while he who devotes himself too exclusively to the practical task of furthering human progress is guilty of neglecting the development of the most precious thing in the universe, human individuality, in the shape of the only individuality which is his to develop—his own.

This brings me to my third point—namely, that in pre-human evolution one mark of progress is a rise in individuality. In early stages this can better be described as increase in physical individuation. Many plants, polyps, corals, and worms, exhibit but the barest beginning of individuation, and in some cases (as in the meandrine corals) the clear-cut individuals found in ancestral types are wholly lost in later evolution. Later, however, sharp physical individuation became established as an indispensable basis for future progress, in the early stages of all the three highest animal phyla—the molluscs, the arthropods, and the vertebrates. And from then on, progress was marked by an increase in the quality and level of the individuality attained, which in its turn depended largely and increasingly upon increase in brain organization. Individuality is thus both a prerequisite for progress and also that type of organization in which progress is made manifest; and biological evolution here again gives us guidance and encouragement concerning the direction and methods of human progress.

I find that Professor Sinnott of Yale has, quite independently, drawn very similar conclusions. Thus, after pointing out that in the human species natural selection has become of secondary importance, and that 'real advance is now on quite another and more active front—the acquisition and transmission of wisdom and experience',[1] he rightly insists that we can and must still obtain guidance as to our own progress from studying the conditions of progress in the biological past: 'My point is that in this new and vastly difficult problem which confronts us we shall succeed only so far as the systems which we frame are still in harmony with . . . evolutionary history. The foundations upon which we build may have been laid in blood, but we can raise on them a noble edifice'.

Sinnott also stresses the paramountcy of the individual. 'There is', he says, 'another respect in which democracy is anchored deeply in man's physical nature—his individuality. Through all the centuries, the measure of his advance has been the growing definition and significance obtained by men as individuals; and in those nations which have been most free, this gain was greatest. . . . We must remember what so many now forget, that persons are of greater worth than any systems which they may compose. In this conclusion we may be assured and comforted by the great fact that protoplasm comes not at wholesale but in individual packages, and that, throughout the vast pageant of evolution, its organising force has fashioned living systems of ever greater and more exquisite complexity till man himself appeared. The infinite variety of man is not expressed in populations but in personalities'.

Finally, Sinnott develops very effectively some of the implications of man's genetic variety. He points out that 'through all the course of evolution, [long-term] advantage still has been with species which were variable, and thus produced a wealth of different types for the great proving-ground of evolutionary competition. With such a premium on variability, it is not strange that mechanisms have been established which ensure its main-

[1] Sinnott, E. W., *The Biological Basis of Democracy.* Yale Rev., 35: 61-73 (1945).

tenance'—namely, mutations of various sorts, and recombination.
If he does not particularly stress the unusual and indeed unique
extent of variability in our own species, he says well that 'the
plain fact is—and let us thank Heaven for it—that the basis of
our divinity is sunk deep in the constitution of living stuff itself.
. . . Human divinity, a stumbling-block for dictators, is the basis
of democracy; for only when each member of a society is free
to develop his native gifts to the utmost will that society reach its
highest efficiency, and its members their deepest satisfaction'. And
he points out that this genetic diversity affords a 'biological
argument (which) can strongly reinforce and justify that high
desire for freedom which we feel'. When asked to justify our
longing for liberty we fall back all too readily on some instinctive
desire for freedom. But 'the answer goes far deeper even than
instinct. It lies in the very architecture of our chromosomes, in
protoplasmic mechanisms which ensure that each of us is different
from his fellows'.

Needham, in his *History Is on Our Side* (1946), also stresses
the reality of evolutionary progress, and the fact that human
evolution depends on social mechanisms quite different from
those operating in biological evolution.

Here I should also like to quote from a very recent article
by another of the few professional biologists who have tried to
see not only the social implications of biological evolution, but
the evolutionary implications of human social organization, C. H.
Waddington.[1] Waddington, after pointing out that man 'has
invented a new mechanism of heredity—the transmission of
civilization to his descendants by writing, teaching, artistic creation: all the techniques which have been made possible by conceptual thought and language', stresses the vital but often unrealized fact that, as a result of this, a new method of evolution
has been initiated. 'The essential feature of human evolution is,

[1] Waddington, C. H., *Human Ideals and Human Progress*. World Review,
29-36. August, 1946.

then, that it is a process dependent on Man's *social* life, which alone makes possible this new substitute for normal heredity. . . . Man's evolution is, in a very important way, different in kind from that of other animals'.

Waddington also supports the idea that human progress has occurred, that it is still possible, and possible to an unpredictable degree, and that it must be related to the biological progress that has occurred during animal evolution. In the last few decades, as he says, 'Progress became to the intellectuals and the bourgeoisie a word of which to be afraid, a subject for sneers and superior smiles. For the Nazis it was the openly-avowed enemy. . . . These are sentimental reactions. The reality, the nature and the direction of human evolution are too important to be dismissed in a fit of pique at the misfortunes of a few decades out of all Man's long history'. As to the guidance to be derived from a study of biological progress, 'the whole evolution of animal life on the earth shows a general tendency for the increase of these two things: the richness of individual experience and, in the late stages of Evolution, the development of Society. If we look at the broad outline of human history, it is obvious that Man has been enormously successful in carrying forward these trends'.

To Waddington's interesting analysis of the relation between these two trends, and its relevance for our problem, I shall return. Here let me quote something of what he has to say on ethics. First, as to ethical origins. 'Long before a baby can speak it is involved in social relations with its parents, nurse, or other members of the family. It begins to pick up the essential paradox on which human social life is founded—the lesson that the enrichment of the individual personality depends on the existence and enrichment of society, and that this in turn demands a certain sacrifice of one's own individual desires in order not to infringe too much on the individuality of others'. As Waddington, as well as myself, has set forth in detail elsewhere, this adjustment is in the first instance made by means of the crude mechanism of psychological repression. Further, 'In our earlier years we cannot, of course, formulate clearly and straightforwardly the lessons we learn. . . . Our ethical beliefs, therefore, tend even in later life to appear as a somewhat uncoordinated jumble of very strong, but sometimes conflicting origins'; and he continues as follows: 'If, however, we look at their origin we see that essentially their function is to enable society to persist' (a conclusion which I should like to extend) by adding that the best ethics are those which in addition enable society to progress.

Here we are back again at what is, after all, only an extension of the Marxist formulation of ethics. It is true that the Marxists assert that morality is an organ of one class within society, while Waddington would make it an organ of society as a whole; but in both cases it is regarded merely as a social organ, whose function is to secure the persistence and success of a social group. On the contrary, I would maintain that morality has also an individual function, negatively in liberating the individual from some at least of his load of guilt, and positively in guiding him towards what the Bible calls righteousness—ethical fulfilment, the achievement of moral nobility of personality, the sense of oneness with something beyond and larger than ourselves, which is itself either moral or transcends and includes morality.

Here let me interrupt the thread of my argument a moment to present some evidence from quite another quarter—namely, from that modern 'prophetic' theology of which the chief proponent is Reinhold Niebuhr. Niebuhr sets out from the presupposition that the scientific approach cannot give an adequate account of ethics; yet, though he employs the language of theology and not of science, he is in point of fact, largely scientific in his own approach, since he is not content with any *a priori* system, but is constantly referring back to facts—in this case the facts of man's spiritual nature and his ethical experience.

Niebuhr's central contention is that both the over-pessimistic attitude of 'orthodox Christianity' and the over-optimistic attitude of 'liberal Christianity' towards sin on the one hand and the possibility of human perfection on the other, are wrong because one-sided. The one leads to a neglect of this world for the next, and tends to turn the Church into 'a support for traditional and historic injustice'; the other leads to an unscientific utopianism which is bound to be disappointed, and tends to discourage interest in the necessary mechanism of social justice at the precise moment in human history when the development of a technical civilization required more than ever that social ideas be implemented with economic and political techniques. . . .'

The two must be combined in what at first sight appears to be an impossible reconciliation. Indeed, Niebuhr himself used the phrase 'impossible possibility' to denote his position. What he means is that man is at one and the same time finite, limited, imperfect, and conditional, but also (through his capacity for abstract thought) capable of grasping the idea of the perfect and the unconditional, and therefore always forced to recognize an ideal beyond reality, before which his best efforts must inevitably fall short.

Niebuhr is not afraid of the unfashionable word *sin*, and attacks the modernist view that sin is merely negative—'nothing but a defect, a gap, a blank, a minus quantity'. Nor does he fear the accusation of pessimism in drawing 'the conclusion most abhorrent to the modern mood—that the possibilities of evil grow with the possibilities of good'. Even if man succeeds in creating more order and more virtue in the world, that increase of orderliness or cosmos itself creates increasing possibilities of disorder or chaos. Accordingly, 'every human advance offers new possibilities of catastrophe. . . . The adventure of life is much more perilous than is assumed by those who imagine that human continuity is a simple guarantee of progressive moral achievement'.

Again, he is constantly opposing the fact of man's finitude and consequent imperfection to his quest for the infinite and the absolute. 'If finiteness cannot be without guilt because it is mixed with freedom and stands under ideal possibilities, it cannot be without sin because man makes pretensions of being absolute in his finiteness. . . . Ideally men seek to subject their arbitrary and contingent existence under the dominion of absolute reality. But practically they always mix the finite with the eternal and claim for themselves, their nation, their culture, or their class the centre of existence. This is the root of all imperialism in man. . . . Thus devotion to every transcendent value is corrupted by the effort to insert the interests of the self into that value'. (Here we may recall the saying of Goethe, that all action involves injustice.)

Nor is Niebuhr afraid of the word *love*. It is for him the supreme virtue and value. Thus 'the ideal of equality is a fact of the natural law which transcends existence. . . . The ideal of love, on the other hand, transcends all law. . . . It is impossible to construct a social ethic out of the ideal of love in its pure form, because the ideal presupposes the resolution of the conflict of life with life, which it is the concern of law to mitigate and restrain'. None the less the ideal of love is the only foundation 'for an ethic which enables men to give themselves to values actually embodied in persons and existence, but also transcending every activity'. Similarly, 'the law of love is involved in all approximations of justice, not only as the source of the norms of justice, but as an ultimate perspective by which their limitations are discovered'.

Finally, Niebuhr is emphatic in the need for an ethic which will issue in social and political action as well as in resolution of inner conflicts or in a sense of salvation. He is on the side of the oppressed, and is fully aware of the dangers of an absolute or perfectionist morality in condoning inaction in the face of injustice. 'Political problems drive pure moralists to despair, because in them the freedom of the spirit must come to terms with the contingencies of nature, . . . another ideal principle must be sacrificed to guarantee its partial realization. [But] for the Christian the love commandment must be made relevant to the relativi-

ties of the social struggle, even to hazardous and dubious relativi-
ties.'

Before attempting to transpose Niebuhr's ideas into the
terminology and the conclusions of evolutionary humanism, I
will pass for a moment to another and very different approach
to the ethical problem—that of the saint and mystic, as ex-
pounded to the western world by such men as Gerald Heard
and my brother.[1]

Aldous Huxley adopts 'the ethic that places man's final end
in the knowledge of the immanent and transcendent Ground
of all being'. This is the ethic of that 'Perennial Philosophy'
which, as metaphysic, 'recognizes a divine Reality substantial to
the world of things and lives and minds'. This must be achieved
through the 'unitive knowledge, the state of "not I, but God in
me",' which arises from love. For 'love is a mode of knowledge,
and when the love is sufficiently disinterested and sufficiently
intense, the knowledge becomes unitive knowledge and so takes
on the quality of infallibility'.

He is strongly opposed to the idea of progress in time. Thus
he speaks of those who in their 'pride and madness, treat it
[discursive reasoning] . . . as at once the means to Progress and
its ever-receding goal in time'. And in another passage he refers
bitingly to progress as a modern idolatry, whose devotees expect
that 'after the harnessing of atomic power and the next revolution
but three, the Kingdom of God will be added'.

He devotes an entire chapter (chapter 21) to this concept
of an idolatry of progress. Modern 'higher idolatry' he classifies
under three main heads. First, technological idolatry—'the most
ingenuous and primitive of the three; for its devotees, like those
of the lower idolatry, believe that their redemption and liberation
depend upon material objects—in this case gadgets'.

'Only a little less ingenuous are the political idolaters. For
the worship of redemptive gadgets these have substituted the

[1] Aldous Huxley, *The Perennial Philosophy*. London and New York, 1945.

worship of redemptive social and economic organizations. Impose the right kind of organizations upon human beings, and all their problems, from sin and unhappiness to nationalism and war, will automatically disappear'.

Finally there is moral idolatry. 'The moral idolaters are realists in as much as they see that gadgets and organizations are not enough to guarantee the triumph of virtue and the increase of happiness.' But they 'cease to be realistic and commit idolatry in as much as they worship, not God, but their own ethical ideals. . . . The idolatrous worship of ethical values in and for themselves defeats its own object—and defeats it not only because . . . there is a lack of all-round development, but also and above all because even the highest forms of moral idolatry are God-eclipsing, and therefore guarantee the idolater against the enlightening and liberating knowledge of Reality'.

I cannot discuss these arguments and points of view in detail, and must content myself with indicating how the truths contained in them can be translated or even transvalued to fit in with the approach I have adopted—as well as indicating some omissions or errors which appear to me important.

In the first place, Aldous Huxley distorts the issue of progress by referring to it as *inevitable* progress. Progress is not inevitable, either in the sense that it always must happen, or that it will happen without human effort.

Next, while he is certainly correct in regarding his 'technological and political idolatries' as errors, and indeed as disastrous errors, he is guilty of error himself if, as is apparently the case, he considers that the idea of progress is necessarily bound up with this sort of belief. As I have elsewhere set forth[1] there are various progress myths as well as a scientifically grounded doctrine of progress. And one chief type of progress myth is the myth of millenary progress—the notion that the Golden Age is round the corner, only awaiting the abolition of priests or kings, or the

[1] *The Prerequisites of Progress.* Unesco Lectures. Editions Fontaine, Paris, 1947.

arrival of universal suffrage or universal literacy, or the imposition of some political system. In the light of scientific analysis, such ideas are immediately seen to be mere myths. But the fact that they are erroneous does not in the least invalidate other theories of progress.

His 'moral idolatry' is in another category. Here he would seem to be insisting on a profound truth—namely that we must beware of narrowness, and of projecting our own self, with all its limitations, upon the universe, but must accept the universe, with all its vast and apparently incomprehensible drama: the self must learn to be humble before the larger reality of not-self.

But to accept the experience of this vaster reality, in all its numinous and mysterious strength, is not necessarily to equate it, or anything within or behind it, with God. Here, and in many other parts of his commentary, Aldous Huxley seems to me to fall into the error against which he elsewhere warns his readers, of adopting an unsatisfactory terminology, and then (doubtless unconsciously) using it as a premiss or base from which to draw important conclusions. When men thought in theological terms, it was inevitable that they should describe the mystical experience of so-called 'unitive knowledge' as union with the Divine. The existence of this particular type of experience, with its sense of enlarged knowledge and union with something beyond self, is an empirical fact. But this does not mean that the 'something beyond self' is God; to explain the fact as union with the Divine is, in scientific terms, only a preliminary hypothesis, and not in any way a proof of the existence of God.

Similarly, it is obvious that these experiences come with a sense of overpowering significance: but this does not mean that they reveal the one and ultimate Reality with a capital R, real in a different way from the reality of other experience. It is also obvious that such experiences confer a sense of timelessness and give intimations of something relatively unchanging; but this is no ground for jumping to the conclusion that what they reveal is actually out of time, still less 'eternal'. Finally, in his zeal, he opposes the self to the not-self or more-than-self, in what would appear to be a far too rigorous and quite unjustified way.[1] He also appears to emphasize the value of the quest for 'unitive knowledge of reality' over against that of striving for social progress, to a degree which seems much exaggerated, and for which he adduces no satisfactory justification.

One final point. Aldous Huxley would seem to have lumped together two types of mystical experience which, in spite of superficial similarities, and in spite of possessing many details in common, are radically distinct because of a difference in quality.[2] Taking the extremes of the two types, the one tends to the destruction of the barriers of selfhood by an annihilation of the self, the other by its transcendence: the first operates by dispersal or disintegration of the self, the second by its concentration or focusing upon a point that takes it beyond selfhood: the first aims at the absence of all desire, the second at the swallowing up of all partial and undesirable desires in one comprehensive and desirable desire. The one is thus essentially negative, with Nirvana as its goal, the other essentially positive, with the goal of Love. And as a matter of historical fact, the former has been chiefly represented in Indian, the latter in Christian mysticism.

The importance of the distinction is that the two types have very different ethical implications, for clearly the second or positive type can much more readily be reconciled with a practical ethic concerned with social progress than can the first or negative type.

This is brought out very clearly by some of the Christian mystics, such as Eckhart, who wrote: 'what a man takes in by

---

[1] Niebuhr is wiser here: as he rightly says, 'No limits can be set where the self ends and either nature or the divine begins'.

[2] This acute distinction was made to me in conversation by Père Teilhard du Chardin, the distinguished human paleontologist, to whom I wish to express my acknowledgments.

contemplation, that he passes out in love'. Here is the enunciation of a fact of experience, a valuable piece of knowledge. We need to apply that knowledge. If so, we must set ourselves seriously to the study of what we may call psychotechnics. Such a study would include the techniques of attaining this type of contemplation, which can, by a spiritual counterpart of the transformation of energy, be converted into love, and of harnessing this love to human progress. To have achieved this would be to have taken a long step forward in one of the major tasks of progress, the control of nature—though in this case the control of our own human nature instead of the external nature around us.

In passing, Niebuhr too seems to have fallen into a semantic confusion in contrasting the finite with the absolute and the eternal. The opposition should rather be between the concrete and the abstract. Man's power of conceptual thought implies the capacity for abstraction, for setting up ideals and general ideas. By their very nature such general ideas can cover an infinite or at least an indefinite number of concrete instances, and before such ideals any concrete achievement inevitably falls short.

Aldous Huxley in one passage (chapter 27) seems to have given away his case against progress by saying that 'in all the historic formulations of the Perennial Philosophy it is axiomatic that . . . the existence of at least a minority of contemplatives is necessary for the well-being of any society'. For this implies that social well-being is a valuable end; and it would, I think, be impossible to deny, with our present knowledge, that social existence can never be static, and that true social well-being must be considered as a process in time, as something which was leading towards some better state, in addition to being in some degree good in itself.

Finally, it appears to me that his denial of validity and importance to any notion of progress in time, especially on the ground that its goal is an ever-receding one, cannot be maintained, and indeed is illogical, even if we were to agree that unitive knowledge of the Divine Reality were the only pure or final end of man. For there was a stage in the temporal history of our earth, a very long stage, extending for over a thousand million years, when the attainment of unitive knowledge by living creatures was impossible, for want of the physical machinery of body and nervous system with which to attain it. Even in the last little span of a million years more or less, during which members of the zoological family of hominids have existed, there must have been very considerable progress in respect of this capacity: the extent, level, and quality of the unitive knowledge potentially attainable (let alone actually ever attained) by *Pithecanthropus* or *Sinanthropus*, and even by the more primitive members of the genus *Homo*, such as Neanderthal man, must have been very low compared with that reached by the saints and mystics quoted in my brother's book. It required a temporal process of improvement in brain-structure to make such experiences possible.

I would go further. I would say that even since civilization began some temporal progress has occurred even in regard to this capacity. After the dawn of civilization in the valley of the Euphrates, centuries or even millennia elapsed before the Indian mystics acquired their techniques of unitive knowledge: and millennia more were to elapse before the great Christian mystics enlarged the scope of mystical experience by fusing it with love. Nor will it be possible to imagine any considerable proportion of the population attaining to this 'final end' of man except on the basis of a good deal more material progress.

In any case, the conflict between individual progress in spiritual matters, and social progress in material and organizational matters, is apparent only, and not only can but must be reconciled.

In this connection, the work of Flugel, notably as summarized in his latest book,[1] is of importance. Flugel deals with the problem of morality both in its individual and in its social aspects. While

[1] Flugel, J. C., *Man, Morals and Society*, London, 1945.

adopting the general standpoint of psychoanalysis, he is not (like some Freudians) narrow or dogmatic, he points out various gaps in psychoanalytic theory, and adopts a refreshingly broad evolutionary attitude towards his subject.

In particular, his detailed discussion of the function and development of the super-ego will be found relevant to our problem. The original nucleus of the super-ego—which I have ventured to call the proto-ethical mechanism—is formed by what the Freudians call the introjection into the child's mind of the authoritarian aspects of its parents. But what is thus introjected is, for various interesting reasons, much more harsh and rigorous than anything in the real parents' actions or character. It is because of this that the first-formed part of the super-ego is so primitive, alarming, and often barbaric. Further, owing to the whole-hearted use of the machinery of repression at this stage, this primitive super-ego is largely unconscious and, in unfavourable circumstances, may remain so throughout life, giving rise to various irrational maladjustments in the field of ethics, and even to neuroses.

The later development of the super-ego can be more conscious and rational, and in any case does not embody so much hate and aggressiveness and is not so severe. These 'upper' or 'outer' layers of the super-ego sometimes merit the title of ego-ideal. The super-ego as a whole is thus a highly complex psychological mechanism, in which indeed conflicts of various sorts can arise between its different elements or levels. And since the prime function of the super-ego is a moral or ethical one, such conflicts will distort or disrupt the individual's ethical attitude.

Flugel also draws attention to the fact that the function of the super-ego proper is preceded by the development of a semi-physiological morality, based on the mother's insistence that the infant shall 'control the processes of excretion, so that they shall occur only at what are, from the adult point of view, convenient times and places'. This 'sphincter morality' is probably the first stage at which anything which can be called guilt is experienced. But even before this, during the earliest period of life, the oral stage of the Freudians, during which sucking is the chief gratification and no control of its impulses is demanded of the infant, it can yet experience deprivation and frustration. These in turn can generate fear and misery and what the psychoanalysts rather inadequately call anxiety, often coupled with impotent but distressing anger and aggressiveness. Further, since at these earliest stages the infant seems incapable of distinguishing between the self and the not-self, between subjective sensation and external objects, and since there is thus 'no clear distinction between such distressful and alarming conditions [as those of overwhelming impotent rage] and the associated outer objects or circumstances, it is easy to see that the first step has been taken towards the creation of an outer "bogy" of ill-defined but intense and almost unimaginable evilness'.

It has often been asked what bearing such infantile and transitory experiences, whether 'oral', 'anal', or 'genital', can have upon the mind and the morality of the adult. It is clear, however, that they are extremely relevant to our problem. For one thing, the general form and balance of the proto-ethical mechanism will in any case persist, however much modified in detail, however much deflected towards other objects, for a considerable time, and may do so throughout life. This will help to determine the load of unconscious guilt to be carried by the individual, the harshness or otherwise of his super-ego or conscience, the strength of his need for salvation or self-justification. The infant's attitude to his parents, though often extremely unrealistic, will help to decide his attitude to all the various parent-substitutes which may be offered to him by adult life—a King or a Führer, a country or a cause, a jealous or a loving God—and will strongly influence his chances of a happy marriage or a successful career.

Furthermore, through the triple properties of memory, association, and abstraction, mental states, persisting indefinitely in the reservoir of unconscious memory, may be elicited thence into consciousness, may become displaced and attached to new objects, may become combined with ideas and imagination in unexpected ways. This is perhaps most obvious with the fear of finding oneself without any external moral support or satisfaction through love or approval. Such a situation would assuredly be difficult to bear: but the intense and irrational fear of it which is so frequent (and in latent form perhaps universal) appears definitely to derive from a peculiarly infantile experience (so characteristic as to have merited the special term of *aphanisis* in the vocabulary of psychoanalysis). In this the young child feels an overwhelming terror of being deprived of its parents' love and the satisfactions consequent upon it—all the love and all the satisfaction that the infant knows. The overwhelming nature of the emotion seems to be due in part to the 'all-or-nothing' nature of so much of the child's mental processes, so that it takes a merited severity for a total change of heart, a temporary absence for a permanent loss. In part, too, it seems to be due to the 'omnipotence of thought' in the infant, who tends to believe that his violent hate-wishes may have actually destroyed the object against which they were directed, or at least something essential in it.

Another point which has been brought out by modern psychoanalysis is that the quality of the aggressive impulses projected by the child changes with his development in time. In the earliest stage, the 'oral phase' of the psychoanalysts, the bogies of evil created by projection out of the raw material of the outer world tend to bite and tear; during the phase of sphinctermorality ('anal' and 'urethral' phases), they tend to be associated with physical filth, or with destructive floodings; and in the protosexual phase they tend to castrate, either literally or often in the transferred sense of mutilating or depriving of some vital organ or property. The emphasis on the different types of projection differs from one child to another; and the fears or phobias associated with them, especially when they have been extreme, tend to colour the individual's emotions and distort his ethical reactions throughout life.

The comment that an outsider might pass on the freudian analysis is that, though it has revealed strange new realms haunted by the grotesque products of our early irrationality, and demonstrated the strength and the persistence of our primitive evil impulses and of the guilty tension which they produce, it does not sufficiently stress the conscious and the positive elements in the developing mind. The child very early begins that process by which elements in the outer world, which are actively or positively enjoyed, become in a sense part of us. The mind goes out to them; they enter the mind and become part of our inner furnishing. That is perhaps most obviously seen in the way in which the physical surroundings of early childhood come to have a strong and peculiar emotional flavour, which often lasts throughout life: in general, the important growth of the mind always takes place by the fusion of some external object with a strong positive impulse, whether of love, of intellectual interest or curiosity, of pleasure in mastery, of pity. This is how our inner microcosm comes to develop a strong cohesive structure.

II

### ETHICS AND THE DIALECTIC OF EVOLUTION

So we draw to an end. In the preceding section and in my introductory historical review, a number of difficulties raised by various authors have been cited, a number of conflicting viewpoints encountered. In this final section I shall attempt to show how the biological approach leads to what I may perhaps call the Dialectic of Evolution, and how in the light of this, the reconciliation of many acute conflicts can be effected, and many apparent opposites organically combined in a new synthesis, many hostile dualities reduced to fruitful unity.

First of all, as already noted, the evolutionary approach undercuts the duality of mind and matter, and leads us to think in monistic terms, of an enduring world-stuff, an $x$ which possesses both material and mental (or 'mentoid') attributes, according as it is experienced objectively or subjectively. And this in its turn makes possible the reconciliation of the opposites of necessity and free-will. With the advent of man, thanks to his novel type of cerebral mechanism, the world-stuff becomes capable of having alternatives presented to it and of effecting a choice between them: these objective facts are accompanied subjectively by a sense of conflict or indecision followed by a conscious effort or act of will.

We can now say that T. H. Huxley's antithesis between ethics and evolution was false, because based on a limited definition of evolution and a static view of ethics. But we can go further. Our final conclusion must be evolutionary in the most radical and thorough-going sense. We can obtain from the past history of the evolution of life not only reassurance as to the basis of some of our ethical beliefs, but also ethical guidance for the future. More than that, we perceive that ethics itself is an organ of evolution, and itself evolves. And finally, by adopting this dynamic or evolutionary point of view of ethics as something with a time-dimension, a process rather than a system, we obtain light on one of the most difficult but also most central problems of ethics—the relation between individual and social ethics, and perceive that the antithesis between the individual and society can also be reconciled.

It is clear enough that social ethics manifests evolution. Human codes of morality change, adapt themselves to local and temporal conditions, become diversified, exhibit long-term trends, whether of specialization, regression, or true progress. The function of social ethics is, in biological terminology, phylogenetic, helping society to persist, to reproduce itself, and in some cases to change and to advance.

The function of individual ethics, on the other hand, is onto-genetic, helping the individual to develop towards moral adaptation, moral growth, moral fulfilment and satisfaction. But although the biologist usually excludes individual development from the category of evolution, it is none the less a truly evolutionary process, with its own dialectic. Furthermore, this is particularly true of all aspects of mental ontogeny in man, since human evolution operates chiefly by means of tradition, and that tradition is the product of individual minds. Social ethics is, of course, not the result of the mere summation of individual moralities, nor indeed any simple function of them, but rather a complex resultant of their interaction; yet nevertheless individual ethical development is an integral part of social ethics, and a necessary cog in moral evolution.

T. H. Huxley opposed the 'cosmic process' to the 'ethical process'. We can perhaps best show how this pair of opposites can be reconciled by thinking of the human individual as a microcosm, that term so dear to the philosophers and writers of the sixteenth and seventeenth centuries. However, since our ideas of the macrocosm have changed a great deal since then, we shall be forced to use the notion of the microcosm also in a rather altered sense. The chief difference is that the cosmos must be looked on not as a static collection of phenomena or a finished mechanism, but as a complex process; so that in so far as the microcosm mirrors the macrocosm, it too must be a process, embodying movements, directions, and trends.

Take as a concrete instance a particular human individual at the stage when he (or she) is about to embark on adult life. Consider what he has already incorporated in his miniature universe, what realms remain for him to bring in and to organize under his sway. And relate this to the complementary processes of individual and of social ethics.

In the first place, our young man, if he approximates to *l'homme moyen sensuel*, will be animated by a number of urges

or psychological driving forces, which are not merely emotionally of different quality but often incompatible with each other.
His simple instinctive drives towards comfort and a full belly
and sexual satisfaction, towards the pleasant exercise of his limbs
and his faculties, will have been built up into complex sentiments
(to use McDougall's convenient term), sublimated, rationalized,
often distorted or displaced from their original objectives. In
particular, they will have been organized in relation to the bi-polar
drive towards self-assertion or its reverse, to the load of guilt
with which his unconscious infancy has been saddled, to the type
of ideals which his emotional nature has built up in interaction
with his powers of abstraction and generalization.

They will also show a marked degree of adaptation to the
current morality of his time, nation, and class. But here again
the adaptation will be a bi-polar one. In some respects the adaptation will be towards uncritical conformity, in others it will be
a reaction (also often uncritical) against current standards. And
both the acceptance and the reaction will usually be tinged with
unexpectedly and indeed illogically strong emotional feeling.
He will also be the possessor of an ethical mechanism (as we
have styled it) for attaching the labels of rightness and wrongness to his own deeds and thoughts, as well as to those of other
people and to things. This ethical mechanism operates partly on
a rational and conscious level; partly in the form of what is
generally called conscience, in which reason is fused with emotional impulse and conscious blend into unconscious processes;
and partly on a purely irrational and unconscious level, in virtue
of the type and quantity of unconscious guilt he is carrying, and
the primitive super-ego mechanism which, long previously, was
built up to deal with that load of guilt. The charge of emotion
associated with conscience, and still more with the unconscious
ethical (proto-ethical) mechanism, is very strong, and colours and
distorts the structure of his psyche in various ways, tending on
the whole to make it illogical and unrealistic. Thus he is certain

to have in his make-up a certain need for punishment, a super-stitious (if often also rather surreptitious!) faith in luck and omens, coupled with an irrational fear of being too lucky or too successful, a tendency to wish-fulfilment, a capacity (quite remark-able when viewed with the cool eye of logical detachment) for self-justification and the projection of his own shortcomings on to circumstances or other people, a bi-polar emotion towards the unfamiliar, manifesting itself in a thirst for novelty and adventure coupled with a dread of the unknown and a dislike of everything 'different', a craving for certitude (whether through religious or political belief, identification with a cause, adherence to a movement, or devotion to a leader or other personal figure), which is often coupled with the need to hate some other belief, cause, movement, person, or group.

In the sphere of knowledge our exemplar will have incor-porated some sort of framework—diagrammatic and often rather inaccurate—of the macrocosm. He will know some elementary facts about astronomy and geography, about physics and chemistry, natural history and physiology. He will also mirror the social aspects of the macrocosm, and will have some knowledge too of history and economics, sport, religion, literature and the arts, though here his microcosm is likely to be more distorted and more relativistic.

He will in some sphere or another be a specialist—that is to say, he will have incorporated some of the capacity of life to understand its environment in detail and to control it. In any particular man, this specialized control may be over the physical world, as with an engineer, a carpenter, or a farmer; or over the social world, as with a lawyer, a schoolmaster, or an economist. He will realize (if he ever troubles to consider the matter) that in being a specialist he is reflecting another aspect of the social macrocosm, namely that society can only operate by means of a division of labour; and accordingly he takes a great deal of his knowledge on trust, and is content to have various human achievements incorporated in his microcosm symbolically, through prominent individuals, from politicians to film stars, rather than concretely, through their actual mastery or understanding by himself.

This is one of the ways in which his microcosm of knowledge and understanding is deflected or distorted from being a faithful miniature of the macrocosm. Another difference, of course, lies in the incompleteness of the average microcosm, and its reduction to a crude and often vague diagram rather than a detailed picture. It is also sure to be distorted ego-centrically, so that the parts of it which directly concern the individual, his nation, and his class or religious group, are magnified relative to the rest. His map of reality is distorted by being drawn on what we may call a relativistic projection.

Still more important is the influence of belief and emotion. The picture of the macrocosm which our average young man carries about inside himself is again distorted (as well as coloured) by various emotional urges and the sentiments and beliefs arising from them. Thus he is almost certain to have a belief in some Power in or behind the universe. This power requires to be placated, and is likely to exact punishment (though often in unexpected and mysterious ways) for transgression; it also provides outlets for our wishes and longings, whether in a supernatural Paradise, a millennary ideal, or a future date (unspecified and usually unrealized) in our own little lives.

Then it must be observed that the organization of the microcosm is very various in its nature. Some parts of the outer world have been taken in and incorporated much more thoroughly than others. This full incorporation always seems to be the result of love in the broad sense—a positive going-out of the mind and the emotions towards selected objects of the outer world, a certain fusion of subject and object in the act of apprehension-with-love or of love-with-apprehension, so that the object, in entering the microcosm, becomes impregnated with feeling.

Thus the essential structure of the microcosm is not made of a series of mere reflections or copies of objects in the microcosm, but is composed of object-copies fused and impregnated with emotions so as to produce a truly synthetic material of construction. The matter is indeed more complex, for the outer components of this material, in addition to object-copies, may consist of relations between objects (such as scientific laws), or of abstract or general ideas about objects; and the internal components may include what one may perhaps call abstract emotions, in the shape of ideals. One of the most important structures formed out of this synthetic 'material' are those which McDougall called the sentiments, which together form an orderly framework that is one of the major elements in the structure of the self.

The converse of this takes place with the negative emotions of dislike and contempt, hate and aggressiveness. These tend to mark off their objects from the self, to reject them from its emotional unity. Thus, though our enemies are in a sense bound to us by our hate, they are not incorporated in our intimate structure.

These facts have an important bearing on ethical development. They first of all help us to understand the implications of the dictum 'tout comprendre, c'est tout pardonner'. We cannot truly understand without a positive outgoing of spirit, a certain incorporation of what is understood with the good and constructive elements in ourselves—which immediately signifies that we find ourselves unable (if the understanding is true and full, not superficial or purely intellectual) any longer to indulge our simple and elementary feelings of vengefulness and desire to inflict punishment, even when the events or persons concerned have been guilty of grave crime or evil.

Furthermore, we find empirically that crime and evil are more effectively reduced by means of the positive effort of understanding, followed by sympathetic treatment and efforts at prevention, than by the negative refusal to understand, followed by revenge and punishment. Thus to reach true, positive understanding is to attain a higher ethical development.

Secondly, they bear on the question of the 'unitive knowledge' of the mystics, and its ethical value. Our young man may have had flashes of this sort of experience, by falling in love, or in relation to his religion; and it will have come to him with a satisfying sense of certainty and assurance which he does not find in any other type of experience. The intensity and assurance inheres in the inner components of the experience—in the fact that, for the time at least, the forces of the *id* and the super-ego, usually hostile, are no longer hindering each other, but to a greater or lesser extent working together, flowing in the same direction. The burden of guilt is for the moment shed, and the whole being suffused with a sense of rightness.

If, later, by dint of spiritual exercises, he succeeds in making this internal adjustment permanent, and at the same time bringing these unified mental forces to bear on his experience of the outer world as a whole, he will have reached a very high ethical level. Since his reaction to the macrocosm is now wholly one of comprehension, acceptance, and love, he is no longer separated from any of it by hate. His microcosm becomes entire, and entirely positive, and the emotional component of its framework is complete, unified and of great strength.

Now let us look at our typical young man in another and more comprehensive way—not as a solid construction, essentially permanent though regrettably subject to a certain amount of alteration; but as a momentary cross-section of a change taking place in time. From this evolutionary angle, the real human being is not a static entity but a process.

The same is true of his ethics. That too is a process, not a fixed system. In the individual ethical process, the developing human being incorporates certain innate tendencies, certain emotional responses towards outer events and objects, a certain amount of knowledge of the outer environment, and various ways of dealing with it in general and with the specific situations which it presents. There is a constant procession of action and reaction, inwards and outwards, between the microcosm and the macrocosm. This interaction does not take place at random but issues in a directed process, which J. M. Baldwin, long before the term had become fashionable, styled 'the dialectic of personal growth'; and it inevitably has an ethical aspect. The process has, of course, not one possible direction only, but (as in evolution in general) many; some are more desirable than others, some more satisfactory in the short term, others in the long.

How does the ethical dialectic work out for the individual? The first move in the fated game is the act of birth, as a result of which the infant, accustomed to the warm Nirvana of the equable womb, is exposed to the accidents of the outer world. The primal desire of the newborn human individual is a desire for an undisturbed tranquillity of mere existence, and the primal reaction to the inevitable deprivations and discomforts which disturb that tranquillity is rage—a literally howling rage which is itself disturbing, for, as Flugel says, in such paroxysm the infant feels 'threatened and overmastered by its own aggressiveness'.

This primal desire for undisturbed existence, for shelter from the hard knocks of the world, however much it may be later overlaid by the joys of action and successful mastery, remains as a permanent component of the individual's emotional set-up. There is always a temptation (yielded to in very different measure by different individuals) to regress towards this infantile or embryonic shelter and peace, or to attain a substitute or equivalent for it, whether in surrender to some real or imagined authority, or in some essentially regressive escape.

Meanwhile the primal reaction of frustrated rage itself provokes a further reaction. At this stage the baby makes no distinction between self and not-self; it confuses the overwhelming and violent evil of impotent but sinister rage with the objects in the outer world which have provoked it, and so takes the first step towards what psychologists call projection; it tinges objects with its own emotional hues, animates them with its own passions.

As the self become demarcated from the world around, the

tendency is for the infant to project its own evil on to outer objects, including other persons, so leaving the self clothed in what is good and pleasant.

At about this stage the first step is taken towards the setting up of our ethical mechanism, in the shape of the 'semi-physiological morality' associated with the restraint of excretions, which I have previously mentioned.

Soon after, as the child's personality becomes more differentiated in itself and more capable of perceiving the differentiations of the outer world, the true proto-ethical mechanism is erected, in the shape of the primitive super-ego in unremitting grapple with the id.

As we have previously set forth, this arises from the conflict of love and hate in the infant's mind, its primal ambivalence towards its mother and soon afterwards its father. As Flugel puts it, 'it is man's unique and inevitable tragedy (due to his long period of helpless infancy) that he is compelled to hate those whom also he most loves—a condition which is to some extent continued throughout life in his relations with his own super-ego, which is a centre to which both love and hate are directed and from which love and hate emanate'. For now the dialectic of growth proceeds by a process the reverse of projection—namely introjection, whereby in this case the qualities of the parents are injected from without, to become part of the structure of the child's mind.

It is characteristic of this first beginning of our ethical mechanism that it is in many respects unrealistic. The parents have to exercise control over the child, and in so doing will be strict, or even harsh, and will certainly sometimes *appear* cruel. But to their actual and real strictness is added an unreal quota and quality of unpleasantness, in the shape of the child's own thwarted aggressiveness. Thus the dialectic of growth succeeds in introjecting a parent-figure very different from the real parent, since it is 'endowed with all the crude and primitive aggressiveness of the child himself. In this way, it would appear, does the super-ego acquire its more alarming and barbaric features', and this is why the semi-conscious or unconscious core of the super-ego (which may persist even throughout life) is so harsh and so unnecessarily severe, calling all the time upon the self to make atonement for its load of primal guilt.

The microcosm of the individual personality incorporates, by inescapable heredity, a swarm of impulses, many of them astonishingly bad and violent. Indeed it is only the helplessness of the infant which prevents us from realizing the extent and strength of the evil which it contains, and it has needed the learned labours of analytic psychology to reveal the amount of badness with which every human nature has to cope during his or her development.

The 'original evil' is part of what theologians call original sin: the rest consists of the load of 'original guilt' produced as part of the super-ego mechanism by the primal conflict.

But, as Freud himself has said, if we are much more evil and immoral than we consciously admit, we are also better and more moral. Not only is the super-ego an exceedingly strict moralist, but our primitive impulses to good are also numerous and strong. The pure joy of a child, its love of what is lovable and lovely, its interest (which in pure form is but intellectuaul love) in the world around it, are as astonishing as its impulses of hate and destructiveness, and in those rare individuals in which they are strongly developed, shine out in a way which leaves the ordinary adult abashed.

Besides the capacity for unwarranted projection, another unrealistic quality of the infant mind is its belief in what Freud styled the omnipotence of thought—the confusion of wish with fulfilment, the feeling that his all-too-powerful impulses, just because they are so powerful, are likely to achieve their aim. When this feeling is associated with violent hate and aggression towards mother or father, the young child is haunted by the half-unconscious fear that he has somehow smashed or destroyed his parent, or something essential in him or her, and so lost the love and support and help which, once his rage is past, he realizes is indispensable. This horror of loss, this fear of withdrawal of external support, may last through life. It will be accentuated by an actual coldness or physical absence of the parent, or later by any disasters which are taken as signs of divine wrath or punishment by impersonal fate.

This infantile 'omnipotence of thought' may also be prolonged in modified form to serve as the basis for belief in magic or superstition and for what in modern jargon is called wish-fulfilment of all kinds.

The microcosm of the young infant begins (like the microcosm in many myths) as chaos; its mind, if not entirely 'without form, and void' is assuredly shapeless and ill-defined. It is more formless than that of adult mammals—partly because the human being is born in such an early stage of development, partly because human impulses are no longer definite and sharply delimited as in lower mammals. This latter fact again has a two-fold cause: partly it is due to the greater fluidity and vagueness of the instincts themselves, partly to their being able to meet in consciousness instead of being kept apart from each other by means of an all-or-nothing mechanism of response, as is normally the case in non-human species. As I have already pointed out, this is the basis for mental conflict, to which man alone is habitually subjected.

The mind of the young infant is thus not only a chaos, but a chaos in conflict with itself. With the formation of the primitive super-ego, it develops a definite and relatively permanent structure.

The developing human being has now reached a stage which is crucial and decisive, above all in the field of ethics. His microcosm has developed a moral structure, and in doing so has introduced morality into the macrocosm—morality, with all its accompaniments of right and wrong, sin and saintliness, vice and virtue, guilt and expiation.

It has introduced morality because its structure is organized around the tension-lines of guilt which fill the field of force between the two foci of love and hate at either pole of the primal ambivalent conflict. In pre-human life, even at its highest, the conflicting chaos of the macrocosm was not mirrored in any true psychical conflict in the microcosm. Differential response to conflicting needs was achieved by the provision of a battery of specific instincts each suitable for a particular range or set of circumstances. Conflict existed only physically and objectively, whether in the form of a struggle against the elements, or in the straightforward sense of a combat or of the capture of prey, or the metaphysical sense of the darwinian struggle for existence. Mental conflict was still absent, or at best negligible and unimportant, and so was conscious and especially moral choice.

The existence of man on earth introduced morality into the cosmos in the same sort of way as it later introduced the so-called Laws of Nature. Things happen in the physical world, and happen in an orderly and regular way, so that the happenings can be subsumed and intellectually grasped in general intellectual formulations. It is these formulations which are the only Laws of Nature; before man there existed no such laws—only happenings which contained the potentiality of being understood in the form of natural laws. So with morality. There is much that is bad and much that is good in the objective happenings of the cosmos and the actions of its living inhabitants. But moral law does not exist until man appears, with his capacity for perceiving badness and goodness and for generalizing about right and wrong. The happenings of the cosmos contain the potentiality of being understood in the form of moral law, in relation to the concepts and feelings of rightness and wrongness.

Here is one essential relation between ethics and evolution—that at a certain point in time, once and for all in the evolution of the species, but repeated afresh in the evolution of each of its individuals, morality appears. The ethical potentialities of the macrocosm are actualized in the moral mechanism of the microcosm; but the microcosm in its turn reacts upon the macrocosm, and so begins ordering events in terms of morality.

\* \* \* \* \*

The dialectic of ethical growth continues. One of its basic methods is the alternation of projection and introjection, whose first cycle we have already noted. The child projects his own cruelty on to the outer world, including his parents; he then introjects the distorted parent-figures which he has thus produced, to form the harsh, punishing elements in his own super-ego. He may then reproject his super-ego, or elements of it, upon the outer world. The most obvious examples are those of jealous gods, vengeful divinities that demand sacrifice, but there are many other possibilities.

Furthermore, the god-figure, clothed with such attributes of power, majesty, or love as the worshipper and his religion permit, may become to a lesser or greater extent re-introjected, incorporated into the individual to form part of the structure of his mind. This occurs obviously enough in religious exaltation when the worshipper feels 'possessed' by a divinity, and also, in a subtler but more satisfying way, through mystic experience, 'unitive knowledge' of the divine, and so forth. Then the primitive father- and mother-figures which the young child remodels for itself around the core of the real parents may be separately re-projected, though usually tinged or fused with other emotional properties and sometimes so overlaid with other objects as to escape detection until they are looked for. Father-projections tend, of course, to embody the idea of power, authority, and punishment, while mother-projection (as in the cult of the earth-goddesses of antiquity, and later of the Virgin) incorporate the ideas of repose and shelter, of abundance and fertility, and in more developed forms, of tenderness and love.

The dialectic does not, however, proceed at random, or merely by means of a mechanical and unselective alternation of projection and introjection. It has its own general direction, determined by the psychological forces operating in the developing mind.

The ethical dynamism of the individual's mind, once the super-ego mechanization has been erected, is in broad outline as follows. In the first place, every normal individual carries a certain load of unconscious guilt, which is unconscious because it has been totally repressed by the primitive super-ego. However, although unconscious, it is not inactive, for guilt is a form of psychological tension and therefore is continually attempting to discharge itself, to reduce its tensional stress. It is hardly necessary at this stage to remind ourselves that this part of our psychological machinery is not open to direct inspection, whether by ourselves or others, and can only be detected by the results of the tensions which it generates.

In the second place, the same type of tension, though here conscious instead of unconscious, can be produced in relation to the events of life, by means of our super-ego or conscience. One of the chief ways in which the super-ego operates is by generating a sense of guilt—an occurrence which takes place when our actions do not square with the results of the super-ego's mechanism for judging and feeling the rightness or wrongness of things and acts. And this conscious guilt can reinforce and be reinforced by the permanent load of unconscious guilt, until in some cases the tension becomes intolerable. The tension can be eased by favourable circumstances, just as it can be increased by all kinds of frustrations, such as loneliness and failure.

These parts of our ethical dynamic are endogenous, arising from forces entirely within the structure of the mind itself. There is, however, a further set of forces which are concerned with the interaction between our internal ethical mechanism and the external world, both natural and social. The ethical relations of the individual inevitably change and grow with his development. As his knowledge of the external world increases, so must the field of his ethical judgments expand and alter. As he finds himself brought into relation with an increasingly large social universe, beginning with his parents and family, up through the tribe (or that modern counterpart of the tribe, the school), the social group, the nation, to radiate eventually to other nations within humanity, so his ethical attitudes to other people are inevitably affected, and the labels of morality become attached to new and more objects.

The forces in this field can be thought of as arising from the tension of the individual's expanding knowledge and experience upon his ethical machinery, pulling out threads of rightness and wrongness to fresh parts of the cosmos; they promote adjustment between the outer and inner components of the microcosm.

It has often been said that morality co-exists in the adjustment of the selfish impulses of the individual to the needs and wishes of other individuals and of the community as a whole. This is in a sense true, since the first step in morality, the formation of the super-ego, is itself an adjustment between the infant and its parents, between its violent selfish impulses and their loving restraint and guidance. But this first step differs from all the others, in that it sets up a special structural mechanism in the mind and charges the individual with a particular kind of enduring moral tension. And in any case the general statement is only true if the adjustment is regarded as a continuing and permanent process, not as a quick or definitive happening.

Looked at in this way, individual ethics is seen to consist of two processes—the attempt to be free from the tension caused by guilt, whether conscious or unconscious; and the adjustment of our ideas of right and wrong to our constantly enlarging horizons of knowledge and action—or in broader terms, the adjustment of the developing individual to the outer world, and notably the human community in which he lives.

The attempt to escape from the tensions of guilt may issue in all kinds of ways. We may be driven to seek discomfort and danger as punishment; we may take refuge in some form of unconscious expiation, for instance, by devoting ourselves to some unselfish or dangerous service in expiation for our repressed selfish aggressiveness; we may project our guilt outwards on to others—the Jews or the Bolsheviks, on to the enemy in time of war, on to other classes, on to 'sinners' who, we thank God, are not as we are; we may, like the Pharisees and others in all ages, try to make up the quarrel which the universe has picked with us (a quarrel which we are sure must be justified because of the guilty feelings we experience), by ritual placation, by sacrifice, by prayer; we mort. the flesh, deprive ourselves of pleasures; we contrive escape mechanisms, some physical like drugs, some psychological like those religions which Marx could call the opium of the people; or we seek perfection.

And, of course, we may seek perfection in different ways, some right, some wrong. In the light of all our knowledge to-day, it seems, for instance, definitely wrong to seek for perfection through undiluted asceticism, or through mere ritual observance. And there is a general agreement among those who have been willing to study or try the various ways that are supposed to lead to perfection that the way of unitive knowledge (to use the terminology of the mystics) is the best, and notably when it is positive and informed by love.

It certainly appears from the testimony of the great mystics themselves, and of those who have studied their lives[1] that after long discipline of the soul, human beings can attain to a state which can properly be described as one of perfection. It is experienced as complete, overwhelming, as a surrender which brings both power and peace, exalting, entirely satisfying, and as involving the transcendence of the self in something immensely larger.

Further, although in certain men and women it has become, however beautiful and satisfying, a spiritual indulgence which has reduced their other capacities, there are many notable examples

[1] Cf., for instance, Aldous Huxley, *The Perennial Philosophy*. London and New York, 1945.

(such as St. Theresa of Avila) to demonstrate that the practical activities of the self can be strengthened and guided into more efficient channels as a result of such experiences.

There must obviously be some special adjustment of psychological mechanism which accompanies such states. Though the precise nature of this 'function of the soul' has not yet been elicited, it is clear that one way in which it operates is by abolishing, at least temporarily, both guilt and conflict. It reduces the 'psychological distance' between the ego and super-ego, and also sublimates some of the forces of the id,[1] so that there is effected a certain fusion of the three main parts of the structure of the psyche, which are usually kept separate by powerful psychological forces. Since these forces are no longer utilized in repression or in other ways to build up a tensional structure in the mind, they become available to give the sense of increased power and scope which accompanies the mystic experience.

My brother, in the book I have already cited, finds in such experience the only final end of man, and dismisses the idea of progress not only as a delusion but as a danger. Further, he distinguishes with great sharpness between such activities and experiences as provide what he calls 'unitive knowledge of the Divine Ground of all being',[2] and others which are universally or generally regarded as good in themselves, but which are incomplete or partial—for instance enjoyment of natural beauty, æsthetic experience, the acquisition of knowledge and understanding, personal love, devotion to an active cause, and so on.

Here the evolutionary moralist has every right to speak. He can

[1] Various mystics describe their experiences as containing elements of acute emotional pleasure and beauty, obviously of the same general type as those experienced when we are 'in love', though directed to other objects, sublimated, and modified by other emotional components.

[2] I have pointed out elsewhere what appear to me to be quite unwarranted assumptions which my brother draws from the undoubted facts of mystical experience—assumptions such as those made in the above-cited phrase, that what is experienced is Divine and the one ground of all being, or that it is eternal, or in some way more real than other types of experience.

tell us that the facts of nature, as demonstrated in evolution, give us assurance that knowledge, love, beauty, selfless morality, and firm purpose are ethically good. They are good objectively in the sense that the more of them there is in the world, the better; and they are good subjectively, in the sense that the experiences of knowing, of loving, of enjoying beauty, and the rest are to be valued for their own sake.

To this general statement we must add two obvious caveats. First, the quality of the actions or experiences concerned must be high. Knowledge means something more than knowledge of isolated or irrelevant facts, and implies insight and illumination; love, as we all know, can be vulgarized or debased; morality must be genuine and not hypocritical; purpose must be directed to right ends, or at least to ends which the individual genuinely believes to be right. And secondly, the pursuit of any one of these aims must not be too one-sided, or the individual will be deflected from a desirable direction into undesirable specialization—the 'one-pointed' activity which Aldous Huxley properly stigmatizes as wrong. This emerges also from what I said above about quality. Knowledge unrelated to the main stream of human activity or to the general comprehension of nature is one-sided; so is love which does not involve beauty and comprehension, together with some tincture, however unconscious, of morality; so is purpose which is directed merely to selfish ends.

In general, not only are such activities and experiences good in themselves, but they are indispensable for the attainment of the fuller experiences, such as unitive knowledge, which we can agree represent the highest attainments possible to the human individual, and indeed to life as a whole.

It might be possible for someone who had from an early age renounced all enjoyment of 'worldly' knowledge and pleasures, including those of physical and mental exercise, and all concern with social activities, to learn how to resolve his inner conflicts sufficiently to enjoy mystical experiences. These might be very satisfying to him personally, but would assuredly be intrinsically of poor quality if they did not incorporate much knowledge and love of nature and his fellow men, much concern for the service of others, much devotion to some social enterprise. The individual microcosm will be derisory if it is too small in size, too poor in range; the unitive knowledge must be knowledge of an adequate extent of the macrocosm if it is to be of much account. A man must have experienced the urgency and intrinsic importance of simple enjoyment and of the values of love and beauty and understanding if the transcendent experience is really to have enough value to swallow up all the rest.

Finally, it must be said that if the mystic becomes so enamoured of his experiences that he withdraws wholly from the world and gives himself up to their satisfactions to the exclusion of any social obligation, then this too is a one-pointed way of life, an over-specialization which is inevitably wrong.

We may sum up the individual aspect of our subject by saying that every human being inevitably evolves in his ethics, that at its best this ethical development consists partly in a resolution of the primal ethical conflict in ever more sane, rational, and complete ways, partly in an adjustment of his selfish impulses and wishes to the community and its prevailing morality, partly in the achievement of activities and experiences which have intrinsic value, such as knowledge, love, and beauty. Furthermore, that the crown of individual ethical evolution consists in the expression of the microcosm until self is transcended, fused with not-self, and in the resolution of all inner moral tensions in a harmonious though dynamic peace. At this level of ethical development, there is no longer any conflict between selfish and social impulses, so that activity will always in the true sense of the word be moral; and at the same time the individual will have the possibility of enjoying experiences of higher intrinsic value than any other, in the shape of unitive knowledge and love.

Next we come to the question of human ethical evolution in

the larger sense, the ethical development not of the individual but of the social group or the entire species. This can be considered from two aspects. In one sense the ethics of the group is merely the sum and interaction of the ethics of its individual members. But in another sense it is better measured and represented by the current code governing moral behaviour and laying down penalties for moral deviations.

On the first aspect, little need be said, save to point out that one inescapable characteristic of man as a species is his variability, and that this applies as much to his ethics as to any other activity. If we continue thinking in terms of man as the microcosm, any one individual will embody a distinctive array and balance of the good and evil aspects of the macrocosm. Different men and women embody different moral choices—one reacts to the inescapable moral conflict of life by hard work, another by despair; one takes refuge in self-abasement, another in psychological escape; one allows the aggressive impulses of the selfish individual free rein, another perseveres until he reconciles the conflict between them and the claims of the rest of the world in self-transcendence. The principle of division of labour governs man's morals as much as his technical and professional accomplishments. Vicarious atonement has a true social significance; the priest and the prophet are society's specialists in holy matters, and even the saint is in part saintly for the community and not merely for himself.

Here is obviously a limitation on the value of individual ethical development. Human nature being what it is, all its varieties cannot, even in the most favourable circumstances, be expected to attain the highest level of individual ethical development. And even among those who do reach this highest level, there are bound to be immense differences in the type of self-transcendence attained; no one individual can imagine that his type of achievement is the only right one, but is only entitled to think of it as his best contribution to embodying and actualizing the forces of the cosmos that make for good.

In addition to the variability due to genetic difference and to the accident of circumstance, there is the deliberate variability imposed by the division of labour within the community. If society is to continue, and still more if it is to progress, men and women must be specially trained as teachers, doctors, administrators, as artisans and agricultural labourers, as engineers, philosophers, scientists, and artists. And this deliberate specialization, while it does not in theory prevent a man from also pursuing an all-round and perfected development, in practice certainly makes it more difficult. Thus, to take but one example, to employ one's intelligence continually and whole-heartedly on concrete phenomena, as many pure and applied scientists must do, may often limit interest in other aspects of existence, such as the æsthetic or the spiritual, and cause an atrophy by disuse of these other faculties (unless, as sometimes occurs, it causes a deliberate compensatory reaction in these directions).

Aldous Huxley holds up Darwin as an example of how 'one-pointed concentration on that which is not the highest may become a dangerous form of idolatry. Darwin wrote to Hooker that "it is a cursed evil to any man to become so absorbed in any subject as I am in mine". . . . Darwin himself records that in later life he was unable to take the smallest interest in poetry, art or religion'.

On this, one may first remind ourselves that what men do for the community is important, as well as what they do for themselves. If Darwin had managed to preserve his delight and interest in poetry, art, and religion, but at the cost of reducing to any important degree his contribution to science and thought, this would have been, in broad perspective, wrong. Further, what my brother fails to point out is that many men of science have been able to continue their interest in other aspects of life and reality, and that Darwin's failure to do so was due, either wholly or at least mainly, to his chronic ill-health. And finally, some of the failure of enjoyment and interest which Darwin and my brother deplore, seems to be merely a normal (though not necessarily an inevitable) consequence of growing older. Thus in later life Wordsworth lamented—how bitterly!—the failure of his capacity for rapture through the contemplation of natural beauty, in spite of his 'one-pointed concentration' on that aspect of existence.

Accordingly, though we are right in deploring specialization which is so one-sided or excessive as to involve atrophy of other vital interests or faculties, it is not true to say that intellectual or æsthetic or any other specialization is always wrong. It cannot be wrong in itself, for it is necessary to the very existence of society, as well as often providing satisfying outlets or experiences for the individual. What we must aim at is the establishment of a general attitude which condemns over-specialization and the neglect of other faculties, and the working out of practical methods by which the specialist can continue to practise his specialism while yet remaining 'many-pointed', and can be introduced to the wide expanses of new satisfaction and adjustment which lie along the road of truly progressive individual development.

The other aspect of ethical evolution concerns us more directly. For though, as pointed out elsewhere, there is a bewildering relativity of social ethics among different groups and different cultures, yet during man's social evolution we find a definite trend in the form or structure of his moral codes.

Let me amplify this point. Every code governing morality, whether it have the form of apparently arbitrary taboos, of ritual actions, of explicit moral commandments, of criminal laws or penal codes, or of high ethical teachings, always under one aspect represents society's collective method of solving the basic moral conflict between love and hate, between the claims of self and the claims of society, which afflicts each developing individual afresh.

This is diagrammatically illustrated by the phenomenon of taboo. As Freud himself pointed out in one of his earliest excursions from psychiatry into more general fields, taboos generally involve an ambivalent attitude—the tabooed object is regarded at one and the same time as both holy and unclean—what the theologian Otto has called 'bad-sacred'—and to be feared as in some way charged with dangerous power. As Flugel pithily expresses it, 'taboos are the socialized expression of conflicts; they are in their nature ambivalent and imply a double attitude of desire and fear, of attraction and repulsion. It is true that the negative or prohibiting elements preponderate. But underneath each prohibition is a real or potential desire, for people do not trouble to prohibit things that no one wants to do'.

This is not the place to discuss particular taboos and their probable origins. However, I may remind my readers that the elaborate taboos that hedge a king in so many primitive societies indubitably arise from his subjects' ambivalent attitude, combining respect and almost worship with envy and fear of his power; that the almost universal taboos of primitive peoples concerning the recently dead are probably due, as Freud ingeniously suggested, to the sense of guilt of those still living, which in its turn derives from their repressed hostility to the 'dear departed' during his life, a hostility which found expression in wishes—again, of course, largely repressed—for his death; that a similar ambivalent attitude towards the wife gives rise to the taboos and taboo-like rituals of the *couvade*; that the only explanation yet given of the linked taboos concerning totem-clams, totem animals, and exogamy is Freud's bold theory that they externalize and socialize the Œdipus complex; and that the strong element of hardship or suffering involved in almost all initiation ceremonies (a trait which, in diluted and modified form, has persisted to the present day in most examination systems) has its origin in the ambivalent attitude of the adults or the initiates towards the young people who are on the threshold of sharing their social and sexual privileges, and in addition enjoy the biological privilege of youth and vigour.

What does concern us is that taboo prohibitions, combined with positive rituals which share the rigid and often apparently meaningless quality of taboos as well as their quality of expressing emotional conflict in institutionalized form, constitute the main ethical framework of all societies at a certain rather modest level of social evolution.

Recent studies have revealed (I once more quote Flugel's valuable summary) 'a pre-totemic layer of culture among the primitive tribes of Central Australia, surviving (chiefly among women and children) as a background to the more official totemism, in much the same way as pagan beliefs and practices often continue to work behind official Christianity in Europe. This "primal religion" takes the form of belief in demonic or spiritual entities of queer shapes and qualities, and often of cannibalistic tendencies'. There seems little doubt that these and similar survivals (perhaps including ritual cannibalism) represent the last trace of a phase still more primitive than taboo in the evolution of social ethics, during which men institutionalized the earliest stages of individual ethical development—the monstrous, destructive, and frequently cannibalistic 'bogies' which, as we have seen, the child projects at the time when it first begins to divide its unitary experience into self and not-self.

The taboo stage of social ethics itself has various levels. Originally the sanctions involved are regarded as the automatic result of an impersonal inherent force or power, the dangerous 'mana' of social anthropologists. At a higher level the penalties attaching to breaking a taboo are supposed to be enforced by spirits or demons—spiritual small fry, but numerous and varied; and as rationalization and the desire for intellectual explanation grows, the power behind the visible world, which is at the same time the dangerous force inflicting sanctions for taboo-breaking, is projected in the form of gods and finally in that of a single Divine Ruler.

Finally, just as the pre-totemic system persists in the form of sporadic survivals in the taboo phase, so it, in its turn, persists in the form of sporadic taboos, often trivialized and degenerated into mere superstitions, in the next higher phase of society's ethical evolution.

This further phase may be called the legalistic. Society is here institutionalizing a more rational level of individual ethical development, in which moral transgression is envisaged primarily in terms of the damage done to the interests of society or of its individual members, and some attempt is made to 'make the punishment fit the crime'.

The legalistic stage of social ethics has itself had a long and elaborate evolution. It begins with the promulgation of brief general codes, often supposedly with Divine authority, of which the Decalogue is a familiar example. These simple commandments may then be complexified by the super-imposition of elaborate and detailed ritual prescriptions. As an example, we need only compare the injunctions which fill the Books of Leviticus and Deuteronomy with the original Ten Commandments. Many of these ritual injunctions are, of course, nothing more than taboos brought up to date and adjusted to the general social and ethical system of the times. During the course of history, however, ritualized taboos tend to drop out of their legal or semi-legal status into that of social or religious observances, while law itself becomes more official, more varied, and more complicated.

What chiefly interests us here, however, is the change in the psychological attitude expressed in the process of law. Legal institutions, like those of taboo, can under one aspect be regarded as the institutionalized expression of moral conflict; the difference is that they express a rather more advanced stage of its resolution.

Briefly and diagrammatically, the primitive super-ego mechanism, with its attached tensions of repression and guilt, tends to produce what has been described as an inner need for punishment. This 'need for punishment' may remain directed upon the self and its imprisoned id, and will then give rise to the concept of a stern or cruel or vengeful God, or to penance, self-accusation, exaggerated reparation, masochistic asceticism, and other forms of self-inflicted penalties which afflict such a considerable part of our poor suffering humanity, and may culminate in or contribute to certain crippling or unsavoury forms of neurosis, such as melan-

cholic 'nervous breakdown' and sexual masochism. In other circumstances, or with other temperamental types, the need for
punishment is projected outwards and directed on to real or
imaginary transgressors—scapegoats, enemies, criminals, sacrificial
victims (of which Christ crucified is the supreme example), or
merely those whom we unconsciously envy for their freedom from
the guilt which obsesses us, or for their good fortune in general.
This tendency again may contribute to neuroses, such as exaggerated puritanism, or the violence of sexual sadism. This need for
punishment, both inwardly and outwardly directed punishment,
becomes institutionalized in various ways in the legal process.

One of the simplest methods is reparation. The offender is
forced to make good the damage he has inflicted, either directly,
or indirectly by means of a payment, or symbolically by means of
a service. A variant on this is the *lex talionis*—'an eye for an eye,
a tooth for a tooth'. This we might characterize as revengeful
substitution: the injured party does not get back the lost tooth,
but at least the aggressor loses one of his. Sacrifice in the material
sense, whether of 'burnt offerings' or of wealth or precious objects,
contains an element of reparation, and continues as part of insti-
tutional ethics so long as religion itself plays an important part
in the social set-up by means of an organized church or a powerful
priesthood.

Confession is another method of relieving the sense of guilt,
and frequently comes to be accepted as some sort of moral equivalent for punishment. Indeed, at one stage of social evolution
confession is regarded as an integral part of the criminal's expiation of his crime, and its extortion, even by extreme torture, as
necessary and justifiable. In this case, there is clearly what the
psycho-analysts call over-determination; and the repressed impulses
of cruelty and aggression, canalized in an outwardly-directed 'need
for punishment', justify their full expression by means of attaching
it to the morally respectable excuse of obtaining confession. Later,
when ethical evolution has reached a stage at which the infliction

of torture, even for ostensibly moral ends, is regarded as wicked, man's outwardly projected guilty aggressivity often continues to demand savage punishment for offenders, and manages to justify its savagery by means of various rationalizations. One of the commonest of these is the assertion that suffering is in some way good in itself, and that human nature is incapable of amendment save through punishment. This attitude has permeated much of the upbringing and education of children: the principle of 'spare the rod and spoil the child', that convenient justification of our guilty unacknowledged sadism, has darkened many nurseries and many schoolrooms. It has also been embodied in the penal provisions of many systems of law. Thus the world's empire-builders frequently assert that 'natives' understand only severity, with the result that many colonial systems still contain penal provisions of a harshness long abandoned in the mother-country.

Another rationalization is that crime can only be prevented through severity of punishment. This, naturally enough, is often combined with the first type—punishment is regarded not only as a necessary safeguard of the social order, but as also good for those on whom it is inflicted. Such severity of penal provisions is, of course, accentuated by fear, as when the governing class is faced with the danger of losing some of their privileges or possessions. An example is afforded by the savagery of the sentences imposed in England in the early part of the nineteenth century— death or deportation for forgery or even for quite small thefts. This rationalization continues to play its part at the present day— for instance in the arguments concerning the need for capital punishment as a deterrent against murder.

Meanwhile man's ethical evolution is slowly entering on a new phase—the replacement of punishment by treatment. It has now been proved beyond any question that severity of punishment does not in point of fact reduce the commission of crimes. Our only hope for reducing criminality lies in the development of a more just and less frustrating social system and of more moral individuals, with more rounded personalities, within it. Treatment, as with physical ills, can be either curative or preventive, either individual or social; and again, as in medicine, in the long run the social and preventive aspects will be the most important.

The replacement of punishment by treatment implies for one thing the partial replacement of legal systems and processes, in so far as they embody the social framework of ethics, by social science and various of its applications. It also implies that the primal inner ethical conflict shall reach a somewhat higher level of resolution before being institutionalized: a level at which the emotionally neutral power of the intellect, supported by experience and the scientific spirit, is exerted to release some of the knotted emotional tensions of the proto-ethical mechanism and the super-ego. This is an essential stage in the passage of the individual to ethical maturity, and involves some degree of inner illumination, some substitution of unconscious by conscious ethical motivation.

It is, of course, obvious that only a part of the current social ethics becomes institutionalized, whether in social or religious ritual, in law or official regulations: a large part remains in the background, a fluid but none the less potent agency shaping men's thoughts and actions.

One such ethical attitude which has played a powerful role during most of the historical period is what certain psycho-analysts have called the Polycrates complex—the fear of too much fortune for oneself (and especially of ostentation or boasting about it), the resentment against too much success in others. Too much good fortune is felt to invite the jealousy of the gods, or God, or Fate, too much success their resentment, so that in either case disaster is to be expected or feared as a punishment. The ancient Greeks employed the special term *Hubris* to denote some of the characteristics likely to bring down this cosmic wrath, or *Nemesis*, upon their possessor. Thus in the *Persæ* Æeschylus finds a major reason for Xerxes' defeat in his *Hubris* in daring to build a bridge across the Hellespont.

The Polycrates complex in general, together with the stigmatization of *Hubris* as wrong as well as dangerous, is naturally more characteristic of periods when men worship strongly anthropomorphic gods, into whom they can project their own need to inflict punishment for their own guilty, selfish, and aggressive urges. However, it still continues to prevail as a superstition— all over the world one finds proverbs like 'pride goes before a fall', and practices of the 'touch wood' type; and it still provides the motivation for a good deal of serious ethical thinking, particularly in religious circles, but also elsewhere. Even Aldous Huxley in his previously-cited book regards the modern aim of controlling the forces of nature as essentially hubristic, and therefore both ethically wrong and likely to bring disaster in its wake. Thus he speaks of 'recent technological advances—or, in Greek phraseology, recent acts of *hubris* directed against Nature'; of *Hubris* as 'the original sin'; and of 'the ancient and *profoundly realistic* (italics mine) doctrine of *hubris* and inevitable *nemesis*'. This, he says, is because 'modern man no longer regards Nature as being in any sense divine and feels perfectly free to behave towards her as an overweening conqueror and tyrant. The spoils of recent technological imperialism have been enormous; but meanwhile *nemesis* has seen to it that we get our kicks as well as halfpence'.

I would say that Aldous Huxley is here confusing two issues. It is perfectly true that ill-considered control of nature pursued to the exclusion of social or spiritual control, and technological advance considered as the most important end, or even as an end in itself, is bound to bring trouble: it is an example of one-sided specialization, and one-sided specialization is always beset with penalities. It is also true that the attainment of a higher level of control of nature brings with it the possibility of greater evil, of a deeper fall: this, as Niebuhr points out, appears to be the inevitable accompaniment of all types of human advance, whether material or spiritual. To this extent, the notion of *Hubris* can be attached to material progress (though only, it must be admitted, in a metaphorical sense), and technological advance can be properly described as 'overweening imperialism directed against Nature'. But when nature is personified (note Aldous Huxley's use of the capital N in writing of Nature), when it is regarded 'as being in any sense divine', and when it is implicitly endowed with some capacity for feeling or expressing resentment against man's *Hubris* and for indulgence in an avenging *Nemesis*—then we are asked to continue thinking in false terms, terms still coloured by an early and primitive attempt at resolution of man's primal ethical conflict, terms which have been outgrown by scientific thought and must sooner or later be outgrown by social ethics.

Lest as a natural scientist I be thought guilty of partiality, I will once more quote from Flugel. 'We are all', he writes, 'at least dimly (some of us acutely) conscious of failing in numerous respects to live up to the standards of our super-ego; hence we all feel guilty, and in turn experience in some measure the "need for punishment" which is the basic method of dealing with guilt. . . . Only through the pain of punishment can [we] get rid of the burden of [our] guilt. If we do not experience sufficient pain, if things go too well for us and we have too much luck, we begin to feel uneasy because our need for punishment has not been met. Hence at bottom the fear of *Hubris*, . . . which the ancient Greeks . . . were able to discern as a fundamental human trait.

'The influence of this fear in retarding human progress is difficult to estimate but has certainly been very great. . . . Man's attitude to nature thus mirrors his attitude to his own super-ego, and this in turn is built up on the basis of the child's moral and physical dependence on its parents, magnified and distorted by the influence of nemesism. It is not surprising then that throughout history those who have sought to increase human power and understanding should have aroused a degree of suspicion and mistrust that has often led to martyrdom, for at bottom it is felt that such pioneers are guilty of Hubris, and that if they got their way they would involve all mankind in the penalties incurred by those who presume "above their station".' The classical example is that of Prometheus, though as Flugel points out, 'of course Christ was guilty—and guilty of Hubris—in the eyes of most of those actively concerned with his death'. A more recent example was the intense disapproval, notably by clerics, of the use of anæsthetics, particularly in childbirth.

Another characteristic of social ethics throughout historic times (if we exclude the ideal ethical systems formulated by great moral leaders such as Jesus or Gautama Buddha and confine ourselves to the actual systems operating in particular societies) has been their provision of an enemy as an outlet for hate, repressed aggression, and outwardly-directed 'need for punishment'. Sometimes the enemy has supernatural status: is not the Devil of old-fashioned Christianity styled 'The Enemy' *par excellence*? Sometimes the enemy is a theological enemy—the members of another sect (as with Protestant and Catholic in Northern Ireland) or of another faith (as with Christian and Infidel throughout the Middle Ages, or Hindu and Moslem in India today). It was the achievement of Hitler to have invented a racial enemy in the shape of the Jews, to serve as outlet for the repressed aggressiveness of the citizens of Nazi Germany. Or again, the enemy is a political enemy, to be hated for dynastic or nationalistic reasons or on other grounds of power politics. In this case, the enemy is not necessarily a permanent one, and the enemy of yesterday may become the friend or ally of today; but, the world being what it is, any power-seeking group or nation can always find some other group ready to hand, to be put into the position of enemy and so to serve in directing the group's aggressiveness outwards while at the same time providing it with greater inner cohesion. So long as the human species is organized in a number of competing and sovereign nation-states, not only is it easy for a group to pick another group to serve as enemy, but it is in the group's narrow and short-term interest that it should do so.

Social ethics is thus conditioned by four rather distinct sets of factors. One is political, and concerns the nature of organized groups; one is practical, and concerns man's control over nature; a third is intellectual, and concerns man's understanding of the macrocosm; and the fourth we may call for want of a better term psychological or spiritual, and concerns man's understanding and control of the microcosm of his own nature, including more particularly his internal ethical mechanism.

Accordingly we may suggest that the achievement of the next major stage in the evolution of social ethics will depend on the following general points. In the first place, the achievement of some sort of political unification of the entire species, which will render group enmity much more difficult; secondly, the achievement, through the applications of science, of a universal minimum standard of freedom from want and disease and of opportunities for education and enjoyment. Thirdly, the achievement of a general evolutionary outlook to serve as the intellectual scaffolding of our life, thus putting a directional theory of progress as the dynamic core of our ethics; and fourthly, the achievement of sufficient psychological understanding and control to enable the bulk of mankind, or at least the leaders in every field, to take the resolution of their intrinsic moral conflict a stage further than before, to a point at which punishment, whether of self or of others, is no longer constantly demanded to appease the tension of inner guilt.

The specific steps which will have to be taken before we can reach this next stage of ethical evolution are somewhat various. There is first the practical political step of discovering how to transfer some of the sovereign power of the several nation-states of the world to a central organization. This has its counterpart in the moral world: for one thing, any practical success in this task will make it easier for men to abandon the tribalist ethics (for tribalist they still are, however magnified in scale) associated with the co-existence of competing social groups. Conversely, however, any success in mobilizing opinion in favour of One World, of a unified instead of a split humanity, will facilitate the political process of unification, just as the widespread public opinion which held that slavery was morally wrong facilitated the actual abolition of slavery as a social practice.

Such a change in public opinion, however, must be accompanied by a much more profound ethical change before the world can feel at all safe from major physical conflicts. Humanity at large must discover what William James called a moral equivalent for war: in more modern and more profound terms, we must find a way of resolving our inner ethical conflict without recourse to a human enemy, in the shape of another nation or organized group, on whom to project our hatred and our aggression. The world at large is assuredly not capable of resolving its conflict between hate and love without the aid of some kind of enemy to serve as a lightning-conductor for the discharge of our aggressive impulses: as yet, only a few rare souls have learnt this art. It thus seems probable that the next step must be the identification of 'the enemy' with disease, poverty, hunger, ignorance, and the other evil products of the hostile forces of nature and of the defects in our social organization. This in turn is closely linked with my previous point about applying our knowledge: once the people at large realize that there is no longer any excuse for anybody anywhere to grow up deprived of the opportunities for a basic standard of physical and mental well-being, we must make the attainment of that basic standard a major aim of social ethics, and the failure to attain it a major social sin.

It is also linked with advance in intellectual understanding. Not only must people realize that it is ethically wrong to continue to resolve their inner moral conflicts by the partial and primitive methods of wiping out guilt by punishment; they must take the positive step of realizing that it is ethically right to try to resolve it by the aid of the dispassionate intelligence, substituting scientific treatment for emotionally-determined punishment. (If they can add love to understanding, so much the better; but the minimum prerequisite for the next stage of ethics is understanding.)

Intellectual understanding has also a more general role to play. The next stage of social ethics will not be attained until the bulk of opinion believes that it is ethically right to increase knowledge, ethically wrong to put obstacles in its path. More specifically, knowledge and understanding of the evolutionary process, and of our unique role in it, is needed before we can substitute a dynamic and directional ethics for the static sterility of past systems.

Finally, and in many ways most difficult of all, the world must be persuaded that its present concentration on action and material achievement is one-sided and therefore in the long run wrong. Control of our own nature is of equal importance with control of external nature, and to achieve this we must look inwards. If we must build Jerusalem in the green and pleasant lands of the physical world, we must also find the Kingdom of Heaven, and we have it on the highest authority, as well as on the testimony of experience, that this is within us. With this, we again come back to the problem of resolving the basic internal ethical conflict. The decisive step to be taken here is that people at large should realize that this can be resolved much more thoroughly and satis-factorily than is usually the case or than is generally thought possible; that if we apply the same degree of discipline to our moral and spiritual activities as many of us willingly do to our brains or our bodies, we may attain not merely a freedom from primal guilt (which is a negative freedom like freedom from actual disease), but a positive state of moral well-being which is of intrinsic and quasi-ultimate value and satisfaction in itself—the moral equivalent of theological 'salvation'. Even if most of us for one reason or another find it impossible to persevere until these heights are reached, we can acknowledge that it is possible for some people, and that it is right for them to devote themselves to their aim, just as we acknowledge that it is possible for some people to develop their intellects to the highest pitch, and that it is right and good that they should do so. And in any case we need to have a general belief that it is ethically right for everyone to develop their internal moral and spiritual structure well beyond the pitch now customarily tolerated.

*        *        *        *        *

The relation of individual to social ethics now begins to be clearer. With the facts of evolutionary progress to guide us, we find that increase of knowledge, increase of control, increase of autonomy, increase in emotional capacity and enjoyment, increase in will and purpose, increase in individualization, are all good, since they all make for progress. They must become part of our ethical goals. On the other hand, there must not be one-sided or exaggerated pursuit of any one of these aims, since one-sidedness is itself bad, as being in the long run always inimical to progress. These were the trends which made for progress in the biological sector of evolution. But in the human sector another criterion has been added—the understanding and attainment of intrinsic values. And just as, with the passage from the lifeless to the living, control and autonomy became more important as an index of progress than mere complexity, so with the passage from the biological to the human, the attainment of values becomes more important than material control or autonomy.

It is only by individuals that values can be actually understood and appreciated. It is thus ethically good for the individual to pursue and to enjoy experiences of comprehension, of æsthetic satisfaction, of moral nobility. To do this, he must evolve: he must develop his potentialities, and must, in the moral sphere, accomplish some considerable degree of resolution of the inner moral conflict which is at the root of his ethical activity. If he is to achieve all-round or what Aldous Huxley calls many-pointed development, he must relate this resolution of inner conflict to all his outwardly-directed activities—of knowledge and understanding, of love, of action, of emotional and æsthetic appreciation. And the only way in which he can do this fully and satisfactorily seems to be the way of the true mystic—the way of acceptance, unitive knowledge, and love. He must merge inner and outer, lose self by transcendence of self, resolve all tensions, both the original intrinsic tensions of his super-ego, and the later developing tensions between different parts of his experience and different sectors of his activity, in a harmonious working whole. In our previous terms, he must build a comprehensive microcosm, in which the facts and forces of the universe (including the facts and forces of life, of society, and of his own nature) are unified and reconciled. This microcosm of his possesses a time-dimension—not merely in the common sense of developing and changing with the passage of time, but in the sense, applying uniquely to man, of combining past and future in the present unity of consciousness. By the same token it is infinite, or perhaps we should say nonfinite, in quality, for consciousness combines the actual and the real with the abstract and the ideal in such a way that the range of the microcosm surpasses the concrete limits of the macrocosm itself.

The microcosm thus combines actuality and potentiality, fact and fancy, the recorded past and the speculative future, external phenomena and internal purpose, all in relation to the polarized psychological forces of good and evil; and at its fullest development combines them in a smooth working-unity.

\*    \*    \*    \*    \*

In the light of experience and intellectual comprehension, the antithesis between individual and community is seen to be largely a false antithesis. The individual is, quite strictly, meaningless in isolation, and the type and degree of his development, ethical or otherwise, is conditioned by the type of community in which he happens to live. Even if he transcends the current morality of his times, this is only possible if the social framework includes some freedom of ideas, some elasticity of ideals.

Furthermore, though the highest products of evolution are individuals, yet the community is the mechanism by which alone large-scale progress can be realized in regard to increase of control and autonomy by life. When we reflect on the advances made in these broad biological criteria of progress between the first beginnings of our own species and the present day, and on the fact that the rate of advance is still accelerating, we perceive that literally unimagined possibilities of further advance in these respects lie before our descendants. From the standpoint of evolutionary ethics, it is one of the moral duties of the individual to further this advance, and this he can only do by devoting some of his energies to working as a cog in the social machine.

But these criteria, however important they still remain, have in the human sector of evolution become secondary to the criteria of increase in understanding and realization of intrinsic values. Here again, though intrinsic values can be experienced only by individuals and not by the community as such, yet the community is still the mechanism through which alone individuals are able to realize these values. A member of a primitive tribe cannot possibly experience the full satisfactions of intellectual or emotional or spiritual experience which are possible to members of a modern civilized nation.

On the other hand, it is in present conditions only a comparatively few favoured individuals who can enjoy these full satisfactions. Accordingly it is one of the moral duties of the individual to further the development of society in such a way that more of its members are able to realize and enjoy more and higher intrinsic values.

Thus from one angle the relation between individual and society is like that between ends and means. Fuller individualization is an evolutionary end; the developed human individual is the highest product of evolution; the experiences which alone have high intrinsic value, such as those of love and beauty and knowledge and mystical union, are accessible only to human individuals. On the other hand, while a wrong or unsatisfactory organization of society can hamper or suppress individualization, can keep down both the average and the maximum level of individual development, and can, all too easily, stand in the way of knowledge and love and beauty and spiritual satisfaction entering the individual microcosm, yet a certain right organization of society is necessary as a means before those ends can be achieved.

Indubitably the next important step to be taken by humanity is its own unification. This is at present beginning, but at different rates in different fields. The unity of scientific research and knowledge is already well advanced. The political unification of man is making its tentative beginnings through the doubtless temporary expedient of the United Nations Organization. Technical improvements in communications are *de facto* bringing the remotest parts of the world together. And conscious attempts are being made to break down barriers to cultural interchange and the free flow of information. The only logical outcome of these various tendencies will be the creation of a single unified pool of tradition, organized politically in a single unified World Government.

This step once taken, the evolving cosmos will have passed another critical point. Here I may perhaps quote from what I have written elsewhere:[1]

'In evolution as a whole, it is obvious that there are two major critical points—the origin of self-reproducing matter or life, and the origin of self-reproducing society or man. But both the inorganic and the biological sector contain minor critical points, decisive not so much because of their immediate effects as for the new possibilities which they open up for the future. The secondary critical point in inorganic

[1] *The Prerequisites of Progress.* (Unesco Lectures, Editions Fontaine, Paris, 1947.)

evolution was the formation of complex giant molecules, rightly termed "organic" since without them living organisms would have been impossible. The secondary critical point in biological evolution was the origin of learning—the formation of mechanisms for profiting by experience. This was of importance partly because without it the evolution of man, with his social heredity based on experience and tradition, would have been impossible; but partly also because it is at the base of all the most successful and developed products of biological evolution, from bee and ant to mammal and bird.

'I would suggest that the secondary critical point in human evolution will be marked by the union of all separate traditions in a single common pool, the orchestration of human diversity from competitive discord to harmonious symphony. Of what future possibilities beyond the human this may be the first foundation, who can say? But at least it will for the first time give full scope to man's distinctive method of evolution, and open the door to many human potentialities that are as yet scarcely dreamt of'.

This is the major ethical problem of our time—to achieve global unity for man. All such questions as the control of the atomic bomb, the effective working of the United Nations, the possibility of a true World Government, the international freedom of science, the encouragement of cultural interchange and the flow of information across frontiers, are merely parts of this more comprehensive problem. Present-day men and nations will be judged by history as moral or immoral according as to whether they have helped or hindered that unification.

Meanwhile, the evolutionary approach to ethics is itself a prerequisite for progress, including ethical progress. An example will show how closely interwoven are the different strands from which the tissue of human progress must be fashioned. The new knowledge amassed by biologists during the last hundred years has demonstrated that increase of knowledge is one of the characteristics of progress, both in the later biological and in the human phase of evolution. Furthermore, the analysis of our knowledge about progress is providing us with definite guidance as to how we should try to plan social and political change to ensure that it makes for progress.

The evolutionary point of view makes it clear that progress is neither a myth nor a will-of-the-wisp, still less a dangerous delusion: it is the desirable direction of change in the world, and desirable ethically as much as materially or intellectually. It also establishes the reassuring fact that our human ethics have their roots deep in the non-human universe, that our moral principles are not just a whistling in the dark, not the *ipse dixit* of an isolated humanity, but are by the nature of things related to the rest of reality—and indeed that only when we take the trouble to understand that relationship will we be able to lay down ethical principles which are truly adequate. Furthermore, while to the evolutionist ethics can no longer be regarded as having any absolute value, yet their relativity is neither chaotic nor meaningless: ethics are relative to a process which is both meaningful and of indefinitely long duration—that of evolutionary progress.

The peculiar difficulties which surround our individual moral adjustment are seen to be largely due to our evolutionary history. Like our prolonged helplessness in infancy, our tendency to hernia and sinusitis, our troubles in learning to walk upright, they are a consequence of our having developed from a simian ancestry. Once we realise that the primitive super-ego is merely a makeshift developmental mechanism, no more intended to be the permanent central support of our morality than is our embryonic notochord intended to be the permanent central support of our bodily frame, we shall not take its dictates so seriously (have they not often been interpreted as the authentic Voice of God?), and shall regard its supersession by some more rational and less cruel mechanism as the central ethical problem confronting every human individual.

Above all, an evolutionary ethics is of necessity a hopeful ethics, however much the justifiable hope is tempered by a realization of the length and difficulty of man's ethical task. Our ethics are rooted in the evolutionary past, though the relations are often indirect and hard to trace. But with the coming of man, and notably with his attainment of highly organized societies based on scientific knowledge, our ethics are being actually incorporated into the evolutionary process. Man's sense of right and wrong has always influenced the course of history, as we call that sector of the evolutionary process that has occurred in our species since written records began. But as our knowledge grows and our capacity for its wise application increases, that influence will certainly grow, and can be exerted more and more to encourage a desirable direction of our evolution.

Man the conscious microcosm has been thrown up by the blind and automatic forces of the unconscious macrocosm. But now his consciousness can begin to play an active part, and to influence the process of the macrocosm by guiding and acting as the growing-point of its evolution. Man's ethics and his moral aspirations have now become an integral part of any future evolutionary progress.